Nancy L. Sowers
Jan. 16, 1993

Nancy L. Sowers
Jan. 16, 1993

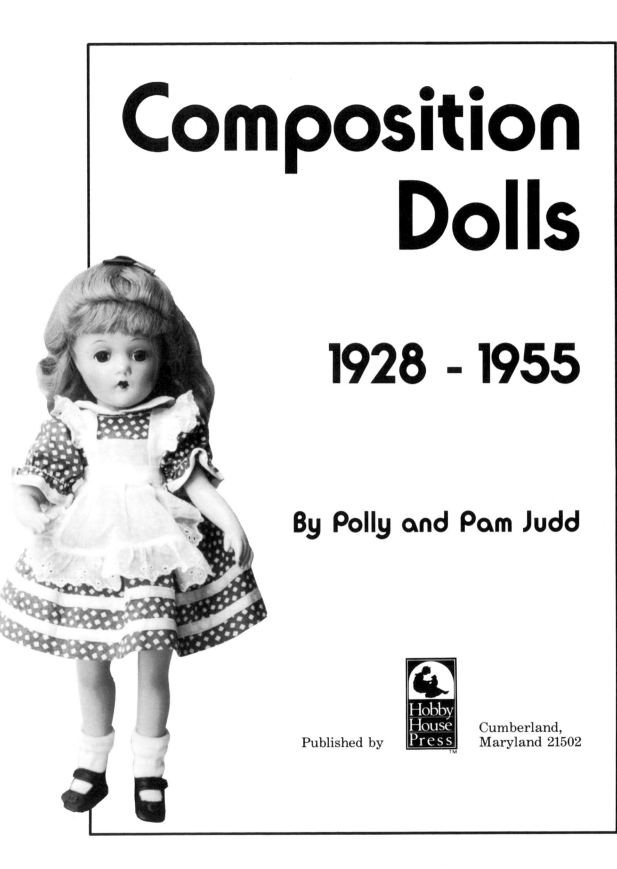

Composition Dolls

1928 - 1955

By Polly and Pam Judd

Published by Hobby House Press   Cumberland, Maryland 21502

Dedication

This book is dedicated to our late husband and father, Wally Judd, and the late Laura May Brown, our cousin, who shared our love of dolls. We love them both dearly.

Acknowledgements

There is a growing concern for the need to preserve and research composition dolls. The authors would like to thank John Axe, Nancy Carlson, Jean Francis of Canada, Ursula Mertz and Pat Schoonmaker for their contributions in this field.

In writing this book, we have found a tremendous interest in composition dolls. People from Arizona, Canada, California, Connecticut, Florida, Georgia, Idaho, Illinois, Massachusetts, Michigan, New Jersey, New York, North Carolina, Ohio, Pennsylvania, Texas and Virginia have contributed pictures and knowledge of these lovely, gentle dolls.

Marianne Gardner has a special touch with composition dolls. She seemed to always know what pictures we needed before we knew it ourselves.

Mary Elizabeth Poole and her sister, Madge Poole Copley, told us wonderful stories of their childhood dolls which are pictured in this book.

Mary Lu Trowbridge has always shared her special collection with us.

Ramona Beard, Kerra Davis and Athena Crowley worked hard to make sure their pictures were very special.

Nancy Carlson's lovely pictures of the *Patsy* family have been shown to doll collectors all over the United States. We are delighted to share some of them with our readers.

Barbara Comienski and Jim Comienski share our love of composition dolls and also share our traveling to find them.

Diane Hoffman's magnificent pre-portrait Alexander dolls were especially photographed for this book.

Connie Lee Martin and Sandra Strater shared their special knowledge of quintuplets.

We also want to thank the following people who sent photographs, allowed us to photograph their dolls or helped in other ways: Kathy Adams, Paula Applegate, Lois Barrett, Frank Biscop, Vivien Brady-Ashley, Camille Brennan, Patricia Buetikofer, Felix A. Cappadona, Nancy Chainey, Ruth Chappell, Cobb's Doll Auctions, Marcia Creswell, Marjorie Merritt Darrah, E. Marilyn Dawe, Nancy Demory, Sandi Dod, Diane Domroe, Caroline Florence, Martha Foster, Jean Francis, Marianne Gardner, Irene Gulick, Lois Janner, Shirley Karaba, Jean Kelley, Carol Kelly, Shirley Kille, Helen Krielow, Penni Lewis, Ruth Lewis, Eleanor Lihit, Priscilla Lynch, Linda Mangold, Elizabeth Martz, Joanne McIntosh, McMasters Productions, Millie Myer, Roslyn Nigoff, Sonia Notaro, Jackie O'Connor, Pat Parton, Dee Percifull, Mary Jane Poley, John Poot, Cynthia Rutherford, Nancy Schwartz, Kathleen Smith, Patricia Snyder, Joyce Stock, Betty Shriver, Jean Strong, Michele Teny, Joan A. Tosko, Jeri Traw, Irene Trittschuch, Marjorie A. Yocum, Joy Putnam Young and Elliot Zirlin.

Title Page Photo: Alexander *Alice in Wonderland* (see page 14).

Table of Contents

Introduction

The first composition dolls are now 80 years old. They were created to give children a "Can't Break 'Em" beautifully molded doll. The last of the old composition dolls made from wood pulp are now 45 years old. Through this 35-year period, children loved the gentle, lovely dolls which usually did not shatter when dropped.

This first book of a two-part series gives an overview of the dolls from 1928 to about 1955 which was the end of an era of hardship in our history. The inexpensive, less breakable dolls helped people forget the Depression and World War II. The dolls portrayed the brighter side of life, and manufacturers often turned to comics and literature for their inspiration.

Research into the doll manufacturers of the time shows an intertwined trail of large and small manufacturers and marketing companies who were using what was inexpensive and available rather than producing and dressing all their own dolls. Doll artists sometimes made contracts for molds with many companies rather than exclusively for one. Doll clothes designers such as Mollye maintained display rooms and made clothes for anyone who could pay the bills.

Old advertisements in *Playthings* and *Toys and Novelties* show that many small companies started production with a "sure fire seller," invented a new composition, bought a mold from a doll artist, rented a garage and set up business. They advertised for a year or two, and they went quietly out of business.

Mail-order companies such as Sears, Roebuck & Co. and Montgomery Ward bought thousands of inexpensive dolls without any marks and sold them through the mail. Accurate records are non-existent.

It is probably not possible to identify all the dolls of the time period. However, the authors hope that collectors and doll lovers will find many of their favorites shown or discussed in these pages.

Themes such as patriotism, comedy, literature and gentle homemaking can be found among the dolls marketed. The short skirts and skimpy dress patterns of adults found their way into the doll industry. The most common doll dress closing was the little gold safety pin rather than the more expensive snaps. Ribbons, trims and colors helped make these dolls attractive, and a piece of elastic in the back of a hair ribbon helped hold the bandeau on the molded hair so that it did not require expensive wigs. Today many doll collectors are again buying these beloved dolls even though they are slightly crazing, and their clothes are fading to a gentler tone.

The authors hope that if you have additional information or pictures of dolls in original boxes or clothes that will help with new identification, you will communicate with us through our publisher, Hobby House Press, Inc. Many people have shared their treasures through these pages, and we hope you enjoy them.

Care of Composition Dolls

Composition dolls have become very popular in the last few years, and that is wonderful. They need protective care to keep them for future generations of children and adults to see and love.

The dolls which doll collectors refer to as "composition" are a mixture of wood pulp, glue and other ingredients. Each company zealously guarded his "other" ingredients, and each tried to produce the ultimate unbreakable doll. They also made varying grades of composition according to the price that customers were willing to pay.

General rules of care do not always work the same on each grade of composition. Therefore, it is necessary to be very careful when working with the dolls and proceed with caution.

1. Composition dolls should not be subjected to sudden changes in temperature. They should not be stored in hot or cold attics or moist basements.

2. When transporting composition dolls, great care should be taken with the packing.

3. Although some manufacturers in the 1920s and 1930s advertised that their dolls were washable, they should not be washed with water or cleaned with any solution that contains water.

4. The best method for cleaning these dolls safely is the method insisted on by the mothers of the children who played with these dolls. They used Ponds Cold Cream or Vaseline which was available then as it is now.

Caution: Always try out *any* cleaner on the back of the neck or a hidden part of the body. Some paints are more soluble than others, and the authors have found that it is best to keep the cream on for a very short length of time, especially around the eyes and mouth. TEST FIRST!

5. Most of these dolls have some form of preservative over the actual composition, and if any water based product is used, it will seep into the almost invisible crazing and lift it.

6. Thought should precede any extensive renovation of composition dolls because modern wood repair compounds and modern paint are quite different from the original, and it does destroy the historical accuracy.

Shattered eyes and some crazing are to be expected. These dolls are part of the most difficult and depressed part of our century, and it is truly amazing that so many have survived so well.

Special Events and Trends

The study of composition dolls is not complete without an understanding of the trends of the period. Along with the regular lines of Mama, baby, celebrity and character dolls, doll manufacturers of the time reacted to special events and trends.

This book has two special sections of newsworthy events which took place in the early

1930s, the Bicentennial of George Washington's birth, and the first live birth of quintuplets in Canada. The dolls produced to celebrate the births were very special then and even more special today.

Because the *Patsy* look-alikes are hard to identify, there is a special section of these dolls in the Identification Guide.

System Used for Pricing Dolls

The oldest dolls in this book are about 80 years old. The youngest dolls are about 40 years old. This places them in the category usually called "highly collectible," and indeed they are *highly* collectible in today's doll market.

There has always been interest in the composition dolls originally called "Can't Break 'Em."

However, as these dolls aged, they developed the fine lines called "crazing," and about ten years ago interest waned. Many people actually sold their composition dolls because of concern about their deterioration. Collectors purchased hard plastic dolls, and there was a severe drop in prices of composition dolls.

Today interest in these dolls, which were used mostly for playthings rather than for display, has intensified. A doll in excellent-to-mint condition is indeed very hard to find. However, it can still be done, but the price will be high. Prices have increased because many of the doll collectors today played with these dolls as children, and the nostalgia surrounding them is high. New collectors are charmed by the beauty of the dolly faces and delighted by the character faces created during this period.

The prices in this book are given for "played-with dolls" to "excellent" dolls in original clothing. The lack of a mint structure of prices reflects the fact that there are practically no dolls without at least some microscopic crazing. An unplayed-with doll with very little crazing can command a much higher price. Dolls with replaced, but clothes "of the period" should be about 30 percent less than the price of a doll with original clothes in the same condition. Dolls in poor condition, but with original clothing, will be about one-half of the lowest price. Dolls in poor condition and replaced clothing will be about one-third of the lowest price.

A Few Words About Crazing

The dolls in this book are made of woodpulp, glue and "secret" ingredients. They will deteriorate as time goes by. However, bisque and china break, and cloth dolls, with their natural fibers, also deteriorate. A *Queen Anne* doll with no arm recently broke an auction record. Composition dolls have reached the point where signs of crazing are acceptable.

As these dolls age, tiny stress lines around the eyes and mouth are very common. They do not detract from the pricing in this book. Other crazing which does not involve deep lines, lifted paint or destruction of the original look is also acceptable.

The same collectors who sold all their composition dolls ten years ago are trying very hard to replace their lovely dolls today. The prices, of course, are much higher.

How To Use This Book

This book is set up in several ways, depending on your knowledge of your doll. If the doll is marked, or if you know the company name, turn immediately to the doll company section and look up the company name which is in alphabetical order. You will find a list of dolls, their characteristics, dates of production if possible and a current price range. Unless otherwise noted, all dolls have original clothes.

If a doll is unmarked, turn to the Identification Guide Table of Contents (see page 183). There you will find many doll characteristics listed and pages which give specific information. Examples include the numbers and abbreviations on dolls, facial and body characteristics, personality dolls of the period, other companies which made dolls, and many others.

Perhaps the section of "look-alikes" will help if you have seen similar dolls. There is a special section with many pictures of *Patsy* "look-alikes."

At the end of many sections which discuss the major composition doll companies, you will find a list of some of their unphotographed dolls and their descriptions.

The authors realize that all the dolls of the period are not listed in this book. Perhaps they were not made during the years covered in this book. In that case they may appear in Book II of the composition series. We hope you have as much pleasure searching through this book as we have had writing it.

Acme Toy Mfg. Co.

The Acme Toy Mfg. Co., was a well-known company from about 1908 until the 1930s. They made dolls in their own factory and sold parts as well as completed dolls. They advertised that they made quality products without a premium price. The quality of their dolls is still excellent today. The composition seems to age better than some of the other dolls. They used "Acme" to mark many of their dolls. The mark "Toy Shop" has also been attributed to them.

Like their competitors, Acme made many *Mama* and baby dolls. In the beginning years, they used composition heads and cloth bodies.

1914-1915 Unbreakable baby character dolls.
1920 Cork-stuffed dolls to other marketing companies.
1922 Walking, talking *Mama-Papa* dolls.
1925 *Peek-a-Boo* infant with a *Grumpy*-type face with a cloth body and celluloid hands.
1928-1930 + *Honey* Baby doll.
1931 *Marilyn, Lovey, Honey Baby* dolls.
They were also reported to have made at least some of the *Kiddiejoy* line for Hitz, Jacobs and Kassler.
SEE: *Illustration 1. (Playthings*, March 1929.)

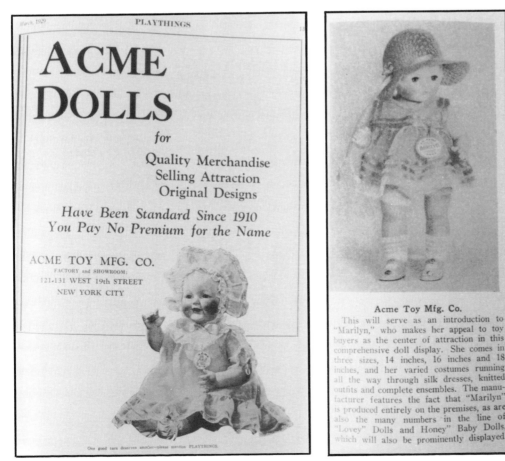

March 1929 **PLAYTHINGS**

ACME DOLLS

for

Quality Merchandise
Selling Attraction
Original Designs

Have Been Standard Since 1910
You Pay No Premium for the Name

ACME TOY MFG. CO.
FACTORY and SHOWROOM:
121-131 WEST 19th STREET
NEW YORK CITY

One good turn deserves another—please mention PLAYTHINGS

Illustration 1.

Acme Toy Mfg. Co.
This will serve as an introduction to "Marilyn," who makes her appeal to toy buyers as the center of attraction in this comprehensive doll display. She comes in three sizes, 14 inches, 16 inches and 18 inches, and her varied costumes running all the way through silk dresses, knitted outfits and complete ensembles. The manufacturer features the fact that "Marilyn" is produced entirely on the premises, as are also the many numbers in the line of "Lovey" Dolls and "Honey" Baby Dolls, which will also be prominently displayed.

Illustration 2.

Marilyn: 14in (36cm); 16in (41cm); 18in (46cm); varied costumes in silk material; knitted outfits; complete ensembles; circa 1931.

Dolls were made on their own premises. The 1931 line included *Lovey* Dolls, *Honey Baby* and *Marilyn*.

For a photograph of *Marilyn*, a *Patsy* look-alike, see Color Section, page 142.

MARKS: "Acme Doll Company" head; "Marilyn" round tag.
SEE: *Illustration 2. (Playthings*, April 1931.)

Alexander Doll Co., Inc.

The first dolls produced by Madame Alexander in the 1920s were cloth dolls. By the mid 1930s, Alexander began dressing and then manufacturing her own composition dolls. The company produced many dolls during a very short period from 1935 through 1948. These dolls are highly collectible today and were made according to very high standards of excellence.

Alexander produced both dolls that used the same face mold over and over to represent many different characters and unique face molds for one specific doll.

There was a large line of many different dolls and characters produced each year during the 1930s. The Alexander company confirmed that they were able to produce a reduced line of dolls during the World War II years.

In 1948 the Alexander Doll Co. began making hard plastic dolls. The *Margaret* face mold was used as a late composition doll and then used as one of the first hard plastic dolls.

Illustration 3.

Small, 7in (18cm) All-Composition Dolls: These very distinctive, small dolls were among the earliest composition dolls that Madame Alexander produced. They have also been referred to as *Tiny Betty* dolls. The dolls have a one-piece body and head with strung arms and legs. The face has painted side-glancing eyes with long, black eyelashes above the eyes. The shoes and socks are molded and painted. These dolls were dressed as characters from fairy tales, nursery rhymes and literature. Others were dressed to represent foreign countries, American life and days of the week. A special group was dressed for each month for the Doll of the Month Club. They were made from 1935 into the early 1940s.
  MARKS: "Mme//Alexander" back.

Fairy Princess: 7in (18cm); for general characteristics, see above; original clothes; circa 1939.
  MARKS: "Mme//Alexander" back; "Fairy Princess" dress tag.
  SEE: *Illustration 4.* (Color Section, page 33.)

Mistress Mary: 7in (18cm); nursery rhyme character; yellow organdy dress, blue flowered apron, blue felt hat, yellow bow; blonde mohair wig; white painted socks; black painted shoes; lamb may have been added later; for general characteristics, see above; circa 1937.
  MARKS: "Mme//Alexander" back; "Madame Alexander" dress tag.
  SEE: *Illustration 3.*

David Copperfield: 7in (18cm); part of the Charles Dickens series; for general characteristics, see above; blonde mohair wig; clothes original circa 1935.
  MARKS: "Mme//Alexander" back; "Charles Dickens//David Copperfield" suit tag.
  SEE: *Illustration 5.* (Color Section, page 34.)

Little Women: 7in (18cm); characters were made for several years, TOP — *Amy* and *Beth; Amy's* dress is blue and white; *Beth's* dress is pink striped; BOTTOM — *Meg* and *Jo; Meg's* dress is red gingham; *Jo's* dress is red calico with a blue border; circa 1937.

    MARKS: "Mme//Alexander" back; "Little Women" dress tags; all dress tags, except *Jo,* also have the name of the doll.

    SEE: *Illustration 6. Barbara Comienski Collection.*

Baking on Saturday: 7in (18cm); part of the *Days of the Week* Series; for general characteristics, see page 8; original clothes; pink and white striped cotton dress; white organdy apron and hat; circa 1936.

    MARKS: "Mme//Alexander" back.

    SEE: *Illustration 7. Helen Krielow Collection.*

Illustration 6.

Illustration 7.

9in (23cm) Composition Doll: all-composition; long, slender body; jointed at neck, arms and legs; painted eyes; painted long black eyelashes; all fingers molded together and slightly curved. This doll was widely used and dressed in foreign costumes, American costumes and as characters from fairy tales, nursery rhymes, *Little Women* and *Days of the Week.* This doll was also dressed as a little girl named *Wendy Ann;* circa 1936 through the early 1940s.

    MARKS: "Mme. Alexander//New York," "Mme.Alexander" or "Wendy Ann" back.

McGuffey Ana: 9in (23cm); painted brown side-glancing eyes; blonde hair in braids tied with blue ribbon; original clothes; circa 1937.

    MARKS: "Mme.Alexander//New York" back; "McGuffey Ana//Madame Alexander N.Y. U.S.A.//Reg. No. 350,781" dress tag.

    SEE: *Illustration 8.* (Color Section, page 33.)
            Illustration 9. (Close-up of face.)

Illustration 9.

Egypt: 9in (23cm); all-composition; for general characteristics, see page 8; part of the foreign series; unusual dark skin tone to match the nationality; white cotton dress and veil; gold sequin belt; leatherette sandals; red Alexander box with a blue and white sticker label; circa 1936.

    MARKS: "Mme Alexander//New York" back; "Egypt" dress tag; "Created by Madame Alexander New York" gold wrist tag.

    SEE: *Illustration 10* and (Color Section, page 34.) *Penni and Ruth Lewis Collection.*

Illustration 10.

Betty Doll: In 1935, Alexander marketed an all-composition doll called *Betty*. The Alexander company probably purchased these dolls and then dressed them. Also in 1935, Alexander introduced one of their own dolls called *Little Betty* which was also all-composition and 13in (33cm). This doll was used for other characters that included the *Little Colonel* dolls, *Princess Elizabeth*, *Doris Keane* and the *Quintuplet Nurse.* One outstanding feature of the early doll is the dimple on each cheek. When referring to this doll, many people call it just the *Betty* doll.

Betty: 13in (33cm); all-composition; jointed at neck, arms and legs; blue tin eyes with lashes; black eyelashes also painted above the eyes; a blonde wig is glued over molded hair; tiny rosebud closed mouth; second and third fingers molded together; curved right arm; very long slender legs; chubby stomach; original clothes; early composition doll believed to have been purchased and dressed by Alexander; 1935.

    MARKS: None; "Betty//Madame Alexander//New York" dress tag.

    SEE: *Illustration 11.* (Color Section, page 34.)

Little Betty Advertisement: In the April 1935 issue of *Playthings* magazine, Madame Alexander introduced "*Little Betty*," a 13in (33cm) all-composition doll. The advertisement also stated, "She is one of the latest creations of Madame Alexander and typifies this company's determination to be known as headquarters for 'What the well-dressed doll will wear.'" Many exquisite outfits were made for this doll.

    SEE: *Illustration 12. Playthings*, April 1935.

Alexander Doll Co.

This winsome little miss goes by the euphonious title, "Little Betty." She is 13 inches high and is quite proud of her most-up-to-date and exquisite costumes. She is one of the latest creations of Madame Alexander and typifies this company's determination to be known as headquarters for "What the well-dressed doll will wear."

Illustration 12.

Betty and Little Betty: Comparison of two early 13in (33cm) all-composition dolls. The left doll's dress was tagged "Betty." This doll face was only used for this early *Betty* doll. The doll and doll face on the right was used for the *Little Betty* dolls, *Little Colonel* dolls and an early *Princess Elizabeth* doll. The doll on the right is often referred to as the *Betty* doll or *Little Betty* doll.
SEE: *Illustration 13.*

Illustration 13.

Illustration 15.

Little Colonel: 16in (41cm); all-composition; jointed at neck, arms and legs; open mouth; brown sleep eyes; blonde mohair wig in curls; jacket is white piqué with blue velvet trim, blue collar and white trim; white and blue velvet hat; blue velvet pants (may not be original); dress tag includes a picture trademark and reads, "Little Colonel//Alexander Doll Co.//New York;" 1935.
MARKS: "Princess Elizabeth" head.
SEE: *Illustration 16. Ramona Beard Collection.*

Princess Elizabeth: 13in (33cm); all-composition; jointed at neck, arms and legs; *Betty*-face mold; blonde mohair wig; sleep eyes with lashes, painted black eyelashes under eye; long slender legs; doll could be purchased with a wardrobe. The coat outfit she is wearing and the white satin dress are original and tagged "Princess Elizabeth;" her crown is missing; the dress on the right appears to be a *Jane Withers* costume; two outfits on top are not tagged and may be hand-sewn; 1937.
MARKS: None.
SEE: *Illustration 14.* (Color Section, page 35.)

Little Colonel Dolls: In 1935, Madame Alexander announced the creation of the *Little Colonel* dolls. She secured the rights to create dolls based on Ann Fellows Johnston's books about a "vivacious Kentucky-bred child" living during the Civil War. The dolls were made in different sizes with beautiful outfits. The smaller size, 13in (33cm) used the *Betty*-face with the dimples. The *Little Colonel* pictured in the advertisement was the registered trademark.
SEE: *Illustration 15. Playthings*, March 1935.

Illustration 16.

Princess Elizabeth: Madame Alexander created a special doll and face in 1937 to represent the little princess at the coronation of her father, King George VI. Later, the same doll mold was used for other types of dolls but was still marked: "*Princess Elizabeth.*" The doll was all-composition and came in sizes ranging from 13in (33cm) through 27in (69cm). The doll had sleep eyes and an open mouth, but a closed mouth can be found in the smaller sizes. Besides *Princess Elizabeth*, the most common other doll was *McGuffey Ana.* Other dolls that used the *Princess Elizabeth*-face were *Snow White* (closed mouth), *Kate Greenaway, Flora McFlimsey* and *Sleeping Beauty.*

Illustration 18.

Illustration 19.

Princess Elizabeth: 13in (33cm); all-composition; jointed at neck, arms and legs; open mouth with two teeth; blue sleep eyes; human hair wig; original clothes; pink socks; silver shoes; circa 1937.
  MARKS: "Princess Elizabeth//Alexander Doll Co." head; "Princess Elizabeth" dress tag.
  SEE: *Illustration 17*. (Color Section, page 35.) *Marianne Gardner Collection.*

Princess Elizabeth: 14in (36cm); all-composition; closed mouth; sleep eyes; blonde mohair wig; print taffeta dress trimmed with black velvet ribbon, white lace collar; black velvet ribbon coronet; pantalets hooked to slip; dress tagged "Madame Alexander;" 1935.
  MARKS: None.
  SEE: *Illustration 18. Marianne Gardner Collection.*

Princess Elizabeth: 19in (48cm); all-composition; jointed neck, arms and legs; blue sleep eyes; open mouth; pink taffeta dress, white organdy sleeves and collar; silver shoes; jeweled crown; circa 1938.
  MARKS: "Princess Elizabeth//Alexander Doll Co." head; "Princess Elizabeth" dress tag.
  SEE: *Illustration 19. Ramona Beard Collection.*

Snow White: 13in (33cm); all-composition; jointed at neck, arms and legs; *Princess Elizabeth*-face mold; brown sleep eyes; black eyelashes under and to the side of the eyes; black wig; original clothes; black leather shoes with turned-up toes and pink bows; closed mouth; 1938.

Dopey: 11in (28cm); composition head; cloth body; painted blue side-glancing eyes with black eyelashes above the eye; painted red lips with a pink molded tongue; original clothes; 1938.

> **MARKS:** Snow White — unmarked; "Snow White" dress tag; Dopey — "Dopey//Madame Alexander//Orig. Walt Disney" back.
> **SEE:** *Illustration 20.* (Color Section, page 35.)

Illustration 21.

Illustration 22.

McGuffey Ana: Advertisement in *Playthings*, October 1939, presenting a very fancy dressed *McGuffey Ana*. This doll used the *Princess Elizabeth*-face mold.
> **SEE:** *Illustration 21. Playthings,* October 1939.

McGuffey Ana: 15in (38cm); all-composition; jointed at neck, arms and legs; open mouth four teeth; brown sleep eyes with lashes; blonde braided hair with red ribbons; red plaid dress, white pinafore, straw hat; original clothes; uses *Princess Elizabeth*-face mold; circa 1938.

> **MARKS:** "Princess Elizabeth//Alexander Doll Co." back; "McGuffey Ana" dress tag.
> **SEE:** *Illustration 22. Athena Crowley Collection.*

McGuffey Ana: 13in (33cm); all-composition; jointed at neck, arms and legs; open mouth with two teeth; human hair wig; *Princess Elizabeth*-face mold; original clothes; no hat on this size doll; unusual dress; circa 1937.

> **MARKS:** "Princess Elizabeth//Alexander" back.
> **SEE:** *Illustration 23.* (Color Section, page 36.) *Marianne Gardner Collection.*

Illustration 24.

Wendy Ann Doll: The *Wendy Ann* doll and face mold was used for many dolls that stretched from 1936 through 1947. These were all-composition dolls ranging in size from 11in (28cm) through 21in (53cm). The doll was dressed as a little girl, named Wendy Ann, in honor of Madame Alexander's granddaughter. There is also a 9in (23cm) composition doll named and marked on the back "Wendy Ann." In addition to the *Wendy Ann* character, this face mold and doll were also used for *Scarlett, Fairy Queen, Fairy Princess, Brides, Bridesmaids, Madelaine de Baines, Carmen,* World War II Armed Forces, *Miss America, Alice-in-Wonderland, Mother and Me, Juliet, Sleeping Beauty* and the special 1945-1946 Portrait Series.

Wendy Ann: 11in (28cm); all-composition; jointed at neck, arms and legs; uses *Wendy Ann*-face mold; tin sleep eyes; human hair brown wig; original clothes; pink skirt and white blouse; pink bow in hair; circa 1938.
    MARKS: None on doll; "Wendy Ann" dress tag.
    SEE: *Illustration 24. Marianne Gardner Collection.*

Wendy Ann: 15in (38cm); all-composition; swivel waist; jointed at neck, arms and legs; brown sleep eyes; black eyelashes painted under the eyes; blonde human hair wig; uses *Wendy Ann*-face mold; closed mouth; hat not original; circa 1939.
    MARKS: "Wendy Ann//Mme. Alexander" back; "Wendy Ann" dress tag.
    SEE: *Illustration 25.* (Color Section, page 37.) *Marilyn Dawe Collection.*

Alice-in-Wonderland: 14in (36cm); *Wendy Ann*-face mold; all-composition; jointed at neck, shoulders, hips and waist; sleep eyes; human hair wig; all original clothes; blue and white print dress; organdy trim on dress; white organdy apron; late 1930s.
    MARKS: "Wendy Ann//Mme. Alexander//N.Y.;" "Alice in Wonderland" dress tag.
    SEE: Illustration on Title Page.

Carmen: 11in (28cm); all-composition; jointed at arms, neck and legs; sleep eyes; black wig; *Wendy Ann*-face mold; all original; dark green velvet skirt trimmed with yellow rickrack and a white ruffle, white apron, pink satin top with colorful braid and rickrack trim; dark green turban with flowers and fruit; gold earrings; circa 1942.
    MARKS: "Carmen" dress tag.
    SEE: *Illustration 26. Ramona Beard Collection.*

Illustration 26.

14

Southern Girl: 11in (28cm); all-composition; jointed at neck, arms and legs; original clothes; *Wendy Ann*-face mold; circa 1941.
MARKS: "Alexander" head.
SEE: *Illustration 27.* (Color Section, page 38.) *Lois Janner Collection.*

Fairy Queen: 14in (36cm); all-composition; jointed at neck, arms and legs; closed mouth; sleep eyes; reddish mohair wig; original clothes; *Wendy Ann*-face mold; 1942.
MARKS: "Alexander" head; "Fairy Queen" dress tag.
SEE: *Illustration 28.* (Color Section, page 40.) *Ramona Beard Collection.*

Scarlett O'Hara: for description of doll, see *Illustration 30*; original clothes; green bodice trimmed with white lace; red floral print skirt, straw hat; 1937.
MARKS: None
SEE: *Illustration 32. Barbara Comienski Collection.*

Madeleine de Baine: 18in (46cm); all-composition; jointed at neck, arms and legs; uses *Wendy Ann* face mold; brown sleep eyes with lashes; painted black eyelashes under eye; long blonde wig with curls; original clothes; circa 1938.
MARKS: "Alexander" head; "Madeleine de Baine" tag on dress.
SEE: *Illustration 29.* (Color Section, page 38.) *Ramona Beard Collection.*

Scarlett O'Hara: 11in (28cm); all-composition; jointed at neck, arms and legs; uses *Wendy Ann*-face mold; green sleep eyes; painted black eyelashes under the eyes; black wig; second and third fingers molded together; both have hoop skirt and white pantalets; 1937.
MARKS: None on dolls; "Scarlett O'Hara" dress tags on both; RIGHT — "Madame Alexander's Scarlett O'Hara" with picture of Scarlett and Tara on wrist tag.
SEE: *Illustration 30.* (Color Section, page 36.)
Illustration 31. (Color Section, page 36 for close-up view.)

Illustration 32.

Scarlett: 14in (36cm); all-composition; black wig; green sleep eyes; red taffeta coat and matching hat; *Wendy Ann*-face; featured in the 1941 John Plain catalog.
    SEE: *Illustration 33. Caroline Florence Collection.*

Miss America: 14in (36cm); all-composition; jointed at neck, arms and legs; *Wendy Ann*-face mold; blonde mohair wig with long curls; one hand is molded in a fist with a small opening in which to place the flag; brown sleep eyes; original clothes; special World War II doll; circa 1944.
    MARKS: "Mme. Alexander" head; "Miss America" dress tag; "An Alexander Product" gold wrist tag.
    SEE: *Illustration 34.* (Color Section, page 36.) *Lois Janner Collection.*

W.A.V.E.: 14in (36cm); all-composition; jointed at neck, arms and legs; blue sleep eyes; black painted eyelashes under the eyes; blonde mohair wig; original clothes; *Wendy Ann*-face mold; 1942.
    MARKS: "Mme Alexander" head.
    SEE: *Illustration 35.* (Colored Section, page 37.) *Marianne Gardner Collection.*

Illustration 33.

Illustration 36.

Wendy: 18in (46cm); all-composition; all original; blonde mohair curled wig; dark pink taffeta skirt and bodice with pink floral pattern; white organdy sheer overbodice; black waist ribbon; pink straw garden-style hat trimmed with flowers; original purchase price at Taylor's in Cleveland, Ohio, $14.95; 1947.

    MARKS: "Mme Alexander" head; "Madame//Alexander//New York U.S.A." dress tag.
    SEE: *Illustration 36. Joan A. Tosko Collection.*

Sears 1946 Catalog, Alexander Doll Grouping: Left to right: Bridesmaid (*Wendy Ann*-face), *Bride* (*Wendy Ann*-face), Margaret O'Brien (*Margaret*-face).
    SEE: *Illustration 37.* (Color Section, page 39.)

Illustration 38.

Margaret: Margaret O'Brien was another very popular child star from whom Madame Alexander secured the doll copyrights. The *Margaret O'Brien* doll came in three sizes: 14in (36cm), 18in (46cm) and 21in (53cm). The doll and face were also used for other dolls including *Alice in Wonderland, Hilda* (a black composition doll), *Karen Ballerina, Margaret Rose* and *Hulda.* The *Margaret* doll mold continued to be used when Madame Alexander switched from composition to hard plastic in 1948. The composition *Margaret O'Brien* doll was introduced in 1946.

Margaret O'Brien: 18in (46cm); all-composition; brown braided hair looped and tied with blue ribbons; original clothes; pink and white gingham dress with white and blue braid; matching straw hat; 1947.
    SEE: *Illustration 38. Mary F. Poole Collection.*

Margaret O'Brien: 14in (36cm); all-composition; jointed at neck, arms and legs; brown sleep eyes with lashes and eye shadow; black painted lashes under eyes; brown braid wig; blue corduroy coat and hat; all original; 1947. The original store tag is stapled to the hem of the coat.
    MARKS: "Alexander" neck; "Margaret O'Brien" clover leaf wrist tag.
    SEE: *Illustration 39.* (Color Section, page 38.) *Joan A. Tosko.*

Alice in Wonderland: 14in (36cm); all-composition; *Margaret* mold; for general characteristics, see page 39; 1947.
    MARKS: "Alice in Wonderland//" dress tag.
    SEE: *Illustration 40.* (Color Section, page 39.) *Joan A. Tosko.*

Montgomery Ward's 1946 Catalog, Alexander Doll Grouping: TOP (left to right): *Princess Margaret Rose (Margaret*-face), *Hulda (Margaret).* BOTTOM (left to right): *Karen Ballerina (Margaret), Sleeping Beauty (Wendy Ann)*

   SEE: *Illustration 41.* (Color Section, page 39.)

Dionne Quintuplet Dolls: Within a year of the Dionne Quintuplet's birth, Madame Alexander had acquired permission to make sets of *Dionne Quintuplet* dolls. The event was recorded in *Playthings* magazine with a stern warning to competitors not to sell dolls in sets of five with a similar name and appearance to their own set (see *Illustrations 319* to *324* in the special Quintuplet Section for more pictures of Alexander and other Quintuplet dolls.)

   SEE: *Illustration 42. Playthings,* April 1935.
   Illustration 43. Playthings, July 1935.

For more information see the Quintuplet Section pages 169-170.

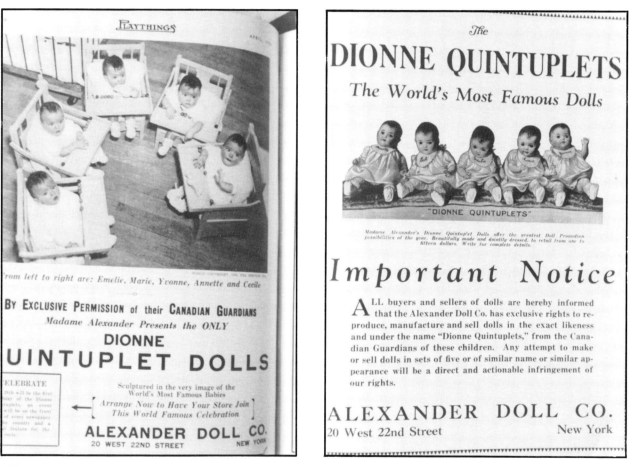

Illustration 42.   *Illustration 43.*

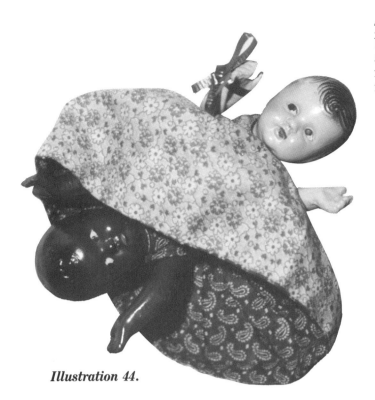

Illustration 44.

Topsy Turvy: 7in (18cm); all-composition; two upper bodies with head and strung arms; one side is white and the other side is black; painted eyes; simple cotton reversible dress; red gingham on one side, blue and red gingham on the other; molded hair; circa 1937.
 MARKS: None
 SEE: *Illustration 44. Cindy Rutherford Collection.*

Snow White Marionette: 12in (31cm); composition head, arms and legs; cloth body; painted brown eyes; molded black painted hair with blue painted bow; original clothes; pink satin dress, blue velvet bodice and cape; 1938.
Alexander made many other Tony Sarg marionettes.
 MARKS: "Tony Sarg//Alexander" back.
 SEE: *Illustration 47. Ramona Beard Collection.*

Illustration 45.

Jane Withers: Jane Withers was a very popular child star of the 1930s. By 1937 Madame Alexander had the rights to produce the *Jane Withers* doll. Two types of face molds were made for the composition doll. One had a closed mouth and the other had an open mouth. A gold name pin came with the dolls. She was dressed in different outfits. She was made in a variety of sizes from 13in (33cm) through 20in (51cm); 1937.
 SEE: *Illustration 45.* Madame Alexander and *Jane Withers* doll, *Toys and Bicycles*, February 1937.
 Illustration 46. (Color Section, page 40.) 13in (33cm); closed mouth. *Diane Hoffman Collection.*

Illustration 47.

19

Sonja Henie: Sonja Henie, from Norway, was one of the best known celebrities during the 1920s and 1930s. She was a world-famous ice skater and Olympic gold medal winner. In the 1930s, Sonja Henie became a professional ice skater and Hollywood movie star. Madame Alexander received the rights to market *Sonja Henie* dolls in 1939 and continued into the early 1940s. A special *Sonja* face was created. The doll came in a variety of skating costumes and other clothes. Gift sets that included *Sonja Henie* and a wardrobe were also sold.

Sonja Henie: This advertisement was taken from *Playthings*, November 1939. Both ice-skating outfits and ski outfits were featured. *Sonja Henie* dolls came in three sizes: 14in (36cm), 18in (46cm) and 21in (53cm).
   SEE: *Illustration 48. Playthings*, November 1939.

Sonja Henie: 18in (46cm); composition; original ice-skating outfit; blonde wig in ringlets; navy blue skirt, white blouse, braid bodice; unique red ice skates made only for the *Sonja Henie* dolls; 1939.
   SEE: *Illustration 50.* (Color Section, page 40.) *Diane Hoffman Collection.*

Sonja Henie: 18in (46cm); all-composition; jointed at neck, arms and legs; special face mold; open mouth with six teeth; brown sleep eyes with lashes; black painted lashes under the eyes; feathered light brown eyebrows; large hands with second and third fingers molded together; dimples on each cheek; blonde mohair wig with ringlet curls; dressed as a skier; blue corduroy trimmed with white fur, red corduroy jacket, white jersey scarf, matching blue pants; came with skis and ski poles; 1939.
   MARKS: None; "Sonja Henie" tag on jacket.
   SEE: *Illustration 49.* (Color Section, page 37.)

Jeannie Walker: 14in (36cm); all-composition; jointed at neck, arms and legs; by holding *Jeannie Walker's* hand, she was able to walk; unusual pin mechanism that goes through her legs; brown sleep eyes; brown wig with curls; red checked dress with white organdy trim and collar; 1942.
   MARKS: "Alexander//Pat.No.2171281" back.
   SEE: *Illustration 51.* (Color Section, page 41.) *Athena Crowley Collection.*

Illustration 48.

Illustration 52.

Special Girl Doll: 22in (56cm); composition head and limbs; cloth body; sleep eyes with lashes; brown braided wig; curved arms and straight legs; pink taffeta dress, black vest; 1943.
  MARKS: None; "Madame Alexander" dress tag.
  SEE: *Illustration 54. Vivien Brady-Ashley Collection.*

Illustration 53.

Jeannie Walker Comparison: 13in (33cm) and 18in (46cm) sizes were the only two available; all-composition; SMALL DOLL (left): slender body and legs; original white tagged outfit; brown wig; LARGE DOLL (right): white dress; chubby size legs; both have pin mechanism for walking; 1942.
  MARKS: RIGHT — "Alexander Doll Co." back; "Jeannie Walker" dress tag;
    LEFT — "Alexander//Pat.No. 2171281" back.
  SEE: *Illustration 52. Ramona Beard Collection.*

Illustration 54.

Mother and Me: 11in (28cm). This was a pair of dolls dressed alike to represent a mother and child. The doll pictured is the child. The mother was a larger size doll using the *Wendy Ann*-face mold; all-composition; sleep eyes; closed mouth; brown mohair wig; navy pleated skirt, red blouse, white collar, matching blue hat; 1942.
  MARKS: "Alexander" head; "Mother and Me" dress tag.
  SEE: *Illustration 53. Ramona Beard Collection.*

21

Little Genius: Composition head and limbs; cloth body; advertisement from *Playthings*, September 1939.

    SEE: *Illustration 55. Playthings, September 1939.*

Baby Genius: 25in (64cm); composition head and limbs; cloth body; closed mouth; blue sleep eyes; brown wig; head inset in cloth body; yellow marquisette dress trimmed with white lace; white bonnet; late 1930s.

    MARKS: "Alexander" head; "Baby Genius" dress tag.

    SEE: *Illustration 56. Mary Jane Poley Collection.*

Baby McGuffey: 20in (51cm); composition head and limbs; cloth body; mohair wig over molded hair; closed mouth; sleep eyes with eyeshadow; red floral dress, white pinafore trimmed with red and white cross-stitch braid; crier in body; circa 1938.

    MARKS: "Madame Alexander" head.

    SEE: *Illustration 57. Sonia Notaro Collection.*

Illustration 55.

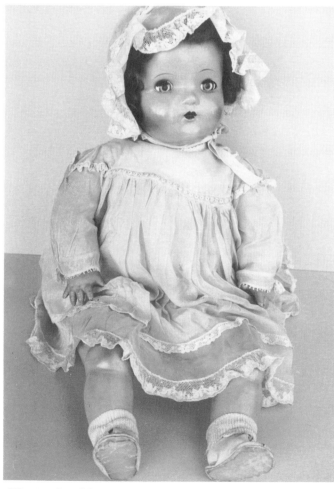

Illustration 56.

Illustration 57.

Pinky: 18in (46cm); composition head and limbs; bent legs; sleep eyes; molded/painted hair; white dress trimmed with white braid, white bonnet, pink ribbons and bows; circa late 1930s.
  MARKS: "Pinky" dress tag.
  SEE: *Illustration 58. Linda Mangold Collection.*

Precious: 12in (31cm); composition; molded/painted hair; blue sleep eyes; closed mouth; dimples on knees and elbow; chubby toddler; white dress and matching bonnet trimmed with white lace; 1940s.
  MARKS: "Alexander" head; "Precious" dress tag.
  SEE: *Illustration 59. Vivien Brady-Ashley Collection.*

Bitsey (doll on left): 11in (28cm) composition head, wrists, hands, legs and feet; cloth body and arms; same molded hair as *Butch* under the wig, but not colored the same; thin eyebrows, real eyelashes; sleep eyes; closed mouth; white sleeveless underdress under a long-sleeved sheer dress; one-piece slip, panties; circa 1940s.
  MARKS: "Mme Alexander" head; "Bitsey//all rights reserved" paper wrist tag side 1; "A Madame Alexander Doll" paper wrist tag side 2.
  SEE: *Illustration 60.* (Color Section, page 41.) *Jeri L. Traw Collection.*

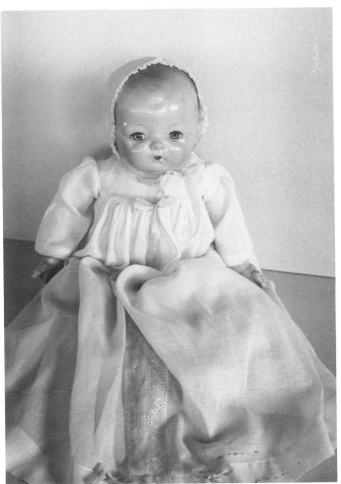

Illustration 58.

Butch (doll on right): 11in (28cm); composition head, wrists, hands, legs and feet; cloth body and arms; painted, molded hair; thick pointed eyebrows; sleep eyes; closed mouth; one-piece romper suit; circa 1940s.
  MARKS: "Mme Alexander" head; "Butch//all rights reserved" paper wrist tag side 1; "A Madame Alexander Doll" paper wrist tag side 2.
  SEE: *Illustration 60.* (Color Section, page 41.) *Jeri L. Traw Collection.*

Illustration 59.

23

Illustration 61.

Portrait Group: After the close of World War II, Madame Alexander created a very special group of composition dolls that have been given the collective name, "Portraits." These beautiful, all-composition, 21in (53cm) *Wendy Ann* dolls were made from 1945-1946. This group of dolls had their beginnings in 1938 with a series of 21in (53cm) *Wendy Ann* Portrait dolls. Some of the 1938 dolls, including *Flavia*, were repeated in the later 1940s series. Each doll in the 1940s series was exquisitely dressed to match its character. Great care was given to the costumes, fabrics, trims, accessories and wigs. Facial features such as fancy eyebrows, long black side eyelashes, beauty marks, lips and eyes were carefully painted. Special attention was given to the eyes. Eye liner, eyelids and eye shadow colors were chosen to blend with the color of the sleep eyes and character of the doll. The price of these dolls was $75 which was very expensive in 1945. The dolls were tagged, but the tags were often hidden in the underwear.

In this section there are seven of the 1945 Portraits pictured; they are *Carmen, Flavia, Ballerina, Lady Windermere, Melaine, Orchard Princess* and *Antoinette.*

    SEE: *Illustration 61.* Close-up of *Antoinette's* face. (*Joan A. Tosko.*)

Carmen: 21in (53cm); all-composition; Portrait series of 1945; *Wendy Ann*-face; Carmen was the tragic figure in Bizet's opera "Carmen"; elaborate Spanish dress trimmed with black lace and red roses; black lace mantilla; gold hoop earrings; unusual black eyebrows; bright red lips and fingernails; star-shaped beauty mark on left cheek; turquoise eyelids and eye liner; brown sleep eyes.

    MARKS: None; "Madame Alexander//New York// U.S.A." tag on underwear.
    SEE: *Illustration 62.* (Color Section, page 41.) *Diane Hoffman Collection.*

Ballerina (Degas): 21in (53cm); all-composition; Portrait series of 1945; *Wendy Ann*-face; reddish mohair wig pulled back in braids coiled in back of head; pink lips and nail polish; lavender eyelids; white net tutu with satin bodice; rose headdress and rose clusters on dress.

    MARKS: None; "Madame Alexander//New York// U.S.A." tag on underwear.
    SEE: *Illustration 63.* (Color Section, page 42.) *Diane Hoffman Collection.*

Flavia: 21in (53cm); all-composition; Portrait series of 1945; *Wendy Ann*-face; Flavia or Princess Flavia was a character from the movie *Prisoner of Zenda*; blonde braided wig wrapped on top of head and over each ear; blue eyes, eyelids, eye liner and eye shadow; red lips; gold braid jeweled crown; patterned satin gown with train; sash gathered with blue jewel; white collar of tatting and sequins; pearl and jeweled earrings.

    MARKS: None; "Madame Alexander//New York// U.S.A." tag on underwear.
    SEE: *Illustration 64.* (Color Section, page 44.) *Diane Hoffman Collection.*

Lady Windermere: 21in (53cm); all-composition; Portrait series of 1945; *Wendy Ann*-face; from the movie *Lady Windermere's Fan*; red wig with curls piled on top of head with three back long curls; turquoise eyelids and eye liner; dark pink lips; taffeta gown with bustle; straw hat trimmed with pink flowers.

    MARKS: None; "Madame Alexander//New York// U.S.A." tag on underwear.
    SEE: *Illustration 65* — front. (Color Section, page 44.) *Diane Hoffman Collection.*
          Illustration 66 — back. (Color Section, page 44.) *Diane Hoffman Collection.*

Melaine: 21in (53cm); all-composition; Portrait series of 1945; *Wendy Ann*-face; brown mohair wig arranged in curls; brown eyelids, eye liner and eyelashes; red lips; white cotton dress with pleated ruffles and lace, sash of embroidered flowers; straw bonnet trimmed with flowers; green velvet hat ribbon; floral bouquet matches flowers in hat; dress tied to wrist by a white ribbon.

    MARKS: None; "Madame Alexander//New York// U.S.A." tag on underwear.
    SEE: *Illustration 67.* (Color Section, page 42.) *Diane Hoffman Collection.*

Orchard Princess: 21in (53cm); all-composition; Portrait series of 1945; *Wendy Ann*-face; blonde mohair wig upswept into curls on top of head; blue-green eye liner, eyelids and eye shadow; brocade gown with long train; dark sash trimmed with flowers; beads interwoven with sash at shoulder; butterfly sleeves.

   MARKS: None; "Madame Alexander//New York// U.S.A." tag on underwear.

   SEE: *Illustration 68* — front. (Color Section, page 43.) *Diane Hoffman Collection.*
      Illustration 69 — back. (Color Section, page 43.) *Diane Hoffman Collection.*

Antoinette (Marie Antoinette): 21in (53cm); all-composition; Portrait series of 1945; *Wendy Ann*-face; elaborate white wig styled in a series of upswept curls in imitation of 18th century France; hair trimmed with satin flowers, paper flower pedals and gold metallic braid; blue taffeta dress with gold rickrack; flowers and braid match those in hair; ruffled lace on sleeve; underskirt of pink cotton trimmed with gathered lace; sequins on dress; star and circle beauty marks; turquoise eye liner and eyelid; brown eye shadow; diamond earrings; star-shaped ring.

   MARKS: None; "Madame Alexander//New York// U.S.A." tag on underwear.

   SEE: *Illustration 70.* (Color Section, page 44.) *Joan A. Tosko Collection.*

The registered trademarks, the trademarks and copyrights appearing in italics//bold within this chapter belong to Allied-Grand Manufacturing Inc.

Allied-Grand Doll Manufacturing Inc.

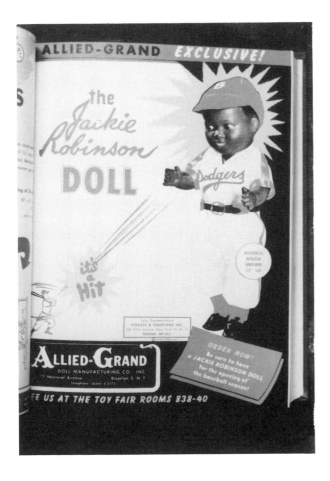

The Allied-Grand Manufacturing Co. made a popular line of inexpensive dolls. They were well-known for their black dolls. One of the most popular was *Jackie Robinson* made in 1950. They were still making composition dolls when most of the other companies had started to make hard plastic dolls.

Jackie Robinson: 19½in (50cm); five-piece all-composition body; molded, painted hair; black side-glancing eyes; open/closed mouth with teeth; wearing Dodgers' uniform; also made in other sizes.

   MARKS "Allied Grand Doll Mfg. Co. Inc//Brooklyn 5 N.Y." paper tag shaped like catcher's mitt.

   SEE: *Illustration 71. Playthings,* March 1950.

Illustration 71.

Amberg, Louis, & Son

The Amberg company was a maker of excellent composition and other dolls. In 1929 they made a line called "It" dolls. These dolls have now become very collectible. In 1930 this line and other composition lines were sold to the E.I. Horsman Company. They were advertised under the Horsman name and manufactured in the Horsman factory. Some of the dolls were renamed which is causing confusion for some collectors today. Horsman eventually marketed their own body twist doll (see pages).

The Amfelt line was sold to the Paul Cohen Company and continued to be sold by them and other marketing companies such as George Borgfelt.

Illustration 72.

"It" Dolls: The center doll (*Sue*) in *Illustration* has the same hair style as the Horsman *Peggy* (see page 129, Illustration 236). *Sue*, a body twist doll, has the same molded hair mold. *Peggy* does not have the twist body. *Sue* was made in 1929 just before the company was sold to Horsman in 1930.

Amfelt Art Dolls: Came in various sizes and styles. They were jointed at the neck, shoulders and hips. The bodies were cloth and the heads came in various materials including composition, European papier-mâché and cloth; their clothes were designed by European artists, and they competed with Lenci dolls.

These dolls were advertised in many catalogs such as Sears, Roebuck and Co. They were inexpensive (usually from 25 cents to $5.00).

Teenies Weenies: All-composition; jointed at neck, shoulders, high waist and hips; molded hair in several styles; 1929.

The illustration shows that there were at least three different types of molded hair on the "It" dolls. *Sue* in the center on the left side has a side part; *Peter Pan* on the right has a wind-swept style with slight bangs. The doll on the left has heavier bangs. The *Little Amby* 8in (20cm) dolls have molded hair. They include a boy's style on the left; a style with a bow in the center; and the third style with a center part on the right.

MARKS "Amberg//Pat.Pend//L.A.S. RCP 1928" body.

SEE: *Illustration 72. Playthings*, April 1929.

Amfelt Art Doll: 17in (43cm); inexpensive composition head that does not easily craze; painted eyes with medium blue eye shadow; brown eyebrows; black straight lines representing eyelashes on outer edges of eyes; dimple on chin; blonde mohair wig; cloth body jointed at neck, shoulders and legs with metal disks; mitt hands; unusual pointed knees; felt dress and matching hat; circa 1928.

UNUSUAL IDENTIFICATION FEATURE: Pompon on toe of shoe (see Identification Guide, page 199, Illustration 395).

MARKS "M//y" on neck; "Head Washable//Amfelt Art Dolls//Trade Mark Reg.//L.A.&S. 1928" paper wrist tag.

SEE: *Illustration 73.* (Color Section, page 83.)

Amfelt Art Doll: 14in (36cm); light papier-mâché type composition head; large painted eyes with medium blue eye shadow; brown eyebrows; black straight lines representing eyelashes on outer edges of eyes; dark mohair wig with bangs; cloth body jointed at neck, shoulders and legs with metal disks; mitt hands; unusual pointed knees; felt dress with appliqued felt flowers; matching bonnet; black shoes with white stitching trim and unusual pompon decoration (see Identification Guide, page 199); circa 1928. Inexpensive but well made.

UNUSUAL IDENTIFICATION FEATURE: Pompon on shoe; artistic facial paint.

MARKS None on doll.

SEE: *Illustration 73.* (Color Section, page 83.)

American Character Doll Company, Inc.

About 1919, the American Character Doll Company sold their first dolls. From the beginning, they were high quality dolls. They made the traditional *Mama* dolls, baby dolls and novelty dolls.

When *Patsy* was introduced, they followed the trend and made a similar doll. They used their own trademarked names *Sally* and *Petite* for this line. They advertised *Sally* widely, and collectors have found that she is one of the nicest *Patsy* look-alikes.

They are known to have purchased some dolls in their line from Ideal. Most of their dolls are marked, but some are not.

Campbell Kids and Puggy: The 1929-1930 line of the American Character Doll Company included the smiling *Campbell Kids*, chubby *Puggy* and other lifelike babies and feminine members of the Petite doll family.
SEE: *Illustration 74. Playthings,* December 1929.

Illustration 76.

Campbell Kid Dolls: 12½in (32cm); all-composition; painted eyes; jointed at neck, shoulders and hips; molded hair with curl in middle of forehead (different from Horsman early *Campbell Kids;* various costumes modeled after cartoon characters in Campbell Soup advertisements; doll has left hand molded into fists, and the right hand fingers are more open; 1929.
    UNUSUAL IDENTIFICATION FEATURE: Curl is in middle of forehead.
    MARKS: "A Petite Doll" doll; "Campbell Kid" label on dress.
    SEE: *Illustration 75. Toy World,* August 1929.

Sally: 12½in (32cm); all-composition; painted face and eyes; closed mouth; beautiful flesh color; molded hair with part in middle of head; third and fourth fingers molded together and curved slightly inward; blush color on knees and backs of hands; jointed at neck, shoulders and hips; toes not well defined; single line on seat; introduced in 1930.
    Sally was in competition with the Effanbee *Patsy* and was widely advertised (see also Identification Guide, page 142; see also Color Section, pages 142 and 186).
    MARKS: "Sally//A//Petite Doll" back.
    SEE: *Illustration 76. Playthings,* July 1930.

Illustration 74.

Illustration 75.

Illustration 77.

Illustration 78.

George Washington Doll: 1932 Bicentennial of George Washington's birth doll (see page 56); (see also Color Section, page 45); doll dressed in blue and pink costume.

George Washington: 1932 Bicentennial of George Washington's birth doll dressed in black costume (see page 56); (see Color Section, page 82).

Bicentennial Costumes on Petite Dolls: Advertisement for 1932 Bicentennial of George Washington's birth doll (see page 57, Illustration 114).

Petite Line of Dolls: 1934 American Character line of dolls included *Sally, Sally Joy, Toodles, Toddling Toodles* and many other innovations.

The *Sally Joy* doll pictured has the same curly *Shirley*-type wig shown in *Illustration 78*.

SEE: *Illustration 77. Playthings*, July 1934.

Sally Joy: 24in (61cm); composition shoulder plate head; limbs; cloth body; sleep eyes with lashes; lashes above eyes; feathered eyebrows; dimple above mouth; open mouth with four teeth; dimples in elbows; white batiste dress with yellow polka dots; yellow ribbon belt; matching hat; front of shoe is scalloped; all original; 1934.

MARKS: "Petite; Amer Char. Doll Co." back of shoulder plate. "Lovable Petite Doll//(drawing of doll)//Sally Joy" dress tag.

SEE: *Illustration 78*.

Sally: 24in (61cm); one of the *Sally Joy* dolls; (for general characteristics see *Illustration 78*); competed with the Ideal *Shirley Temple* doll; red and white "Stand Up and Cheer" look-alike costume.

American Character advertised in 1934 that "Sally's in the Movies." The doll was in the Columbia Movie *I'll Fix It Up* starring Shirley Jean Rickert and Jack Holt.

SEE: *Illustration 79. Playthings*, October 1934.

Doll Souvenirs of the Bicentennial of George Washington's Birth: See Special Bicentennial Section, page 56; see also Color Section, page 82, 83.

Illustration 79.

Petite W.A.V.E.: 15½in (39cm); all-composition; light brown mohair wig; no molded hair on head; metal sleep eyes with real eyelashes; painted eyelashes above eyes; open mouth with four teeth; dimple on each cheek next to mouth; pink cheeks; molded mouth; second and third fingers molded together; early 1930s-type of composition which is not as glossy as later composition; dressed in W.A.V.E. uniform; overseas cap and shoulder bag have eagle insignia; leatherette shoes scalloped across front; circa early 1940s. During World War II, American Character and other doll companies used earlier parts during shortages.

MARKS: "Petite" back of doll.
SEE: *Illustration 80.* (Color Section, page 45.)

Illustration 81B.

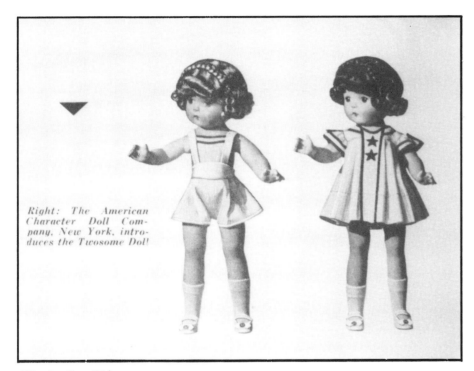

Right: The American Character Doll Company, New York, introduces the Twosome Doll!

Illustration 81A.

Carol Ann Berry was the adopted daughter of the famous Hollywood actor Wallace Berry. She had a role in one of his movies, *China Seas*, in 1935.

The *Twosome* doll is a *Patsy*-type doll.

Carol Ann Berry, The Hollywood Twosome Doll: Created for the 1935 line. Each doll has a distinctive wig and a "Twosome" Costume. According to the advertisement, "The twosome costume is really two costumes in one — a little playsuit — a little dress-up dress — interchangeable at will — and each doll is sold with two costumes so that the little child can dress her doll to suit her moods." A special group of costumes was created for this doll. A special all-wood, lift-top trunk could be purchased to hold the clothes; 13in (33cm); blonde mohair wig over molded hair; brown sleep eyes; lashes.

MARKS: "Petite" back of doll.
SEE: *Illustration 81A. Playthings,* June 1935.

Carol Ann Berry, The Hollywood Twosome Doll: 16½in (42cm); all-composition; blonde mohair wig with distinctive braid on top of head; yellow lawn dress and teddy with brown polka dots; trimmed in chocolate brown; cream leather shoes; all original except socks and hair bow; 1935.

MARKS: "Petite//Sally" head; "Petite" back.
SEE: *Illustration 81B. Barbara Comienski Collection.*

Toddle-Tot: Life-size; fully-jointed; could turn its head, hands and legs in different directions; sleep eyes; open mouth with teeth; walked when the child held its hand; crier in body; part of the Petite doll line; came with knitted suits or frilly dresses; 1929 into the 1930s.

    SEE: *Illustration 82. Playthings,* January 1930.

Chuckles: 17in (43cm); composition head, arms and legs; cloth body; mohair wig; sleep eyes; open mouth with teeth.

    This type of baby doll was made from the early 1920s into the 1930s.

    MARKS: "Amer.Char" head; "Petite---Chuckles" paper tag.

    SEE: *Illustration 83.* (Color Section, page 45.) *Kerra Davis Collection.*

"TODDLE-TOT"

is our greatest contribution to the world of fine dolls . . . It establishes the highest level of excellence . . . . the nearest approach to life in winsome expressiveness . . . We invite you to judge for yourself.

Illustration 82.

Illustration 85.

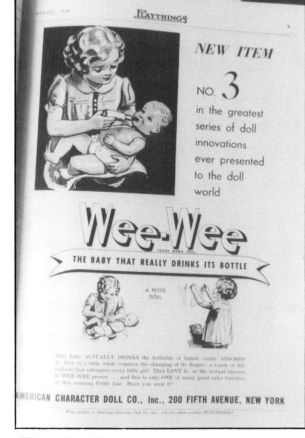

Illustration 84.

Wee-Wee: Advertised as the baby that really drinks its bottle.

    "This doll ACTUALLY DRINKS the bottleful of liquid — really absorbs it — then in a little while requires the changing of a diaper — a touch of life realism that entrances every little girl."

    SEE: *Illustration 84. Playthings,* August 1935.

Mama Doll: 22in (56cm); composition head, lower arms and lower legs; wire around molded ridge holds head to body; individual fingers; voice box; sleep eyes with real eyelashes; eyelashes under eyes; open mouth with two large upper teeth; molded hair under mohair wig around the edges only; no molded hair on upper part of head; molded hair on forehead only.

    MARKS: "Am. Char. Doll" neck.

    SEE: *Illustration 85. Pat Parton Collection.*

Paratex Dolls: American Character advertised in 1935 that their dolls were made of "Paratex" and would not break or peel and could be washed. Each doll was guaranteed for a full year against injury.

    The authors do not recommend that these dolls be washed now in spite of American Character's claim in 1935.

American Character Composition Dolls
1928 to End of Composition Era *

1928 **Puggy** 1928-1930 +: Chubby, all-composition boy doll.
Toddle-Tot 1928-1935 +: Baby doll in Petite Line.

1929 **Campbell Soup Kids;** Composition shoulder plate; composition arms with very fat legs.
MARKS: "Petite AM.Character Doll Co."

1930 **Tottle-Tot:** New model that could turn head, hands and feet in any direction; walk;
upper teeth; wore knitted suits or frilled dresses.
Baby Dolls: Continued with many types in line through the 1930s.
Marked Petite Girls: Continued all through the 1930s.
Marked Petite Mama dolls: Continued all through the 1930s.
Chuckles: Baby doll.
Perfect Beauty: 24in (61cm); 1920-1937; human hair wigs; composition head, arms and
legs; open mouth with teeth; sleep eyes; in 1930 Sears catalog; *Mama*-doll type.
MARKS: "Petite";"Amer.Char.Petite".
Sally Petite: *Patsy* look-alike; continued into the mid 1930s.

1931 Continued line with new outfits.

1932 **Bicentennial Dolls:** Dressed as Martha and George Washington.

1934 **Sally Petite: Sally Joy: Toodles: Tottletot Tottling Tootles** continued.
Toodles: New type of sleep eyes.

1924 **Twosome Doll** (Carol Ann Berry): Extra clothes and trunk could be purchased.
Paratex, a new type of unbreakable and washable composition was introduced into
line; added weight to dolls.
Girl Doll with shoulder plate and swivel head.
Wee-Wee: Drinking, wetting baby.

1936 **Toddle Petite:** 13in (33cm); composition head; rubber body; sleep eyes; molded yellow
hair. MARKS: "Petite//Doll/Toddles."

1937 **Baby:** 18in (46cm); composition head; all rubber body.

1939 **Debutante:** Heavy walker; open mouth with four teeth and felt tongue; large cryer in
middle of stomach.

1940 **Wee Girl:** All-composition; painted brown eyes; black hair.

1941 Wartime restrictions limited line; continued some production with whatever materials
were on shelves.
Petite Wave with metal eyes.
Black doll with curly hair. MARKS: "AC" head.
Little Love: Two teeth and felt tongue.

1945 Returned to doll making full time and quickly turned to hard plastic dolls.

* Not a complete list.

Arranbee Doll Co.

The Arranbee Doll Co. began to make dolls about 1922, and they continued production until 1958 when the company was sold to Vogue Doll Company. For a short time, Vogue continued the Arranbee line as a subsidiary of their company.

Arranbee sold quality dolls which were popular with the customers of the period and with collectors today. Some of their dolls were purchased from the Ideal Novelty and Toy Co., and that is why it is often difficult to identify their dolls. They used the name *Nancy* as a trade name when they made both *Patsy* and *Shirley Temple* look-alikes. *Nancy* was also sometimes dressed in a costume similar to the Alexander *McGuffey Ana*.

The Hedwig dolls were basic *Nancy* dolls dressed in the special costumes described in the books by Marguerite de Angeli (see *Illustration 228*), also see Color Section, page 129.

Mama Doll: Made under "Dream Baby" trade name along with a complete line of novelty, baby and other *Mama* dolls; dressed in complete dress and matching coat and hat costume; 1930.
 MARKS: "Arranbee Dolls" tag.
 SEE: *Illustration 86. Playthings*, March 1930.

Nancy: 20in (51cm); all-composition; jointed neck, shoulderpiece is separate; jointed arms and legs; tin sleep eyes with real eyelashes; painted eyelashes above and below eyes; open mouth with molded tongue; two teeth; cloth body with crier; slightly wavy molded hair combed to one side; second and third fingers molded together; long straight legs with two lines below kneecap; red, blue and white original print dress; original leatherette shoes with scallops above toes; *Patsy* look-alike; mid 1930s.
 MARKS: "Arranbee" head.
 SEE: *Illustration 87. Laura May Brown Collection.*

Nancy: 12in (31cm); all-composition; *Patsy* look-alike (see Identification Guide, page 187).
 MARKS: "Arranbee//Doll Co." back.

Nancy in a Trunk: 14in (36cm); all-composition; dressed in bathing costume of the mid 1930s; other clothes include a short dress, a long dress, playsuit, coat and hat; slip, extra hat, low and high shoes; 1936.
 SEE: *Illustration 88. Mary Merritt Museum.*

Illustration 87.

Illustration 86.

32

Illustration 88.

RIGHT: *ALEXANDER* Fairy Princess *(see page 8, Illustration 4).*

ALEXANDER McGuffey Ana *(see page 9, Illustration 8).*

ALEXANDER Egypt *(see page 10,* Illustration 10*)* Penni and Ruth Lewis Collection.

ALEXANDER Betty *(see page 10,* Illustration 11*).*

ALEXANDER David Copperfield *(see page 8,* Illustration 5*).*

ALEXANDER Princess Elizabeth (see page 11, Illustration 14).

ALEXANDER Princess Elizabeth (see page 12, Illustration 17). Marianne Gardner Collection.

ALEXANDER Snow White and Dopey (see page 13, Illustration 20).

ALEXANDER Scarlett O'Hara *(see page 15,* Illustration 30).

BELOW: *ALEXANDER* Scarlett O'Hara *close-up (see page 15,* Illustration 30).

ABOVE: *ALEXANDER* McGuffy Ana *(see page 13,* Illustration 23). Marianne Gardner Collection.

ALEXANDER Miss America *(see page 16,* Illustration 34). Lois Janner Collection.

ALEXANDER
W.A.V.E. *(see page 16,*
Illustration 35*).* Marianne Gardner Collection.

ABOVE: *ALEXANDER* Wendy Ann *(see page 14,* Illustration 25*).* Marilyn Dawe Collection.

ALEXANDER Sonja Henie *close-up (see page 20,* Illustration 49*).*

RIGHT: *ALEXANDER* Margaret O'Brien *(see page 17*, Illustration 39). Joan A. Tosko Collection.

ALEXANDER Southern Girl *(see page 15*, Illustration 27). Lois Janner Collection.

ALEXANDER Madeleine de Baines *(see page 15*, Illustration 29). Ramona Beard Collection.

RIGHT: *ALEXANDER* doll grouping, *Sears, Roebuck & Co. 1946 catalog (see page 17,* Illustration 37*)*.

ALEXANDER doll grouping, *Montgomery Ward 1947 Catalog (see page 18,* Illustration 41*)*.

ABOVE: *ALEXANDER* Alice in Wonderland *(see page 17,* Illustration 40*)*. Joan A. Tosko Collection.

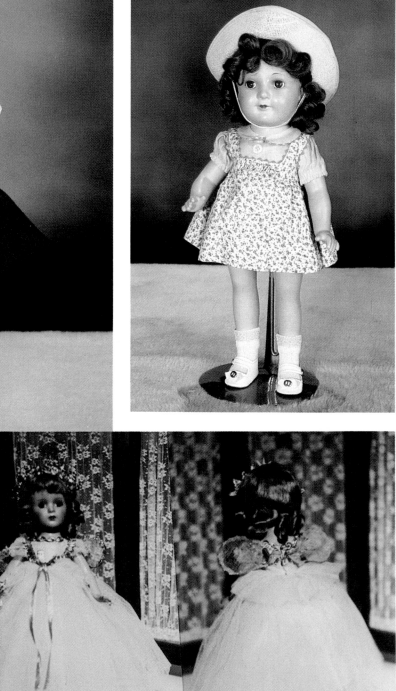

BELOW: *ALEXANDER* Jane Withers *(see page 19*, Illustration 46*)*. Diane Hoffman Collection.

ALEXANDER Sonja Henie *(see page 20*, Illustration 50*)*. Diane Hoffman Collection. Neal Eisaman, Photographer.

ALEXANDER Fairy Queen *(see page 15*, Illustration 28*)*. Ramona Beard Collection.

LEFT: *ALEXANDER* Bitsey and Butch *(see page 23*, Illustration 60*).* Jeri L. Traw Collection.

ALEXANDER Carmen *(see page 24*, Illustration 62*).* Diane Hoffman Collection. Neal Eisaman, Photographer.

ALEXANDER Jeannie Walker *(see page 20*, Illustration 51*).* Athena Crowley Collection.

INSET: *ALEXANDER* Degas Ballerina *(see page 24, Illustration 63)*. Diane Hoffman Collection. Neal E. Eisaman, Photographer.

ALEXANDER Melaine *(see page 24, Illustration 67)*. Diane Hoffman Collection. Neal Eisaman, Photographer.

INSET: *ALEXANDER* Orchard Princess, *back (see page 25*, Illustrations *68 and 69)*. Diane Hoffman Collection. Neal Eisaman, Photographer.

ALEXANDER Orchard Princess, *front (see page 25*, Illustrations *68 and 69)*. Diane Hoffman Collection. Neal Eisaman, Photographer.

RIGHT: *ALEXANDER* Lady Windermere, *fronnt (see page 24, Illustrations 65 and 66)*. Diane Hoffman Collection.

FAR RIGHT: *ALEXANDER* Lady Windermere, *back (see page 24, Illustrations 65 and 66)*. Diane Hoffman Collection. Neal Eisaman, Photographer.

BELOW: *ALEXANDER* Flavia *(see page 24, Illustration 64)*. Diane Hoffman Collection. Neal Eisaman, Photographer.

ALEXANDER Marie Antoinette *(see page 25, Illustration 70)*. Joan A. Tosko Collection.

ABOVE: *AMERICAN CHARACTER* Petite W.A.V.E. *(see page 29,* Illustration 80).

LEFT: *AMERICAN CHARACTER Bicentennial* George Washington *(see page 57,* Illustration 112).

ABOVE LEFT: *AMERICAN CHARACTER* Chuckles *(see page 30,* Illustration 83). Kerra Davis Collection.

ARRANBEE Nancy *(see page 49, Illustration 90) and Ideal* Shirley Temple *(see page 145, Illustration 256).*

ABOVE: *ARRANBEE* Pirate *(see page 50, Illustration 92)*.

ABOVE RIGHT: *ARRANBEE* Debuteen *(see page 50, Illustration 96)*.

RIGHT: *ARRANBEE* Girl from Southern Series *(see page 49, Illustration 90)*.

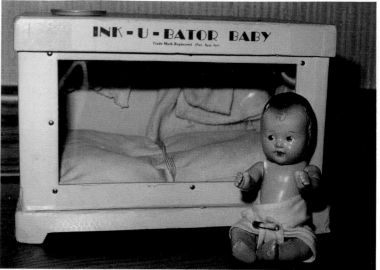

ABOVE: *ARRANBEE* Ink-U-Bator Baby *(see page 51,* Illustration 99). Mary Lu Trowbridge Collection.

LEFT: *ARRANBEE* Dutch Twins *(see page 50,* Illustration 93).

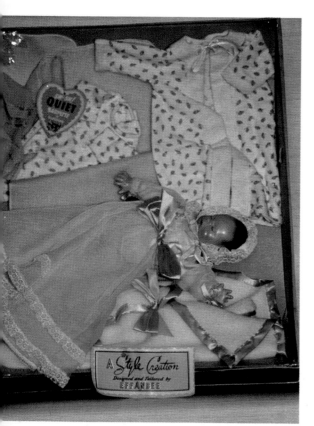

ABOVE: *ARRANBEE* Mary Had a Little Lamb *(see page 50,* Illustration 95).

LEFT: *EFFANBEE* Sleeping Babyette *(see page 73,* Illustration 160). Mary Lu Trowbridge Collection.

Comparison Between the Arranbee Nancy and the Ideal Shirley Temple

Nancy (doll on left): 17in (43cm); all-composition; jointed at neck, shoulders and hips; second and third fingers molded together; sleep blue eyes with real eyelashes; other eyelashes painted under eyes; open mouth with tongue and four teeth; beautiful flesh color composition; blush on back of hands, elbows and knees; white, $\mathcal{Y}$ on lower back; typical Arranbee leather strap shoes with open work on each side; circa mid 1930s; (see Identification Guide, Illustration 395).

Arranbee used this material and color to make clothes for several types of dolls in their line (see also *Illustration 100*).

 UNUSUAL IDENTIFICATION FEATURE: The shoes of more expensive Arranbee dolls often have cutwork on the sides; less expensive dolls often wear shoes with rounded edges on the front of the shoes.

 MARKS: "Nancy" head.

 SEE: *Illustration 89.* (Color Section, page 46.)

Shirley Temple: (see Ideal section, page 145 and Color Section, page 46).

 SIMILARITIES: Almost the same body, limbs, $\mathcal{Y}$ on lower back, height, open mouth with tongue, sleep eyes with eyelashes painted under eyes, eyebrows, fingers, round stomach with a line underneath it.

 DIFFERENCES: *Nancy* has four teeth. *Shirley* has six teeth. While both have excellent quality facial color, it is a different shade. *Nancy* has blue eyes. *Shirley* has hazel eyes. *Nancy* has no dimples, *Shirley* has two dimples.

Girl from Southern Series: 17in (43cm); sleep eyes with real lashes; eye shadow above eyes; blonde human hair wig; oval shaped face with pointed chin; blue striped dress which has faded to lavender; blue felt hat; 1939-1940.

 UNUSUAL IDENTIFICATION FEATURE: Arranbee dolls often have eye shadow above the eyes.

 MARKS: "R & B" head.

 SEE: *Illustration 90. Barbara Comienski Collection.*

Girl from Southern Series: 14in (36cm); all-composition; jointed at neck, hips and shoulders; sleep eyes with real lashes; eye shadow above eyes; auburn mohair wig; late 1930s.

 MARKS: "R & B" head.

 SEE: *Illustration 91.* (Color Section, page 47.)

Illustration 90.

Nursery Rhyme Series (pictures of characters on boxes):
1. *Little Bo Peep*
2. *Mary had a Little Lamb*
3. *Jack Be Nimble*
4. *Little Red Riding Hood*
5. *Sing a Song of Sixpence*
6. *Jack and Jill*
7. *Queen of Hearts*
8. *Little Boy Blue*
9. *Mary, Mary Quite Contrary*
10. *Humpty Dumpty*
11. *Rub a Dub Dub*
12. *Little Jack Horner*
13. *Mother Goose*
14. *Jack, Jack the Piper's Son*
15. *Goose Which Laid the Golden Egg*
16. *Bye Bye Blackbird*
17. *The Cow Jumped Over the Moon*
18. *Old King Cole*
19. *Puss in Boots*
20. *Little Miss Muffet*

Illustration 94.

Pirate: 9in (23cm); all-composition; jointed at neck, shoulders and hips; slightly wavy molded hair combed to one side; slightly puffy wave above ear; small pin-type curls at neckline in back; second, third and fourth fingers molded together; thumb and fifth finger molded separately; dressed in dark blue short pants and bolero; white shirt with no buttons; black tie shoes and socks; felt pieces simulate boots; *Patsyette* look-alike; late 1930s and early 1940s.
   MARKS: "R & B//Doll Co." in raised letters middle back.
   SEE: *Illustration 92*. (Color Section, page 47.)

Dutch Twins: 9in (23cm); all-composition; for general characteristics, see *Illustration 92*; late 1940s.
   MARKS: "R & B//Doll Co." raised letters on back.
   SEE: *Illustration 93*. (Color Section, page 48.)

Mary Had a Little Lamb: 8in (20cm); all-composition; for general characteristics, see *Illustration 94*; pictures of nursery rhyme characters printed on elaborate box; circa late 1930s.
   MARKS: "R & B" back.
   SEE: *Illustration 95*. (Color Section, page 48.)

Little Bo-Peep: 9in (23cm); all-composition; jointed at neck, shoulders and hips; molded hair; painted eyes; closed mouth; smiling face; pink cotton skirt; pink and blue flowered cotton print top and panniers; pink net hat with blue ribbon trim; green metal crook with blue ribbon; white tie; leatherette shoes; white socks; organdy pantalets with lace trim; flannel and papier-mâché lamb tied to right wrist; nursery rhyme characters in suitcase-type box; circa late 1930s-early 1940s.
   MARKS: "R & B//Doll Co." raised letters on back.
   SEE: *Illustration 94*.

Debuteen: 17in (43cm); composition shoulder plate head, limbs; cloth body; fully jointed; sleep eyes with real lashes; eye liner above eyes; closed mouth; red cheeks; human hair wig; very long slender legs; matching purse; suede shoes; circa late 1930s and early 1940s.
   UNUSUAL IDENTIFICATION: Arranbee used lace and ribbon wrist bands.
   MARKS: "R & B" head; "This doll//has a//human hair wig" wrist tag.
   SEE: *Illustration 96*. (Color Section, page 47.)

Illustration 100.

Illustration 97.

W.A.A.C.: 14½in (37in); attributed to Arranbee but the composition is inferior to marked Arranbee dolls; painted eyes; small, closed mouth; slightly wavy hair combed to one side; small pin-type curls at the neckline in the back of head; right arms slightly bent; long straight legs with two lines below the kneecap; right arms and legs have a large metal pin on outside joint; left arm and leg have only a nail; straw-filled cloth body; W.A.A.C. uniform; molded shoes and socks painted khaki color to match uniform; dimples above fingers; early 1940s. Dolls sold during World War II were often of inferior quality.
    MARKS: None
    SEE: *Illustration 97. Laura May Brown Collection.*

Drink'N Babe (The Doll that Drinks Like Magic): Advertisement for baby that "..actually drinks milk and, then-presto-the bottle magically refills itself and is ready for another feeding. Any doll can be fed from this ingenious bottle. This unique Drink'N Babe set consists of a magic milk bottle, pillow, rattle, hot water bottle, dress and bonnet."
    In 1935 the Arranbee line included *Nancy* dolls, *Mama* dolls, Baby dolls and wardrobes for them all.
    SEE: *Illustration 98. Playthings,* July 1935.

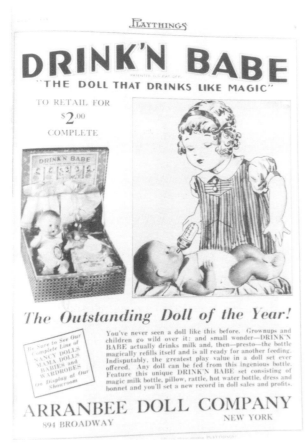

Illustration 98.

Quintuplet Toddlers: 7in (18cm) all-composition (see Quintuplet Section, page 170).

Ink-U-Bator Baby: 7in (18cm); all-composition; came in box that represented an incubator; inside there is a hooded cape, blanket, undershirt, booties, rattle and rubber funnel with rubber tube; metal thermometer on top of box; doll has molded hair with curl in the middle of the forehead; fully jointed; late 1930s.
    This doll was also used for a set of quintuplets.
    MARKS: "R & B" doll; metal thermometer on top of box says, "Mfg. by R & B Doll Co."
    SEE: *Illustration 99.* (Color Section, page 48.) *Mary Lu Trowbridge Collection.*

Toddler Boy: 16in (41cm); composition head, arms and legs; cloth body; crier inside body; brown mohair wig; closed mouth; sleep eyes with real lashes; blue pants held up by straps; blue and white striped shirt with bias trim of the same material as the pants that are original; circa late 1930s. Arranbee often used the same material for clothes for different dolls in their line (see also *Illustration 89*).
    MARKS: "R & B" head.
    SEE: *Illustration 100. Athena Crawley Collection.*

Averill Mfg. Corp., Georgene Novelties, Inc., MME. Hendren, Georgene Averill, Brophy Doll Company (CANADA)

Georgene Averill designed many dolls and clothes. She and her husband owned doll companies, and she occasionally designed dolls for other companies, including Borgfeldt.

She made many composition dolls, especially in the 1920s. Today these dolls are very collectible. In the 1930s she seemed to concentrate on cloth dolls, but she continued to meet the composition competition and issued dolls yearly.

From 1928 until the end of the decade, her line included the Sunny Line; *Sunshine* dolls; *Dolly* and *Bobby; Baby Brite; Nize Baby* (cartoon character); *Snookums* (with a laughing mouth and teeth); *Kiddie Karakters, Dimmie* and *Jimmie; Rufus* (black doll).

In the 1930s the composition dolls included *Chickie; Bobby Bounce; Baby Hendren; Mama* dolls, *Peaches* (*Patsy* look-alikes); *Polly* and *Polly Peaches; Harriet Flanders; Yawn Baby; Baby Blue Eyes; Tear Drop Baby* and others.

For more information about *Peaches*, see Identification Guide (page 187, *Illustration 372*).

Illustration 101.

Kiddie Karakters: Characters from Mother Goose; *Little Bo Peep; Mary Had a Little Lamb; Mother Goose; Little Boy Blue; Captain Kidd.*

SEE: *Illustration 101. Playthings,* October 1929.

Whistling Cowboy: 14in (36cm); molded hair with row of curls in the back; painted eyes; puckered mouth with slight hole for sound of whistle; composition arms; third and fourth finger molded together; cloth body; legs have springs inside cloth as part of whistling mechanism; dressed in cowboy suit with tan shirt and blue pants with tan fringe; all original; introduced in 1927 and made during most of the 1930s. Other Whistlers included *Dan* (boy doll), *Sailor, Soldier, Cop, Dutch Boy* and possibly an *Aviator.*

MARKS: "U.S.A." head; "I whistle when you dance me on one foot and then the other. Patented Feb. 2, 1926, A Genuine Madame Hendren Doll" tag.

SEE: *Illustration 102.* (Color Section, page 81.)

Illustration 103.

Illustration 106.

Illustration 107.

Dimmie and Jimmie: 14in (36cm); for characteristics, see *Illustration 104*; body twist dolls; 1929.
MARKS: None.
SEE: *Illustration 103. Playthings*, February 1929.

Dimmie: 14in (36cm); all-composition; jointed at neck, shoulders, breast, waist and hips; molded hair; painted eyes with large pupil; eye shadow above eyes; pink dotted swiss romper suit and matching bonnet; pink socks; black shoes; all original; circa 1929.
MARKS: None.
SEE: *Illustration 104.* (Color Section, page 81.) *Sandra Strater Collection.*

Peaches: *Patsy*-type (See Identification Guide, page 187, *Illustration 373*).

Val-encia: 15in (38cm); composition shoulder head and limbs; cloth body; face flocked to resemble felt and imitate Lenci dolls; closed mouth; eye shadow around eyes; unusually vibrant, painted eyes; curly mohair wig; voice box; 1928-1929.
    In 1926, Averill experimented with a new type of slimmer *Mama* doll which could walk due to limber joints and a low center of gravity. *Val-encia* was one of these early *slender Mama* dolls.
    The *Mama* dolls were dressed in felts or combinations of felt and organdy costumes. The name, itself "Val-encia," indicated the competition.
    MARKS: "Genuine//Madame Hendren//Doll//1714 Made in U.S.A." stamped on the cloth body in the middle of the back; "Madame Hendren//Everybody Loves Them" dress tag.
    SEE: *Illustration 105.* (Color Section, page 81.)

Little Sister and Little Brother: composition shoulder plate head and limbs; cloth body with voice box; both have felt coats and berets; girl wears flowered print cotton dress with lace trim around neck; boy wears two-piece suit with large buttons at waist; other costumes were available; 1927-1930.
    The popular dolls were designed by Grace Corry, a popular doll artist of the period.
    MARKS: "©//By//Grace Corry"
    SEE: *Illustration 106. Playthings*, January 1929.

Baby Hendren: Averill Co. Inc., advertised in 1929 that stores should Hendrenize their doll departments. They featured the *Baby Hendren* dolls, *Babs*, *Dimmie* and *Bunchy*.
    SEE: *Illustration 107. Playthings*, March 1929.

Harriet Flander (doll on right): 12in (31cm); all-glossy composition; jointed at neck, shoulders and hips; molded yarn hair on side of head; open mouth with painted tongue inside mouth; painted eyes with three eyelashes above each eye; red, white and blue felt dress and matching hat; 1937.

Georgene Averill often dressed her dolls in felt and organdy clothes. She was competing with Lenci.

Kewpie Lamp (doll on left): *Kewpie* look-alike from the 1920s.

MARKS: "Harriet © Flander//1937" doll.
SEE: *Illustration 108. Kathleen Smith Collection.*

Yawning Baby: 19in (48cm); composition head; molded hair; eyes closed; open mouth with teeth; cloth body and limbs; body made of blue and white checked flannel; matching bonnet; circa 1946.

MARKS: "Georgene//Doll" tag. Some dolls were marked "Georgene//1946 Ỵ" in raised letters on head.
SEE: *Illustration 109. Lois Barrett Collection.*

The registered trademarks, the trademarks and copyrights appearing in italics//bold within this chapter belong to Beehler Arts Co.

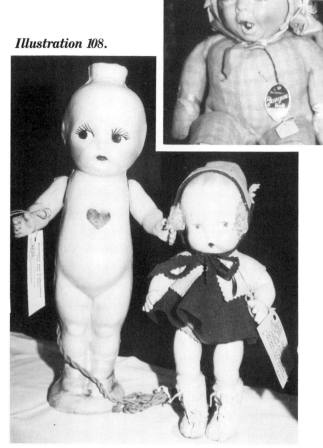

Illustration 109.

Illustration 108.

Beehler Arts Co. (VIRGA DOLL)

Girl: 7in (18cm); all-composition; one-piece head and body with strung arms and legs; painted blue eyes; no eyelashes; unpainted molded socks; painted black shoes; *Nancy Ann Storybook Doll* competitor; white satin dress trimmed with red and blue ribbon; flag paper decal on bodice; white felt hat with pink boa trim; circa early 1940s.

MARKS:: "M.B.C." back.
SEE: *Illustration 110.*

Illustration 110.

Berwick Doll Company
(See also *European Doll Company*)

During the 1920s and into the 1930s, the Berwick Doll Company distributed the *Famlee* doll sets. Each set included at least one body and several heads which could be screwed on the dolls. The company advertised that these dolls walked and talked.

Through the years they came in sets containing one to 18 heads and one or two bodies. Costumes that matched the heads were included in the set. As late as 1931, the company advertised that they were making new heads and costumes for dolls made previously.

Characters included:

1. *Baby*
2. *Chinese Boy*
3. *Indian Girl*
4. *Dutch Girl*
5. *Dutch Boy*
6. *French Girl*
7. *Sailor Boy*
8. *Sailor Girl*
9. *Susie Bumps*
10. *Dolly Dimple*
11. *Nurse*
12. *Commander*
13. *Crying Baby*
14. *Indian Boy*
15. *Pierrette*
16. *Clown*
17. *Colored Girl*
18. *Colored Boy*

In 1931, the company was taken over by the European Doll Company. See page 103.

Illustration 111.

Famlee Doll: 16in (41cm); composition head, shoulder plates, arms; cloth body stuffed with straw; five heads including *French Girl, Crying Baby, Clown, Indian, Colored Girl* and one body; all original; circa 1925-1931.

SEE: *Illustration 111. Betty Shriver Collection.*

MARKS:: "A Whole Family of Dolls in One//Three to eighteen entirely different//dolls from one just by changing faces and costumes//Walks//Talks// and is unbreakable//Berwick Doll Company// N.Y., N.Y.//8010//Patented April 12, 1921" box.

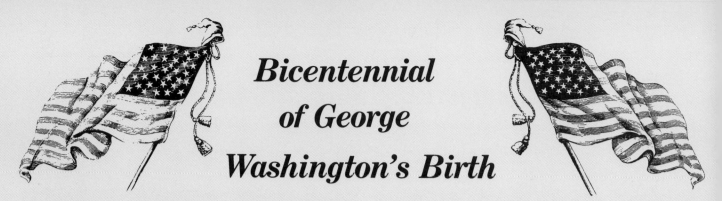

Bicentennial of George Washington's Birth

February 22, 1932, was the bicentennial of the birthday of George Washington, and the United States celebrated his birthday with enthusiasm. President Herbert Hoover addressed a joint session of Congress and led a pilgrimage to Mt. Vernon. The entire nation followed the proceedings by radio.

For weeks before the great event, the traditional souvenirs were purchased by the general public. Department stores advertised furniture reproduced in the authentic spirit with details of Mt. Vernon. Washington plates with scenes from his life sold well.

Doll companies also caught the spirit of the great occasion, and souvenir dolls were eagerly purchased. Many of these dolls were sold in Washington D.C. as crowds descended on the capital for the festivities. However, other bicentennial dolls could be purchased in doll stores around the country.

Many of these dolls were well made and dressed handsomely. They included Martha as well as George. Because they were intended to sit on a shelf for everyone to enjoy, many of these dolls have survived in excellent condition.

The registered trademarks, the trademarks and copyrights appearing in italics//bold within this chapter belong to American Character Doll Company, Inc.

American Character Doll Company, Inc.

George Washington: 16½in (42cm); all-composition; slightly molded hair under wig; painted eyes with eyelashes above eyes; narrow black line above eye; closed mouth; left arm straight; right arm curved; second and third fingers curled; dressed in colonial costume; 1932.

UNUSUAL IDENTIFYING FEATURE: Joint lines on inside of fingers are very bumpy.
MARKS:: None on doll: "George Washington" printed on ribbon across chest.
SEE: *Illustration 112.* (Color Section, page 45.)

Bicentennial Beddoll

Martha Washington: 25in (64cm); composition head, arms and feet; straw-stuffed body and legs; painted features; blonde colonial style wig with two curls in front; painted fingernails; molded fingers with separate thumb; molded high-heeled shoes; 1932.

This is a Judd family doll which belonged to Donna Judd's relatives in Pennsylvania. They owned a furniture store in Craley during the 1930s. For the bicentennial of George Washington's birthday, they gave these dolls with the purchase of furniture. Recently, it was found in a drawer of a dresser belonging to members of the family.
MARKS:: None
SEE: *Illustration 113.* (Color Section, page 82.)

American Character Doll Company, Inc.

George Washington Bicentennial Doll: 14in (36cm); all-composition; unusual molded hair with deep waves; painted eyes with slender, dainty eyelashes above eyes; closed mouth; one dimple under mouth; right arm curved at 90 degree angle; left arm unusually straight; second and third finger molded together with a wide space between first and second finger; black pants and coat; black stockings and shoes; costume not complete; 1932.
MARKS:: "A C INC" head.
SEE: *Illustration 113.* (Color Section, page 82.)

American Character Doll Company, Inc.

Bicentennial Costumes on Petite Dolls: The American Character Doll Company made dolls dressed in what they advertised as "Authentic and Exclusive George Washington Bicentennial Costumes." They were approved by the Bicentennial Commission at Washington as shown by the ribbon in the left hand bottom corner of the advertisement.

SEE: *Illustration 114. Toys and Novelties*, February 1932.

Illustration 114.

Effanbee Doll Corporation

Illustration 115.

Suzette Martha and George Washington: 11½in (29cm); all-composition; girl has painted brown eyes; boy has painted blue eyes; girl dressed in pink two-piece colonial costume; boy dressed in orange felt pants and vest; lace jabot; blue felt colonial coat lined with orange felt; all original clothes; colonial powdered wig; gold heart on wrist chain; circa early 1940s.

MARKS:: "Suzette//Effanbee Doll Co." neck.
SEE: *Illustration 115. Barbara Comienski Collection.*

Effanbee Doll Corporation

Bicentennial George and Martha Washington Patsyette: 9in (23cm); all-composition; jointed at neck, arms, and legs; painted brown eyes; painted black eyelashes above the eye; second and third fingers molded together; both dolls have gold heart bracelet; all original; 1932.

MARKS: "Effanbee//Patsyette//Doll" back.
SEE: *Illustration 116.* (Color Section, page 82.)

Toy Products

George Washington Dolls: 12½in (32cm); all-composition; spring jointed at neck, shoulders, hips; molded hair under powdered wigs that are similar to molded hair of Toy Products marked dolls; all original; (doll on left) white pants; blue coat with pink trim; brass buttons; black stockings and shoes; (doll on right) dark blue suit with lace trim; white shirt and tie; white socks and black shoes; 1932.

UNUSUAL IDENTIFICATION FEATURE: Spring strung.
MARKS: None
SEE: *Illustration 117.* (Color Section, page 82.)

Borgfeldt, George

My Playmate: (see *Illustration 73*, Amberg Section); pressed cardboard head; cloth body; late 1920s and early 1930s.

After Amberg merged with Horsman in 1930, George Borgfeldt began to sell the Amfelt imported dolls under their "My Playmate" line. The dolls came in various sizes and styles. The Borgfeldt label was found on the dolls' boxes and tags. The heads were made of composition or pressed cardboard depending on the price of the doll. The faces were artistically painted. Their shoes often had a pompon on the toe (see Identification Guide, page 199, *Illustration 395*, doll on right).

MARKS:"My//Playmate//Trademark//Doll// Reg.U.S.Pat.Office//Germany" tag. "My Play-mate//Borgfeldt" box.

Bouton Woolf Co., Inc.

Phyllis: 11½in (29cm); all-composition; jointed at neck, shoulders and hips; *Patsy* look-alike (see Identification Guide, page 187, *Illustration 374*); black and white dolls were made in their own factory.

Bobby Boy: 14⅓in (37cm); dressed in romper-type suit with large collar; genuine hair wig.

MARKS:: "Phyllis" on some dolls; none on others.
SEE: *Illustration 118. Playthings*, April 1931.

Phyllis: *Patsy*-type (see Identification Guide, page 187, *Illustration 374*).

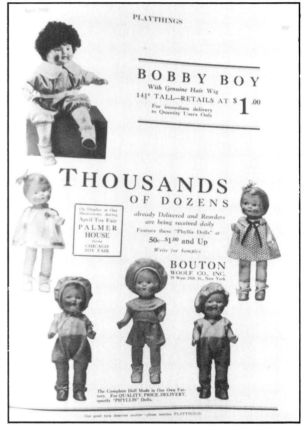

Illustration 118.

Illustration 119.

Burgarella

Woman and Man Dressed in 18th Century Clothes: 19in (48cm); composition; sexed; woman wears pink dress with elaborately trimmed pink organdy top and panniers; man wears blue brocade coat and pink knee britches; lace bow; all original; circa 1927-1929.

SEE: *Illustration 119. Jean Strong Collection.*

Cameo Doll Company

Joseph Kallus was associated with the manufacturing of dolls for most of his adult life. In 1916 he founded the Rex Doll Company which made composition dolls including *Kewpies*. These were distributed by the George Borgfeldt Company. This relationship with Borgfeldt lasted for many years.

He also was associated with the Mutual Doll Company from 1919 through 1921. They manufactured *Kewpies* and *Baby Bundie*.

In 1921 he established the Cameo Doll Products Company which he operated until 1970 when he sold the business and many of the patents and copyrights. He then established Cameo Exclusive Products, Inc., and continued making *Kewpies*.

During the composition period, he modeled and made doll heads for other companies including Ideal Doll and Toy Co.

Rose O'Neill designed dolls for him for many years.

Joy: 10in (25cm); composition head with molded hair with loop for bow; made in several versions; the first was jointed at neck, shoulders, elbows, wrists, hips, knees and ankles; arms, legs and feet made from wood; painted eyes; watermelon mouth; circa 1932.
   MARKS: "Joy" seal on front of body.
   SEE: *Illustration 120. Athena Crowley Collection.*

Margie: 12in (31cm); composition head with molded hair; wood segments and composition body; elastic strung; circa 1929.
   MARKS: "Margie//Des & Copyright//By Jos. Kallus" on front of body.
   MARKS: "Margie//Geo. Borgfeldt & Co//New York//Distributors Cameo Doll Co.//New York//Manufacturers" box.
   SEE: *Illustration 121. (Color Section, page 84.) Linda Mangold Collection.*

Illustration 122.

Illustration 120.

Baby Adele: Lightweight dolls; composition head with molded hair; straight legs; supposed to represent a two-year-old toddler; wore toddler clothes with bonnets.
Margie: Fully jointed; dressed in many beautiful styles.
Ginger, Bones and Streak: three popular breeds of dogs; fully jointed; can be placed in many postures; wood toys.
   SEE: *Illustration 122. Playthings,* June 1930.

Illustration 123.

Scootles: 7½in (19cm); 10in (25cm); 12in (31cm); 13in (33cm); 15in (38cm); 16in (41cm); individual dolls have painted eyes either side-glancing or straight ahead; a few have sleep eyes (see *Illustration 125*); both black and white versions; usually jointed only at shoulders, but some had joints at neck, shoulders and hips; the black version was only 12in (31cm); designed by Rose O'Neill; circa early and mid 1930s.
   SEE: *Illustration 123. Playthings*, June 1935.

Scootles: 12in (31cm); jointed at neck, shoulders and hips; molded hair with curls on forehead; starfish hands; crocheted clothes not original; mid 1930s.
   MARKS: None.
   SEE: *Illustration 124. David M. Cobb Auction Services.*

Scootles: 12in (31cm); all-composition; molded hair; rare side-glancing sleep eyes; starfish hands; costume not all original but appropriate to period; designed by Rose O'Neill; circa 1935.
   SEE: *Illustration 125. Shari McMasters Collection.*

Illustration 124.

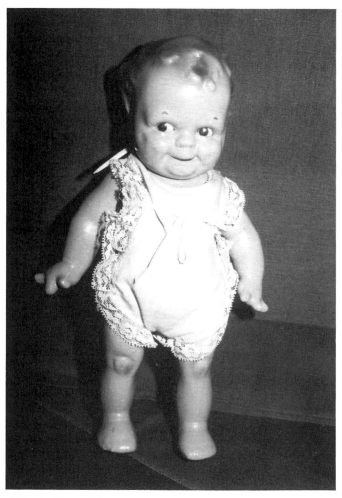

Illustration 125.

Saucy Scootles and Kewpies: Sears, Roebuck & Co. 1946 Christmas catalog.
   SEE: *Illustration 126.*

Kewpies: 11in (28cm); all-composition; jointed at shoulders only; blue wings on back; molded hair; starfish hands; circa late 1930s-late 1940s.
   MARKS: "Kewpie//Des & Copyright//by//Rose O'Neill" printed on heart seal placed in middle of chest.
   SEE: *Illustration 127.*

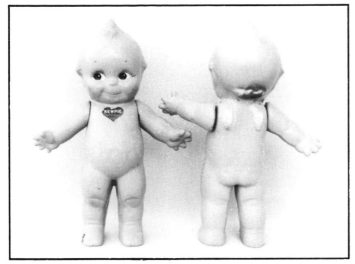

Illustration 127.

Giggles: 12in (31cm); all-composition; molded hair with bangs; starfish hands; original clothes; circa 1947 to mid 1950s. *Kewpie* box original to this doll; purchased new by owner.

    MARKS: "Giggles//Designed and Copyrighted// Rose O'Neill//Cameo Doll Co." on tag.
    SEE: *Illustration 128.* (Color Section, page 83.) *Lois Janner Collection.*

Pop-Eye: 17in (43cm); constructed of wood segments and composition molded head; can be placed in countless positions; finished in bright colors; faithful reproduction of the cartoon Pop-Eye; 1935.
    SEE: *Illustration 129. Playthings*, September 1935.

Illustration 129.

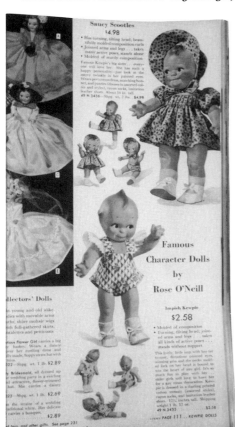

Illustration 126.

Dolls Not Pictured

1927
Baby Blossom: 20in (51cm) and may have come in other sizes; composition shoulder plate head, arms and legs; cloth body and upper legs; bent limb character baby; side-glancing eyes; small nose; some later models may have been flock sprayed; 1927 until after World War II.
    MARKS: "Baby Blossom" on tag; "Des & Copyright//by J.L. Kallus// made in U.S.A." on shoulder plate.

1928
Sissy (possibly *Sissie*): All-composition with joined shoulders and hips so it could stand alone; painted hair and face; distributed by Butler Brothers.

1929-1930
Bandy: 18in (46cm); composition head; wood body; jointed at neck, shoulders and knees; advertising doll for General Electric radios.
    MARKS: "Mfg Cameo Prod. Inc.//Port Allegany Pa//Des & by J.L.K." on foot; "GE Electric//Radio" on hat.

1930
R.C.A. Radiotron: Made for R.C.A. company; could assume many positions; black and white dolls made.

1932
Betty Boop: 12in (31cm); all-composition; molded black hair; ball-jointed body.
    MARKS: "Betty Boop//Des & Copyright by Fleischer//Studios."

1932
Pete the Pup.

1933
Marcia: All-composition; molded hair; painted side-glancing eyes; shoes and socks molded and painted; French-style clothes.

1940
Crownie: composition and wood; segmented; caricature of king.

61

Cohen, Herman and the House of Puzzy

Illustration 131.

Puzzy: 15in (38cm); all-composition; jointed at neck, shoulders and hips; molded and painted head; red hair; large eyes; freckles; open mouth with painted teeth; original white shirt, black pants, red tie; 1948.

> MARKS: "H. of P. U.S.A." head.
> SEE: *Illustration 130. Elliot Zirlin Collection.*

Sizzy: 15in (38cm); all-composition; jointed at neck, shoulders and hips; molded painted features; red hair; probably not original clothes; 1948.

> MARKS: "H. of P. U.S.A." head.
> SEE: *Illustration 131. Frank Biscop Collection.*

Illustration 130.

Illustration 132.

Ⓧ Circle X

Girl in Green Dress: 15in (38cm); jointed at neck, shoulders and hips; mohair wig; sleep eyes with lashes; painted eyelashes under eyes; open mouth with four teeth and tongue; no dimples; ⅄; excellent composition; green organdy dress and slip trimmed with tiny pink rickrack; mid-to-late 1930s.

The Ⓧ dolls are very similar to the Ideal *Shirley Temple* and the Arranbee *Nancy* dolls. They have been attributed to many companies. They have been seen in original Arranbee and Sayco boxes. They are typical of the dolls made by Ideal and sold to other companies to dress.

> MARKS: " Ⓧ " head.
> SEE: *Illustration 132.*

Confetti Dolls, Inc.

Alpine: 6in (15cm); all-composition with strung arms; painted brown eyes; black painted long eyelashes; brown mohair wig; felt costume; painted black shoes; an elaborate blue box with an alpine background picture and an alpine border in front of the doll; *Nancy Ann Storybook Doll* competitor; 1940s.

MARKS: "Confetti//Doll" back.
SEE: *Illustration 133.* (Color Section, page 84.)

Crown Toy Mfg. Co., Inc.

Pinocchio: 12in (31cm); all-composition; jointed at neck, shoulders and hips; all original pants and shirt; pressed felt hat with feather; clothes can be removed for washing; all original; 1939.

MARKS: "Walt Disney Pinocchio, Mickey Mouse, Ferdinand the Bull, & Dopey Banks" one side of tag; "Crown Toy" other side of tag.
SEE: *Illustration 134. Beatrice Campbell Collection. Playthings,* September 1939.

Illustration 135.

Illustration 134.

Dopey Puppet: 13in (33cm); composition head; cloth puppet body; molded, painted Dopey character face; licensed by Walt Disney; purple coat with yellow trim; missing his hat; 1938.

MARKS: "Walt Disney Ent// Crown Toy" head.
SEE: *Illustration 135.*

Dee and Cee Company Ltd. (CANADA)

This Canadian company was started in 1932 as the Amusement Supply Company in the midst of the Depression. In 1938 the company name was changed to Dee and Cee. The name has also appeared as D & C, DeeanCee and DEE & CEE. Many of their composition dolls are unmarked. Often they purchased molds or the rights to molds from the larger toy companies in the United States. They manufactured the dolls in their factory in Canada. One such doll was *Campbell's Kid*.

Campbell Kid: 12in (31cm); all-composition; molded hair with curl in middle of the forehead; bow stapled into composition on the top of the head; tiny embossed eyebrows; painted face; side-glancing eyes; tiny, smiling, watermelon-type mouth; jointed at head, shoulders and hips; painted black shoes and white socks; dressed in blue and white checked dress trimmed in rickrack and organdy collar and cuffs; circa late 1940s. This is the same mold as Horsman's *Campbell's Kid* of the same time period (see page 85); also see cover picture.

SIMILARITIES BETWEEN THE DEE AND CEE AND THE HORSMAN CAMPBELL SOUP KID: Same size and body mold; both unmarked.

DIFFERENCES BETWEEN THE DEE AND CEE AND THE HORSMAN CAMPBELL'S SOUP KID: Dee and Cee doll has a coarser composition than the Horsman doll; painted eyelashes of Dee and Cee doll are thicker than the Horsman doll; the hair of the Dee and Cee doll has more detailed lines actually molded into the hair; the Dee and Cee doll hair is an orange color while the Horsman doll is muted brown.

MARKS: None on doll; "Campbell's Kid//A//DeeanCee Doll//Made in Canada//Permission of Campbell Soup Company Ltd" tag.

SEE: *Illustration 136.* (Color Section, page 85.)

Doll Craft

For many years collectors have been speculating about a group of 8½in (22cm) and 13in (33cm) composition dolls. They were made for the mass market and during the late 1930s, they were often purchased in the "$1.00" stores. This type of store carried slightly higher price merchandise than the "5 and 10 cent" stores. Dolls with labels from these stores can still be found.

There were different lines of dolls including an international group, a group of American vocational dolls and storybook characters. The faces of the different sets were not always painted alike, and the yellow tags were often a slightly different shape. However, the dolls were all made of an inexpensive composition and probably came from the same factory. Undoubtedly, they were purchased by different marketing firms, dressed and sold to different stores and catalog companies which sold the cheaper dolls.

The authors have collected this type of doll for years, and only one doll carried the label "Doll Craft." However, all the dolls in this book will be shown under this label for convenience.

The dolls are colorful, and both adults and children loved them. They taught geographical, vocational and literary lessons, and they are plentiful and inexpensive for collectors. Polly has her collection under her Christmas tree every year, and Pam tries to add to that collection each Christmas. It is one of the delights of collecting together.

The large majority of these dolls wear costumes from around the world. There are interesting variations of costumes from individual countries depending on which marketing country dressed the dolls.

A collector can group these dolls according to the shapes of the tags and costume variations.

These dolls have also been found to have the familiar yellow tags with the "Joy Doll Company" printed on them.

For another pictures of these dolls, see Identification Guide, page 188, *Illustration 375.*

Scarlet: 9in (23cm); all-composition; jointed at neck, shoulders and hips; *Patsy* look-alike; molded hair underneath wig; painted face; white, red and green printed dress with lace collar; black velvet sash; stiff red hat trimmed with rickrack; 1930s.

This is a very unusual doll because it is called "Scarlet," spelled with only one "t." Most other *Scarlett* dolls were made by Alexander. This is also unusual because it has a company label.

MARKS: "Scarlet//A Doll Craft Product" tag; none on doll.

SEE: *Illustration 137.*

From Left to Right: For general characteristics, see Illustration 137.

Girl of the Golden West: Cowgirl costume; mid-to-late 1930s.

Emine of Turkey: Harem costume; mid-to-late 1930s.

Edith the Nurse: Nurse uniform; mid-to-late 1930s.

MARKS: None on doll

MARKS: "I am//The Girl of the//Golden West" paper tag. "I am//Emine//of//Turkey" paper tag. "I am//Edith//Your Nurse" paper tag.

SEE: *Illustration 138.* (Color Section, page 84.)

SEE: Identification Section, page 188, *Illustration 375.*

Dolls Not Pictured

Lone Ranger: 11in (28cm); 13in (33cm); 15½in (39cm), 20in (51cm) and 25in (64cm); dressed in cowboy costumes; late 1930s.

MARKS: "Dollcraft NYC © TLR INC." back of some dolls

Tonto: 20in (51cm); fringed Indian costume; late 1930s.

Illustration 137.

Dream World Dolls

International dolls have always been popular with children and parents. Doll companies such as Alexander, Averill, Mollye and others produced lines of dolls dressed in bright, pretty ethnic costumes. Dream World made and sold such dolls by the thousands. They were made of inexpensive composition. Their costumes were made of cheap, but sturdy material. However, today many of these dolls remain bright and undamaged. Their small size, pretty colors and surprisingly lasting composition make them a favorite of collectors.

Carmen Miranda Look-alike: 12in (31cm) all inexpensive composition; jointed at neck, shoulders and hips; oval, pointed face; molded hair; painted side-glancing eyes; tiny closed mouth; fingers molded together; slim legs; heavy red cotton skirt with green fringe around skirt; green belt; gray satin top; red velvet turbin with fruit and flower trim.
MARKS: None.
SEE: *Illustration 139.*

Spanish Doll (Doll on Left): 12in (31cm); all-composition; for general characteristics, see *Illustration 139*; late 1930s.

Chinese Doll (Doll on Right): 12in (31cm); all-composition; for general characteristics, see *Illustration 139*; painted eyes have an Oriental slant; late 1930s.

The Dream World box can be seen behind the dolls.
MARKS: None on doll; "Dream World Dolls//Makes Dreams Come True" tag.
SEE: *Illustration 140.* (Color Section, page 85.) *Barbara Comienski Collection.*

Illustration 141.

Bride: 14½in (37cm) all-composition; for general characteristics, see *Illustration 139*; white rayon bride dress with beautiful net and lace overdress; wide sash; matching veil with flowers.

This larger size is rarer than the 12in (31cm) size.
MARKS: None.
SEE: *Illustration 141. Barbara Comienski Collection.*

Eaton's Beauty Dolls

Some of the most delightful dolls in Canada are called Eaton's Beauty Dolls. Beginning in 1900 one special type of doll was advertised during the year by T. Eaton, Limited, a Canadian department store. It was a popular doll of the time, and it was sold at a special price. Often the doll came with a ribbon across its chest. These specials were not offered every year, and they are not all documented. However, today these dolls are among the most highly prized dolls in Canada. Composition dolls include:

Reliable Girl Dolls: 18in (46cm); composition; metal eyes; open mouth with teeth; fully jointed; advertised with a wardrobe which could be purchased separately; included a Red Cross nurse's outfit. 1940-1941.

Reliable Girl Doll: 18in (46cm); composition; metal sleep eyes; fully jointed; wardrobe which could be purchased separately included party dress, ski suit and pajamas; 1942-1943.

Reliable Girl Doll: One other composition doll is known to have been featured between 1943 and 1945.

Illustration 139.

Effanbee Doll Corporation

Bernard Fleischaker and Hugo Baum met each other when they operated adjoining shops on the boardwalk of Atlantic City. Bernard watched Hugo clowning while selling the hand puppets he had made. Soon the two men created the firm of Fleischaker and Baum with their head full of ideas for dolls that would make them a fortune.

By 1913, they were ready to manufacture their own dolls "Made in America for American children." They combined their names and created the trademark "EFFANBEE."

At first they made rag dolls and crude composition dolls, but they continued to experiment and finally arrived at a suitable, durable composition formula. Over the years, they perfected their beautiful flesh-colored mixture of wood pulp, glue and other secret ingredients, and their business flourished.

Their first composition doll was *Baby Dainty* and by 1928, they were ready to market the "It" doll of the pre-World War II era.

This book starts with *Patsy* who created a sensation at a time when the United States was plunged into a deep depression. Effanbee turned to movies and comic strips to make dolls like *Patsy* and *Skippy*, inexpensive, well made, but bringing pleasure to millions when there was little to laugh about.

This section of this book gives only an overview of their later composition doll production. Each line had hundreds of variations. Hugo died in 1940, but he had prepared others to continue to produce some of the best composition dolls ever made during the crisis years before and after World War II. The *Little Lady* doll with her smooth golden composition "skin" which is so loved by collectors is the last of the wonderful Effanbee composition era.

Anne Shirley and Little Lady Dolls: Various sizes; all excellent composition; lovely hands have individual fingers; human hair; closed mouth; sleep eyes with lashes.

This doll was Effanbee's answer to the movie star craze which started when Ideal made *Shirley Temple*. *Little Lady* was a pretty doll and sold well. The body was also used for the Historical Series and the *Little Lady* Series.

F.A.O. Schwarz, the famous toy store in New York, placed magnets in the hands of some of these dolls so they could hold metal toys and miniatures and American flags.

During World War II, when supplies were limited, the *Little Lady Doll* had yarn hair (see *Illustration 167*).

The dolls dressed in the short versions of the Historical Dolls also used this model (see *Illustration 150*).

MARKS: (Early) "Effanbee//Anne Shirley."
(Later) "Effanbee//U.S.A."

Mary Lee (left): 17in (43cm); all-composition; jointed at neck, shoulders and hips; sleep glassene eyes; open mouth with teeth; soft caracul wig; pink dress; original except shoes; 1930-1935.

Doll also was made with cloth body.
MARKS: "Mary Lee" head; "Effanbee//Patsy Joan" body.
SEE: *Illustration 142. Nancy Carlson Collection.*

Mary Ann (right): 20in (51cm); composition head and limbs; brown sleep eyes; human hair wig; open mouth with teeth; human hair wig; cloth body; pink organdy dress; large pink hair ribbon; wears golden heart bracelet; all original; 1928-1937.
MARKS: "Mary Ann" head.
SEE: *Illustration 142. Nancy Carlson Collection.*

Illustration 142.

Illustration 143.

Dewees Cochran designed a set of dolls which was called *Portrait Children* when Effanbee advertised them in *Playthings*. They are also known as *American Children*. *Life* showed the four basic types of dolls in their issue of April 3. All the dolls are on an *Anne Shirley* body. Each different doll had a paper tag with her name on it and a metal heart.

1. **Peggy Lou:** 19in (48cm); bow mouth; painted eyes.
   MARKS: "American Children" head.
2. **Barbara Lou:** 21in (53cm); sleep eyes; tall, heavy child body; wig has bangs and hair braided and pulled to the back of the head with a big bow.
   MARKS: "American Children" head.
3. **Gloria Ann:** 19in (48cm); delicate features; sleep eyes; closed mouth.
   MARKS: "Effanbee//American//Children" head; Effanbee//Ann Shirley" body.
4. **Girl Scout:** circa 20in (51cm); painted eyes; slimmer body than other dolls; "pageboy" style wig; wears Girl Scout uniform.
   MARKS: "American Children" head.

Gloria Ann of the American Children Series: 20in (51cm); all-composition; jointed at neck, shoulders and hips; sleep eyes with lashes; closed mouth with slight smile; individual fingers; all original; 1936-1940.
   MARKS: "EFFANBEE//AMERICAN//CHIL-DREN" head; "EFFANBEE//ANN SHIRLEY" body.
   SEE: *Illustration 143. Barbara Comienski Collection.*

Pennsylvania Dutch Dolls: Family groups of Amish, Mennonite and River Brethren; *Baby Grumpy* mold was used for *Father* and *Mother*; children may not be Effanbee dolls and are not marked.

Amish Mother: 12in (31cm); painted face which does not emphasize *Grumpy* characteristics; red mohair wig with braid in back of head; closed mouth; composition head, arms and legs; cloth body; jointed at arms and legs only; circa 1936.
   MARKS: "EFFanBEE//DOLLS//WALK-TALK-SLEEP" in oval.
   "KIMCRAFT//AMERICAN TYPE//DOLLS//Independence Mo." cloth label sewn to flannel petticoat.
   SEE: *Illustration 144.* (Color Section, page 86.)

Amish Father: 12in (31cm); painted face which emphasizes frowning *Grumpy* face; lines on forehead and next to eyebrows; composition head and arms; molded-on shoes; cloth body and legs; dark brown wig and beard; circa 1936.
   MARKS: "EFFanBEE//DOLLS//WALK-TALK-SLEEP" in oval.
   SEE: *Illustration 144.* (Color Section, page 86.)

Amish Girl: 9in (23cm); painted face which resembles *Mother*; all-composition; brown wig with pigtails tied at ends with brown cloth; clothes match *Mother's* in style and color; double bonnet like *Mother*; circa 1936.
   MARKS: None on doll; "KIMCRAFT//AMERICAN TYPE//DOLLS//Independence, Mo." tag.
   SEE: *Illustration 144.* (Color Section, page 86.)

Amish Boy: 9in (23cm); painted face; all-composition; brown short wig cut with bangs; clothes match *Father* in style and color; circa 1936.
   MARKS: none on doll or clothes.
   SEE: *Illustration 144.* (Color Section, page 86.)

Pennsylvania Dutch Dolls - continued

In 1936 Marie A. Polack advertised Pennsylvania Dutch Dolls wearing the authentic religious garb of the "Plain People" of York and Lancaster County. She sold Amish, Mennonite and River Brethren costumed dolls.

The Mennonite and Amish costumes are similar, but the River Brethren ladies wear gray dresses and bonnets. The men wear a coat with an attached cape.

Black Grumpykins: 12½in (32cm); black composition; three black floss pigtails inserted in head; jointed at neck, shoulders and hips; original red polka-dotted dress; shoes and socks not original; early to mid 1930s.
MARKS: "EFFANBEE" back.
SEE: *Illustration 145. Linda Mangold Collection.*

Button Nose (Dutch Boy and Girl): 8in (20cm); all-composition; molded hair; jointed at neck, shoulders and hips; toddler; *Tinyette* body with slightly larger head mold; all original including shoes and socks; 1938-1949.
MARKS: "EFFANBEE" back
SEE: *Illustration 146. Nancy Carlson Collection.*

Illustration 145.

Illustration 146.

Effanbee Historical Dolls

In 1939 Effanbee decided to make three sets of very unusual dolls. Dewees Cochran, a famous doll designer, designed a set of over 30 American historical fashion dolls which were exhibited around the country. These dolls depicted many important changes that have taken place in our American life.

Along with the three original very ornate sets of dolls, Effanbee issued replica dolls with similar costumes. They were sold in selected toy departments around the United States.

The original dolls were about 20in (51cm) and used *Ann Shirley* bodies and *American Children* heads. They had painted eyes. The materials used in the costumes were expensive and ornate. The replica dolls were 14in (36cm). They also had painted eyes and their costumes, while accurate in each detail, were made of cotton. Each doll wore the metal Effanbee bracelet.

Today it is difficult to collect a complete set of these dolls because very few original buyers could afford all 30 dolls. It is also difficult to find the dolls in good-to-excellent condition because their composition is inclined to craze. The first doll was a topless Indian, and the last doll was dressed in a 1939 Chanel evening gown.

1. 1492 Indian.
2. 1565 St. Augustine Settlement.
3. 1607 Indian.
4. 1608 Virginia Colony.
5. 1620 Plymouth Colony.
6. 1625 New York Settlement.
7. 1632 Maryland Colony.
8. 1658 Carolina Settlement.
9. 1666 Massachusetts Baby Colony.
10. 1682 Quaker Colony.
11. 1685 Later Carolina Settlement.
12. 1711 Colonial Prosperity.
13. 1720 Pioneering Spirit of America.
14. 1740 Benjamin Franklin's Influence.
15. 1750 Development of Culture.
16. 1760 Pre-Revolutionary Period.
17. 1777 Revolutionary Period.
18. 1804 Louisiana Purchase.
19. 1816 Monroe Doctrine.
20. 1840 Covered Wagon Days.
21. 1841 Pre-Civil War Period.
22. 1864 Civil War.
23. 1868 Post-War Period.
24. 1872 Economic Development.
25. 1873 Industrial South.
26. 1888 Settling the West.
27. 1896 Unity of Nation Established.
28. 1908 Women's Suffrage Movement.
29. 1938 Modern Miss America.
30. 1939 Today (Chanel Gown).

MARKS: None head; "Effanbee Ann Shirley" body.

Illustration 147.

70

1492 Primitive Indian: 14in (36cm); all-composition; jointed at neck, arms and hips; painted eyes; dressed in white leather; outfit designed with no top; 1939.
MARKS: "Effanbee Anne Shirley" body.
SEE: *Illustration 147* (doll on left). Barbara Comienski Collection.

1620 Plymouth Colony: 14in (36cm); all-composition, jointed at neck, arms and hips; painted eyes; dressed in traditional Pilgrim soft gray costume decorated with dark purple; detachable white collar and apron; 1939.
MARKS: "Effanbee Ann Shirley" body.
SEE: *Illustration 147* (doll on right). *Barbara Comienski Collection.*

1896 Unity of Nation Established: 14in (36cm); all-composition; jointed at neck, arms and hips; painted eyes; red wig styled in Gibson Girl upsweep; large sleeves; peplum at waist; 1939.
MARKS: "Effanbee Anne Shirley" body.
SEE: *Illustration 148* (doll on left). (Color Section, page 89.) *Barbara Comienski Collection.*

1840 Covered Wagon: 14in (36cm); all-composition; jointed at neck, arms and hips; painted eyes; wig styled in ringlets of the period; 1939.
MARKS: "Effanbee Anne Shirley" body.
SEE: *Illustration 148* (doll on right). (Color Section, page 89.) *Barbara Comienski Collection.*

1720 Pioneering American Spirit: 14in (36cm); all-composition; jointed at neck, arms and hips, painted eyes; hair piled on top of head; 1939.
MARKS: "Effanbee Anne Shirley" body.
SEE: *Illustration 149.* (Color Section, page 88.) *Barbara Comienski Collection.*

Carolee and Gaye, Little Lady Dolls: 14in (36cm); all-composition; jointed at neck, shoulders and hips; beautiful wigs; sleep eyes with lashes; closed mouth; clothes are shortened versions of the long dresses of the Historical Dolls.
Carolee of Covered Wagon Set (doll on left): All original; Golden Heart tag says, "I am Carolee of 1840//A Little Lady Doll."
Gaye of Unity of Nation Established Set (doll on right): All original; Golden Heart tag says, "I am Gaye//A Little Lady Doll". There are two other dolls in this series; 1939-1940.
MARKS: "Effanbee//Ann Shirley" body of both dolls.
SEE: *Illustration 150.* (Color Section, page 89.) *Sandi Dod Collection.*

Illustration 151.

Portrait Doll: 12in (31cm); all-composition; sleep eyes; jointed at neck, shoulders and hips; dark red wig with bangs; pink striped cotton skirt and bolero jacket with large puffed sleeves; attached white blouse; missing boater-type hat.
These dolls included *Little Bo Peep, Bride and Groom, Gibson Girl, Kate Greenaway Boy and Girl, Ballerina*; circa 1940s.
MARKS: None.
SEE: *Illustration 151. Barbara Comienski Collection.*

Suzette Martha and George Washington: 1932 Bicentennial of George Washington's birth doll (see page 57.)

Suzanne: 14in (36cm); all-composition; jointed at neck, arms and legs; brown sleep eyes; painted black eyelashes under the eyes; painted arched eyebrow; second and third fingers curved and molded together; blonde mohair wig curled in ringlets; clothes are not original; 1940.
MARKS: "Suzanne//Effanbee//Made in//USA" back.
SEE: *Illustration 152.*

Illustration 152.

Illustration 156.

Suzanne Nurse: 14in (36cm); all-composition; for general characteristics, see *Illustration 152* ; F.A.O. Schwarz special; wears gold heart Effanbee bracelet; yellow paper bell-shaped tag that reads "Doll With Magnetic Hands//Manufactured by F.A.O. Schwarz"; dressed in white cotton nurse outfit with additional red hat, blue nurse cape, matching blue skirt, white blouse; accessories include gauze, swabs, hot water bottle, thermometer, manual which has magnetic tape to fit into her magnet hands; 1940.
    MARKS: "Suzanne//Effanbee//Doll" back.
    SEE: *Illustration 153.* (Color Section, page 88.)

Honey: 21in (53cm); all-composition; jointed at neck, shoulders and legs; flirty sleep eyes with real lashes; 1946.
    A composition *Honey* was last advertised in the 1946 Montgomery Ward catalog. In late 1946 and 1947 they started to make *Honey* in hard plastic.
    MARKS: "Honey" paper Gold Heart tag. "Effanbee" body and head.
    SEE: *Illustration 154.* (Color Section, page 88.) *Sandi Dod Collection.*

Lovums: 18in (46cm); composition head which swivels and is attached to the shoulder plate; light brown molded hair; tin sleep eyes with real lashes; open mouth with two upper teeth, two lower teeth and molded tongue; curved composition arms; third and fourth fingers molded together; straight composition legs with two lines under knees painted pale pink; cloth body with heavily stuffed bottom for easier sitting; came with metal Effanbee gold heard wrist bracelet; round dimple on chin; original dress; 1928 - early 1940s.
    MARKS: "EFFANBEE//LOVUMS//c//PAT.NO.1 1,283558."
    SEE: *Illustration 155.* (Color Section, page 92.) *Ruth Chappell Collection.*

Lovums: 18in (46cm); for general characteristics, see *Illustration 155*; light brown caracul wig (over molded hair); sleep eyes with real lashes; dimple on chin; golden heart bracelet; dress not original; doll made in several sizes; 1928 into 1940s.
    MARKS: "Effanbee//Lovums//©//Pat.1 1,283558."
    SEE: *Illustration 156.*

Lovums Heartbeat Baby: 18in (46cm); for general characteristics, see *Illustration 155*; molded hair; heartbeat mechanism has windup key in body; doll came with a stethoscope; 1942.
    MARKS: "Effanbee//Lovums//©//1,283558."
    SEE: *Illustration 157. Eleanore Lihti Collection.*

Dy-Dee the Almost Human Doll: "Dy-Dee drinks water from a bottle (the only doll in the world of this kind) and then wets her diaper." The doll is dressed in romper suit and hat suitable for the beach.
    SEE: *Illustration 158. Playthings,* June 1935.

Illustration 157
a & b.

Sweetie Pie: 24in (61cm); caracul wig; composition head with flange for attaching body; composition curved arms and legs; dimple on chin; flirty sleep eyes with real eyelashes; flesh-colored cloth body; white dress; 1938-1948.

This type of doll was also called *Touslehead*.

MARKS: "Effanbee" head.

SEE: *Illustration 159. Linda Mangold Collection.*

Sleeping Babyette: 11½in (29cm); layette set never removed from the box; doll wearing Christening dress and bonnet; white blanket with blue trim; white robe with tiny flowers; pink sacque; the box measures 18in (46cm) by 21in (53cm); circa 1942.

During World War II Effanbee is reported to have run out of eyes. So they made sleeping dolls.

MARKS: "F & B//Babyette" head.

SEE: *Illustration 160. (Color Section, page 48.)*
Mary Lu Trowbridge Collection.

Baby Bright Eyes Mold: Just before World War II, Effanbee brought out a new line of baby dolls called *Baby Bright Eyes*. They advertised her and companion dolls widely. An advertisement said, "Just look at Baby Bright Eyes//The New member of the Effanbee Doll Family has flirting Eyes//A REAL HEART-breaking flirt is the newest Effanbee Doll. Large expressive eyes, satin-smooth skin, dainty clothes make *Baby Bright Eyes* a precious playmate." *Tommy Tucker* was made from this mold and was considered a member of the *Bright Eyes* family; 1930-1945.

MARKS: "Effanbee//Made in USA" head.

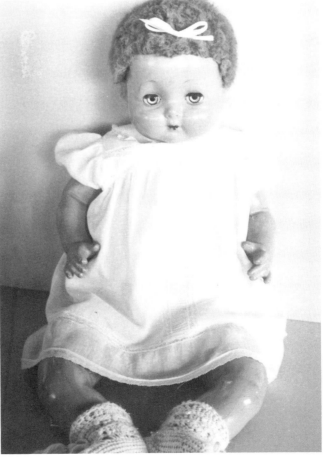

Illustration 158.

Illustration 159.

73

Tommy Tucker: Approximately 17in (43cm); all-composition; original human hair wig; flirty sleep eyes; original clothes; tan corduroy overalls and matching cap; blue and white striped shirt; leatherette shoes; circa 1939-1946.

This doll was given by the present owner to her mother for Christmas. He stayed in the closet and was brought out when children visited her. The doll was well made and today has bright and shiny uncrazed composition and sparkling clothes.

   MARKS: "Effanbee//Made in USA" head; "I am Tommy Tucker with moving eyes//An EFFANBEE Durable Doll" tag.

   SEE: *Illustration 161. Mary Elizabeth Poole Collection.*

Candy Kid: This doll was released in 1946, just after World War II, and was an instant success. Its winsome, American-toddler look appealed to children and adults. It came as a girl or a boy. It was also issued as a pair in matching costumes.

Montgomery Ward featured an Easter doll dressed in yellow. Their Christmas catalog showed the same doll in a trunk with a wardrobe.

Effanbee made a set in red checked gingham. The boy had a wooden yo-yo. The girl had a small stuffed monkey.

The June 2, 1946 issue of the *Pittsburgh Press* showed a photograph of the pair dressed for school carrying a slate, report card, eraser and pencil. The boy was dressed in overalls, matching cap and a white blouse. The girl was dressed in a pinafore, white blouse and matching bonnet. Both wore the tie shoes shown in *Illustration 162* (Color Section, page 89).

Other costumes included matching cowboy costumes, a majorette dress for the girl; wardrobe sets which included a girl's coat and hat, play and dress clothes.

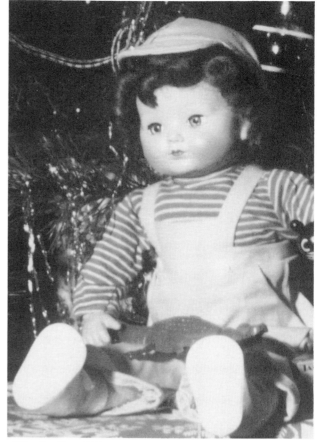

Illustration 161.

Candy Kid: 13in (33cm); all-composition; jointed in neck, shoulders and hips; chubby child figure; closed mouth; sleep eyes; pointed eyebrows; painted eyelashes under eyes; molded hair; real leather boxing gloves; leatherette shoes; 1946.

   MARKS: "EFFANBEE" on head; "EFFANBEE" on body.

   SEE: *Illustration 162.* (Color Section, page 89.)

Sister: 18in (46cm); composition head and hands with dimples above fingers; cloth stuffed body, arms, legs and feet; composition neck piece between head and body; painted face; distinctive eyes outlined with thin brown line; floss wig; companion to *Brother*; not original clothes; circa 1942-1944.

Sister was one of the dolls made during the wartime shortages of World War II when the company used whatever material was available to supply children with dolls.

   MARKS: "Effanbee" on back of head.

   SEE: *Illustration 163. Cobb Auctions.*

Little Lady: 18in (46cm); all-composition; jointed at neck, shoulders and hips; individual fingers; sleep eyes with real lashes; feathered eyebrows; red dots at corner of eyes; eyelashes under eyes; closed mouth; all original wavy floss hair substituted during World War II. Circa 1942-1945.

   MARKS: "Effanbee//U.S.A." head; "Effanbee//U.S.A." body.

   SEE: *Illustration 164* (doll on right). (Color Section, page 87.)

Illustration 163.

Little Lady: 22in (56cm); (for general characteristics, see *Illustration 164*); blonde human hair wig with long curls; gold Effanbee sandals; late 1940s trimmed with black lace; black velvet belt at waist; long taffeta slip; white socks; gold Effanbee sandals; all original; late 1940s.

    MARKS: Effanbee//Anne Shirley" back.

    SEE: *Illustration 164* (doll on left). (Color Section, page 87.)

Illustration 165.

Little Lady Doll Pattern: McCall #1015; included a U.S.O. Volunteer and Red Cross nurse pattern; long party dress with flying birds appliqued on skirt and short coat and matching tam with plaid pleated skirt and white blouse patterns. Circa 1941-1945.

    SEE: *Illustration 165.*

Anne Shirley in Original Box: 32in (81cm); jointed at neck, shoulders and hips; all-composition; blue organdy dress with pink ribbon sash; white stockings; black Effanbee sandals; 1939 into the later 1940s.

    Some *Little Lady* dolls in smaller sizes had magnets implanted into their hands to hold flags, household utensils, brooms, and so forth (see Identification Guide, page 196, *Illustration 394*.)

    MARKS: "Effanbee" box.

    SEE: *Illustration 166. Carol Kelly and Priscilla Lynch Collection.*

Illustration 166.

Little Ladies: 18in (46cm); for general characteristics, see *Illustration 164.*

Majorette: Yarn hair used during World War II; red and white majorette uniform; gold trim; brass buttons; high hat with gold trim; white boots with red trim; early 1940s.
    MARKS: "EFFANBEE" head.
    SEE: *Illustration 167. Barbara Comienski Collection.*

Scottish Costume: mohair wig; black velvet coat; lace jabot; yellow, red, green and black plaid pleated skirt; red stockings; black Effanbee sandals; late 1930s and early 1940s.
    MARKS: "EFFANBEE" head.
    SEE: *Illustration 167. Barbara Comienski Collection.*

Girl in Long Blue Dress: Organza dress with pink braid trim; flower in hair; wears Golden Heart bracelet. Late 1930s and early 1940s.
    MARKS: "EFFANBEE" head.
    SEE: *Illustration 168. Barbara Comienski Collection.*

Girl in Raincoat: tan coat and matching hood with red and blue plaid trim; over-the-shoulder matching plaid pocketbook; 1939 into late 1940s.
    MARKS: "EFFANBEE" head.
    SEE: *Illustration 168. Barbara Comienski Collection.*

Dolls Not Pictured

Happy Birthday Musical Girl: 18in (46cm); all-composition; fully jointed; key wind in back causes music box to play works and music.
    MARKS: "Effanbee U.S.A." back.

Emily Ann Marionette: 13in (33cm); composition head with braided, molded hair; composition hands and feet; wooden body.
    MARKS: "©//Emily Ann//V. Austin//Effanbee."

Illustration 167.

Illustration 168.

Patsy, The Doll That Warmed The Depression With Her Golden Heart

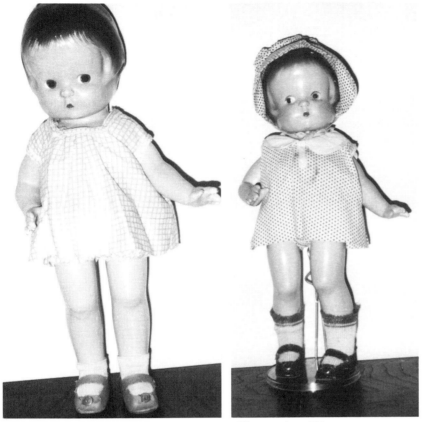

Illustration 170.   *Illustration 170.*

Illustration 169.

Patsy was one of the most popular dolls of the 20th century and the most important doll of the depressed early 1930s. She was first made in 1924 with a stuffed cloth body and head and limbs of composition.

The all-composition doll was put on the market in 1928 and was the most popular doll of the year. She had molded hair, a curved right arm, a wardrobe which could be purchased at the store and a wonderful expression on her tiny face.

Soon the *Patsy* family came along, and sleep eyes and hair were added to members of the family. They wore the golden heart pendant or bracelet which was added to Effanbee dolls in 1923. *Patsy* was still popular in 1938, but World War II soon put an end to both *Patsy* and the metal golden hearts.

In 1946, two *Patsy* dolls were back on the market, but the metal heart was gone. *Patsy* never really regained her popularity with the post-war baby boom generation. By 1950 the winsome little *Patsys* were no longer manufactured.

The hard plastic dolls took over, and the vinyl dolls followed, but *Patsy* was never forgotten. Today the collectors are scrambling for the few available. Because they were play dolls, they are often not in good condition. It has become customary when pricing these dolls to add the words, "Dolls may have some crazing and original or appropriate clothes." Patsy was, and still is an old friend with a "golden heart."

Patsy Has "It": In January of 1928, Effanbee advertised a new doll which was to be introduced at the Toy Fair in February. "It" was to be a simple doll with a revolutionary style and body. They called her the "Personality Doll." To keep the secret, they only showed the back of the doll. This was also a new idea in advertising.

SEE: *Illustration 169. Playthings,* January 1928.

Early Patsy (Doll on Left): 14in (36cm); for general characteristics (see *Illustration 179*); this is one type of simple clothes worn by the first *Patsy* dolls; blue and white checked dress with simple braid trim on collar and sleeves; all original including shoes; childhood doll of Mary Elizabeth Poole; 1928.

SEE: *Illustration 170. Mary Elizabeth Poole Collection.*

Patsy (Doll on Right): 14in (36cm); during the early years of *Patsy*, Effanbee offered a service which fixed *Patsy* dolls. If a doll was broken or cracked, it could be sent back to the factory for refinishing.

This is the childhood doll of Madge Poole Copley, and it was refinished by the Effanbee Company. It has its original clothes.

SEE: *Illustration 170. Madge Poole Copley Collection.*

Wee Patsy Twins: 6in (15cm); all-composition; painted facial features; molded hair with molded hair band; fully jointed; all original sailor matching costumes in blue and white; molded painted socks and shoes; 1934.
    MARKS: "Effanbee//Wee-Patsy" back.
    SEE: *Illustration 171.*

Patsy Tinyette Doctor: 7in (18cm); for general characteristics, see *Illustration 174*; all original; circa 1933.
    MARKS: "Effanbee//Baby Tinyette" back; "Patsy Doctor" label on hat.
    SEE: *Illustration 173.* (Color Section, page 90.) *Nancy Carlson Collection.*

Illustration 171.

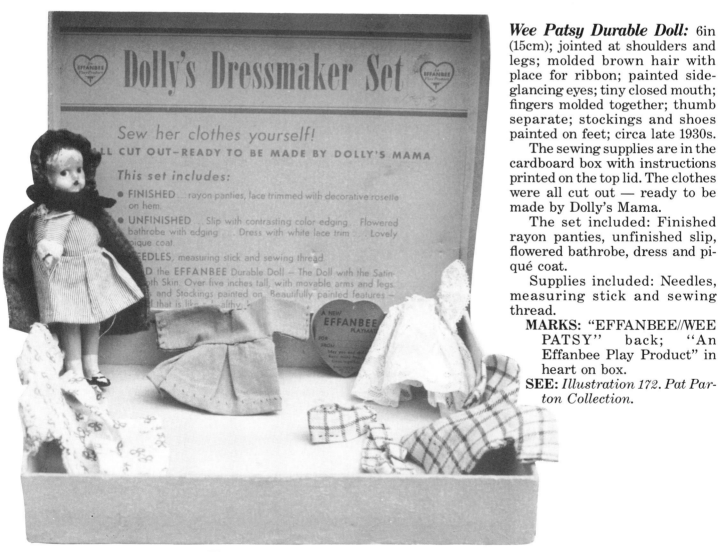

Wee Patsy Durable Doll: 6in (15cm); jointed at shoulders and legs; molded brown hair with place for ribbon; painted side-glancing eyes; tiny closed mouth; fingers molded together; thumb separate; stockings and shoes painted on feet; circa late 1930s.

The sewing supplies are in the cardboard box with instructions printed on the top lid. The clothes were all cut out — ready to be made by Dolly's Mama.

The set included: Finished rayon panties, unfinished slip, flowered bathrobe, dress and piqué coat.

Supplies included: Needles, measuring stick and sewing thread.
    MARKS: "EFFANBEE//WEE PATSY" back; "An Effanbee Play Product" in heart on box.
    SEE: *Illustration 172. Pat Parton Collection.*

Illustration 172.

Illustration 174.

Baby Tinyette as a Dutch Boy:
7in (18cm); all-composition; molded hair; painted eyes with tiny eyelashes above eyes; toddler legs; Dutch costume; black cotton pants with two buttons; red cotton shirt; black tie; felt hat with gold rope trim as decoration; wooden shoes; circa 1933-1936.

MARKS: "Effanbee//Baby Tinyette" back; "Effanbee" head.

SEE: *Illustration 174.*

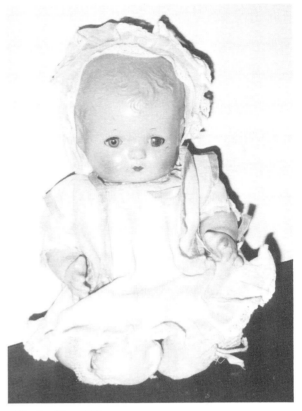

Illustration 175.

Patsy Baby (also called Patsy Babykin): 9in (23cm); all-composition; molded blonde hair; fully jointed; curved baby legs; sleep eyes with lashes; tiny eyebrows above eyes; closed mouth; 1932. The owner recalls from her childhood that the doll came only with a diaper, but baby clothes could be purchased separately. The white dress and bonnet were purchased for this doll. Sunsuits and sweaters were available. When this doll was broken, it was returned to the factory for repairs. It was returned with blonde molded hair.

MARKS: "Patsy Baby" back.

SEE: *Illustration 175. Madge Poole Copely Collection.*

Patsyette: 9in (23cm); various costumes used for *Patsyette* when she was newly introduced. These were similar, or even exactly the same designs, as used for their other dolls in the *Patsy* line; example is the boy's suit used for *Patsy Joan* (see *Illustration 185*); 1931.

SEE: *Illustration 176. Playthings*, May 1931.

Patsyette Hawaiian Twins: 9in (23cm); authentically dressed in Hawaiian clothes; composition tinted to reflect Hawaiian skin tone.

MARKS: "Effanbee//Patsyette//Doll" back.

SEE: *Illustration 177.* (Color Section, page 90.) *Nancy Carlson Collection.*

Illustration 176.

Illustration 181.

Patsyette George and Martha Washington: 1932 Bicentennial of George Washington's birth doll (see page 57 and Color Page 82.)

Patsykins (Patsy Jr.): 11in (28cm); all-composition; molded hair bangs and center part; molded hair band; sleep eyes with lashes; petite painted eyelashes under eyes; tiny closed mouth; curved right arm; straight left arm; gold heart bracelet; 1930.
 MARKS: "Effanbee//Patsy Jr." back.
 SEE: *Illustration 178.* (Color Section, page 93.)

Patsy: 14in (36cm); all-composition; jointed at neck, shoulders and hips; body has new neckline extension which allows head to be easily supported; right arm curved at almost 90 degree angle; left arm straight; third and fourth fingers molded together; chunky body and legs; painted face and eyes; molded hair with molded hair band; all original including shoes and socks; circa 1928.
 MARKS: "EFFanBee//PATSY//PAT.PEND.// DOLL"
  body; none on head.
 SEE: *Illustration 179* (doll on right). (Color Section, page 91.)

Patsy: 14in (36cm); for general characteristics, see *Illustration 179*; all original dress and hat; mohair wig covering molded hair; sleep eyes with real lashes; lashes painted around eyes; closed mouth; circa 1933.
 MARKS: "Effanbee//Patsy" head; "Effanbee// Patsy//Doll" body.
 SEE: *Illustration 179* (doll on left). (Color Section, page 91.)

Patsyette: 9in (23cm); all-composition; fully-jointed; bobbed wig over molded hair with bangs; curved right arm at about 90 degree angle; straight left arm; painted brown eyes; petite lashes painted above eyes; long slender legs; dress original; shoes and socks not original; 1931.
 MARKS: "Effanbee//Patsyette//Doll" back; "EFFanBEE"//Durable//Dolls (in a Golden Heart outlined with red)//Made in U.S.A." cloth tag on dress.
 SEE: *Illustration 179* (doll in center). (Color Section, page 91.)

Patsy and Friend: For the children of the 1930s, money was scarce. *Patsy* was a doll to be loved, played with and dressed in homemade clothes. Today's collectors still enjoy sewing the sweet, simple styles of this charmer. This is Pam's doll and at Christmas, Polly still enjoys making a new outfit for the beloved doll of her own childhood. The "Friend" is a homemade gift.
 SEE: *Illustration 180.* (Color Section, page 94.)

1946 Patsy: 14in (36cm); all-composition; jointed at neck, shoulders and hips; darker composition than on the earlier *Patsy*; painted side-glancing eyes; molded hair; red checked pinafore; red and white ruffled trim; 1946.
 This doll was only made for one year, and it did not sell well. The composition was a cheap quality, and it has not held up well. This is a hard-to-find example of the *Patsy* doll in excellent original condition.
 MARKS: None; "Patsy" paper gold heart.
 SEE: *Illustration 181. Dee Percifull Collection.*

ABOVE: *AVERILL* Val-Encia *(see page 53*, Illustration 105*)*.

ABOVE LEFT: *AVERILL* Whistling Cowboy *(see page 52*, Illustration 102*)*.

LEFT: *AVERILL* Dimmie *(see page 53*, Illustrations 103 *and* 104*)*. Sandra Strater Collection.

BELOW: *AMERICAN CHARACTER* Bicentennial George Washington *(see page 56, Illustration 113) and* Bicentennial Beddoll *(see page 56, Illustration 113).*

ABOVE: *TOY PRODUCTS:* George Washington *(see page 57, Illustration 117).*

LEFT: *EFFANBEE* Bicentennial George and Martha Washington *(see page 57, Illustration 117).*

RIGHT: *CAMEO* Giggles *(see page 61*, Illustration 128*)*. Lois Janner Collection.

BELOW: *AMBERG: Two* Amfelt Art Dolls *(see page 26*, Illustration 73*)*.

DOLL CRAFT Girl of the Golden West, Emine of Turkey and Edith the Nurse *(see page 65*, Illustration 138).

BELOW: *CAMEO* Margie *(see page 59*, Illustration 121). Linda Mangold Collection.

CONFETTI Alpine *(see page 63*, Illustration 133).

RIGHT: *DEE AND CEE* Campbell Soup Girl and *Horsman* Campbell Soup Boy *(see pages 64, Illustration 136).*

DREAM WORLD Spanish and Chinese Dolls *(see page 66, Illustration 140).* Barbara Comienski Collection.

EFFANBEE Pennsylvania Dutch Family *(see page 68, Illustration 144)*.

EFFANBEE two Little Lady *dolls (see pages 74 and 75, Illustration 164).*

BELOW: *EFFANBEE* Historical Doll 1720 Pioneering American Spirit *(see page 71*, Illustration 149*)*. Barbara Comienski Collection.

ABOVE: *EFFANBEE* Honey *(see page 72*, Illustration 154*)*. Sandi Dod Collection.

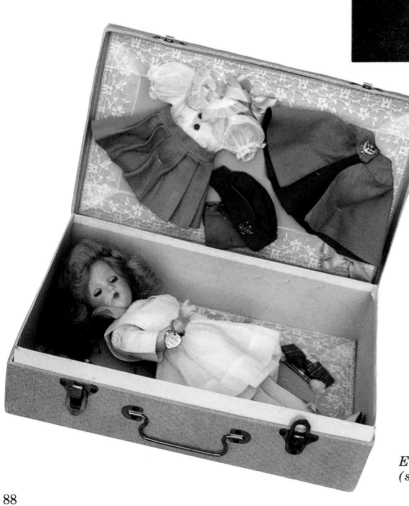

EFFANBEE Suzanne Nurse *(see page 72*, Illustration 153*)*.

BELOW: *EFFANBEE* Candy Kid *(see page 74, Illustration 162).*

ABOVE: *EFFANBEE* Historical Dolls, Unity of Nation Established *and* Covered Wagon *(see page 71, Illustration 148).* Barbara Comienski Collection.

LEFT: *EFFANBEE* Carolee and Gaye, Little Lady Dolls *(see page 71, Illustration 150).* Sandi Dod Collection.

ABOVE: *EFFANBEE* Tinyette Doctor *(see page 78,* Illustration 173*).* Nancy Carlson Collection.

ABOVE RIGHT: *EFFANBEE* Aviator Skippy *(see page 100,* Illustration 192*).* Mariane Gardner Collection.

RIGHT: *EFFANBEE* Hawaiian Twins *(see page 79,* Illustration 177*).* Nancy Carlson Collection.

LEFT: *EFFANBEE Wigged* Patsy, *molded hair* Patsy *and* Patsyette *(see page 80, Illustration 179)*.

BELOW LEFT: *EFFANBEE* Patricia as Anne of Green Gables *(see page 97, Illustration 183)*. Nancy Carlson Collection.

BELOW: *EFFANBEE* Patricia *(see page 97, Illustration 184)*. Nancy Carlson Collection.

ABOVE: *EFFANBEE* Lovums
(see page 72, Illustration 155).
Ruth Chappell Collection.

ABOVE RIGHT: *EFFANBEE*
Patsy Joan *(see page 98*, Illustration 187).

RIGHT: *EFFANBEE* Patsy
Anns *(see page 98*, Illustration 188).

EFFANBEE Patsykins (Patsy
Jr.) *(see page 80*, Illustration 178*)*.

RIGHT: *EUGENIA* Girl in Pink Dress *(see page 102*, Illustration 195). Joyce Stock and Kathy Adams Collection.

FAR RIGHT: *EFFANBEE* Patsy *and* Friend *(see page 80*, Illustration 180).

BELOW: *UNKNOWN* Cuban Dancers *(see page 104*, Illustration 201).

ABOVE: Gaucho from Argentina *(see page 104, Illustration 199).* Shirley Karaba Collection.

RIGHT: *UNKNOWN* Swedish Boy in Folkloric Costume *(see page 105*, Illustration 207*)*.

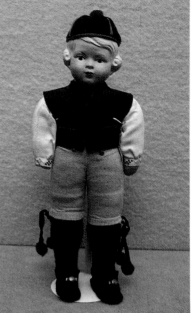

BELOW: *FREUNDLICH* Red Riding Hood, Grandmother and Wolf *(see page 107*, Illustration 212*)*.

FREUNDLICH Baby Sandy *(see page 108*, Illustration 216). Sandra Strater Collection.

IDEAL Shirley Temple *(see page 145*, Illustration 257). Athena Crowley Collection.

BELOW: *HOLLYWOOD* Cowboy and Cowgirl *(see page 114*, Illustration 230).

HORSMAN Toddler *(see page 119*, Illustration 239).

Anne Shirley: picture of the movie actress Ann Shirley with the new *Anne Shirley* doll.

SEE: *Illustration 182. Toys and Novelties*, August 1936.

Patricia as Anne Shirley: 14⅗in (37cm); all-composition; jointed at neck, shoulders and hips; body more slender than *Patsy*; sleep eyes with lashes; closed mouth; human hair wig with blonde wig; clothes all original; wears the Golden Heart bracelet; circa 1936.

This is one of the rarer *Patsy*-type Effanbee dolls. She was advertised as a grown-up *Patsy*. *Patricia* dressed as *Anne of Green Gables* came with either red or blonde hair. There were several variations of this costume.

Patricia had a variety of other costumes including school dresses, party dresses and others.

This doll can be found with either molded hair or a wig. Variations of bodies and heads with different markings have been found.

MARKS: "Effanbee//Patricia" back; "I am//Anne Shirley//Anne of Green Gables" paper wrist tag.

SEE: *Illustration 183.* (Color Section, page 91.) *Nancy Carlson Collection.*

Illustration 185.

Meets Her Namesake

Fleischaker & Baum, 200 Fifth Avenue, New York, launched a successful promotion on the Anne Shirley doll, inspired by R. K. O.'s star of that name. Seldom has such an appeal been made to mothers and daughters as the charmingly naive portrayal of the unsophisticated girl in "Anne of Green Gables."

Illustration 182.

Patricia: 14⅗in (37cm); for general characteristics, see *Illustration 183*; unusual blonde mohair wig; dressed in colonial-type costume; all original. This doll's costume is comparable to the quality of the historical dolls. It does resemble the *Aunt Patsy* costume.

MARKS: "Effanbee//Patricia" back.

SEE: *Illustration 184.* (Color Section, page 91.) *Nancy Carlson Collection.*

Patsy Joan: 16in (41cm); all-composition; jointed at neck, shoulders and hips; molded hair without band; sleep eyes with lashes; one-piece blue and white sailor suit; matching tam; braid trim; belt with silver buckle; buttons on sides of pants; all original except socks and shoes; 1928-1936.

MARKS: "Effanbee//Patsy Joan" back.

SEE: *Illustration 185.*

Patsy Joan: 16in (41cm); all-composition; for general characteristics, see *Illustration 185*; wig; dress with ruffled skirt; pink ribbons at yoke line; all original including shoes and socks; printed blue organdy dress with ruffled skirt; circa 1928-1936.
    MARKS: Effanbee//Patsy Joan" back.
    SEE: *Illustration 186. Madge Poole Copley Collection.*

1946 Patsy Joan: 17in (43cm); all-composition; color of composition is a more ivory shade than the original rosy *Patsy*; molded hair with part on left hand side with right side wavy and deep on forehead; protruding curls at hairline on back of head; sleep eyes with real lashes; small closed mouth; jointed at neck, shoulders and hips; second and third fingers molded together; curved right arm; straighter left arm; dimples in back of elbows; Ƴ on backside; long legs with dimples at back of knees; green organdy dress with large white collar; tiny yoke; high skirt with deep hem with hemstitching for trim; tiny flowers on skirt and matching hat; 1946.
    This doll was made for only one year and crazes easily. While different from the original, it is beautiful in its own right. It is difficult to find, and a doll in excellent condition and all original is rare. The marking is unusual, and some of the dolls are unmarked.
    MARKS: "EFFANBEE" back.
    SEE: *Illustration 187.* (Color Section, page 92.)

Illustration 186.

Patsy Ann with Wig: 19in (48cm); for general characteristics, see *Illustration 188*; blue sleep eyes; human hair wig over molded hair; all original including shoes; circa 1928.
    MARKS: "EFFANBEE//'Patsy-Ann'//©// Pat.#1283558" back.
    SEE: *Illustration 188* (doll on left). (Color Section, page 92.)

Patsy Ann with Molded Hair: 19in (48cm); all-composition; molded hair without hair band; blue sleep eyes with lashes; eyelashes under eyes; red dots in corner of each eye; tiny closed mouth; jointed at neck, shoulders and hips; right arm curved; left arm straight; all original including shoes and socks; introduced in 1928.
    MARKS: "EFFANBEE//'Patsy-Ann'//c// Pat.#1283558" back.
    SEE: *Illustration 188* (doll on right). (Color Section, page 92.)

Patsy Ann: 19in (48cm); for general characteristics, see *Illustration 188*; dressed in green silk dress with beautiful smocking; all original including shoes and socks; doll came in box at left; 1928.
INSET AT TOP LEFT: traditionally the *Patsy and Family* clothes were fastened with safety pins; most original clothes do not have other closings.
INSET AT TOP RIGHT: Many *Patsy* dolls had hair ribbons on their molded hair. To keep the ribbon on the doll, most original ribbons had elastic in the back. The inset shows how this was made.
    MARKS: "EFFANBEE//'Patsy-Ann'//c// Pat.#1283558" back.
    SEE: *Illustration 189. Marianne Gardner Collection.*

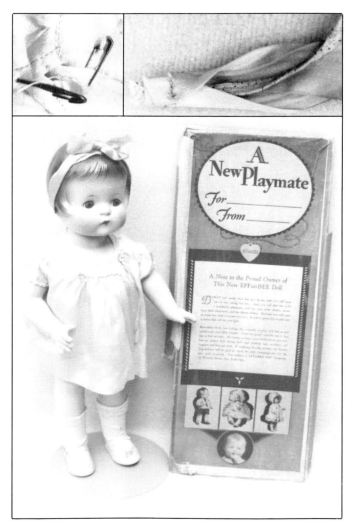

Illustration 189.

Patsy Lou: 22in (56cm); all-composition; molded hair with no molded hair band; fully jointed; sleep eyes with lashes; yellow print dress with white collar; black trim around bottom of skirt; made from 1930 to 1940.
  SEE: *Illustration 190. Roslyn Nigoff Collection.*

Patsy Ruth (Doll on Left): 27in (69cm); composition head, arms and legs; cloth body; wig covering molded hair; sleep eyes with lashes; yellow and white print dress with ruffle around the bottom.

Patsy Mae (Doll on Right): 30in (76cm); largest of *Patsy* family; composition head, arms and legs; *Lovums*-type body; circa 1934.
  MARKS: "Effanbee//Patsy Ruth" head.
  MARKS: "Effanbee//Patsy Mae" head.
  SEE: *Illustration 191. Betty Shriver Collection.*

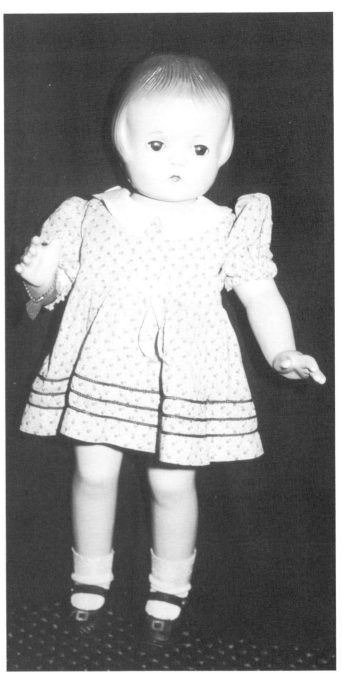

Illustration 190.

Illustration 191.

Skippy

In January 1929, Effanbee advertised in *Playthings* "...The Famous Mischievous Skippy. Millions of children and parents follow with delight the antics and adventures of Skippy in the leading newspapers and magazines of the country. This perfect doll reproduction of Skippy will make an instant appeal to them. He will equal Patsy's popularity. We have secured the exclusive rights for doll reproduction of Skippy from his creator, Percy Crosby."

In May 1929 *Playthings* published a photograph of a line of *Skippy* dolls. *Skippy* was costumed as a cowboy, farmer, little boy in short pants, baseball player, little boy in long pants with suspenders and little boy in short pants with suspenders.

Illustration 192.

Skippy: 14in (36cm); all-composition; jointed at neck, shoulders and hips; black version with black molded hair; brown eyes; all original.
>   MARKS: "Patsy//Pat.//Pending" body; "I am Skippy//The All American Boy" pin on front of shirt.
>   SEE: *Illustration 192. Nancy Carlson Collection.*

Aviator Skippy: 14in (36cm); cloth body and upper legs; composition arms; composition legs to just above knee; shoes and socks molded on leg; molded hair with lock low on forehead; painted eyes; widely spaced eyelashes above eyes; tiny arched eyebrows; dressed as aviator; all original; circa 1940s.
>   MARKS: "Effanbee//Skippy//C.P.L.—" back; "Keep 'em Flying" wing patch.
>   SEE: *Illustration 193.* (Color Section, page 90.) *Marianne Gardner Collection.*

Skippy: Advertisement in *Toy World*, February 1929; store window with picture of Jackie Cooper and *Skippy* dolls in various outfits.
>   SEE: *Illustration 194. Toy World*, February 1929.

Skippy Body Variations: There are three basic types of *Skippy* bodies:
1. All-composition; jointed at neck, shoulders and hips.
   MARKS: "Patsy//Pat.//Pending" body.
2. Composition head, arms and legs; cloth body.
3. Composition head and arms; cloth body and upper legs; composition legs to just above knees which were molded to show socks and shoes. These bodies were used for the military dolls during the 1940s.
   MARKS: "Effanbee//Skippy//c//P.L. Crosby" head.

Patsy Chart

Although there were dolls called *Patsy* as early as 1924, the all-composition best-seller with the "It" personality was introduced in January 1928. The *Patsy* "family" of dolls includes:
I. ***Wee Patsy:*** 6in (15cm); eyes were round, regular or almond-shaped.
   A. Sets include a *Fairy Princess* in Colleen Moore's Fairy Castle box and a boxed sewing kit.
   B. Boy and girl matching costumes.
   C. Special costumes such as Naval Officer's uniform (advertised in *Home* magazine, December 1932).

Illustration 194.

D. Regular clothes included one-piece play-suits, short checked dress with wide pleated panties, organdy dress with lace at hem.

II. **Baby Tinyette:** 7in (18cm); introduced in 1933.
    A. Came with molded hair or wigs.
    B. Came as separate babies, twins, triplets and quintuplets in suitcase; also came as a doctor.
    C. Came with curved baby legs or straight legs.
    D. Foreign costumes often used on dolls with straight legs.

III. **Patsy Babyette:** 8in (20cm); introduced in 1933.
    A. Frequently sold as boy and girl twins.
    B. A few dolls had yarn hair.

IV. **Patsyette:** 9in (23cm); introduced in 1931; excellent seller; well-made doll that has held up well through the years.
    A. Many dolls dressed in traditional *Patsy* outfits.
    B. Sewing kits.
    C. Dressed in foreign and historical costumes.

V. **Patsy Baby (also called Patsy Baby-kin):** 10in (25cm); introduced in 1932.
    A. Some had caracul wigs.
    B. Black babies inspired by Amosandra of the "Amos and Andy" radio program; had molded hair with a head band and three tufts of hair.

VI. **Patsykins (also called Patsy Jr.):** 11in (28cm); introduced in 1930.
    A. Marked *Patsy Jr.* but sold as *Patsykins* because Effanbee felt the name was too masculine.
    B. One of rarest of *Patsy* dolls.
    C. Most often dressed in short dresses.

VII. **Patricia-kin:** 11in (28cm); introduced in 1932.
    A. Different face.
    B. Hard to find doll.

VIII. **1924 Patsy** 14in (36cm) — 15in (38cm); did not look like later dolls.

IX. **Patsy:** 14in (36cm); name registered on October 14, 1927; first advertised in January 1928.
    A. Similar to Armand Marseille *Just Me*.
    B. Costumes included foreign, historical, brother and sister combinations.
    C. Play and party clothes often were variations of same style or material.
    D. Dolls had molded hair until wigs added in 1933.
    E. Many of the first dress tags and advertising had the NRA (National Recovery Act) label.
    F. One of first dolls to have modern-type wardrobe for sale in stores and patterns for home sewing.
    G. In 1936 a new fingernail of colorless celluloid inserted on cuticle of some dolls.

    H. In 1938-1939 magnets put in some of *Patsy's* hands by F.A.O. Schwarz.
    I. Some dolls sent to Hawaii to be dressed for tourists.
    J. Special dolls included:
        1. *Chinese Patsy* with oval eyes and black hair with bangs.
        2. *Patsy* in riding habit with jodhpurs as advertised in *Home* magazine, December 1932.
    K. Elastic used to hold hair ribbons on molded hair.
    L. *Patsy* discontinued during World War II; reissued in 1946; quality poor; doll crazes easily.

X. **Patricia:** 14⅛in (37cm); introduced in 1932.
    A. Advertised as *Patsy's* grown-up sister; slimmer body; tiny breasts.
    B. Dressed in play clothes, party clothes and costumes of *Ann of Green Gables*.
    C. Two different faces on same body; both dolls marked the same; one face had green eyes; other face had blue eyes; both had human hair wigs.

XI. **Patsy Joan:** 16in (41cm); made from 1928-1936.
    A. No molded headband like *Patsy*.
    B. Reissued in 1946 only; 17in (41cm); different mold.

XII. **Patsy Ann:** 19in (48cm); introduced in 1928.
    A. Advertised as *Patsy's* big sister.
    B. Fingernail added on some dolls.
    C. Costumes included traditional *Patsy* clothes.
    D. Special costumes made including snowsuit with zippered boots shown in *Home* magazine in December 1932.

XIII. **Patsy Lou:** 22in (56cm); made from 1930-1940.
    A. Had either molded hair or wig.
    B. Wore traditional *Patsy* costumes.

XIV. **Patsy Ruth:** 27in (69cm); introduced in 1936.
    A. Some dolls all-composition; some dolls had shoulder plate.
    B. Hair molded but wig sometimes used over molded hair.

XV. **Patsy Mae:** 30in (76cm); introduced in 1934.
    A. Largest of the *Patsy* family.
    B. *Lovums*-type body.

XVI. **Skippy:** 14in (36cm); introduced in 1929.
    A. Advertised as *Patsy's* boyfriend.
    B. Most dolls came with all-composition body; some came with cloth body.
    C. Outfits included cowboy, farmer, baseball player, aviator, Tyrolean, play and dress-up boy clothes.

The Patsy Doll Club had 275,000 members at its height. "Aunt Patsy" (and there truly was such a lady) traveled all over the country to visit her little friends. She is often pictured with a costume similar to the *Patricia* costume in *Illustration 184*. She kept in touch with doll owners by mail with the club's own newspaper, *The Patsytown News*, and through another publication called *My Doll's Magazine*.

Eugenia Doll Company

In the late 1930s, through the 1940s and into the early 1950s, the Eugenia Doll Company marketed nice dolls which they purchased from Ideal and sold through Montgomery Ward and possibly other mail-order houses. The excellent quality dolls were dressed in well-made costumes. In the early 1950s the company changed from composition to hard plastic. They continued to produce excellent dolls in this new medium.

Illustration 196.

Girl in Pink Dress: 15in (38cm); all-composition; jointed at neck, shoulders and hips; sleep eyes; closed mouth; unusually arched eyebrows; long real eyelashes; round face that is easily recognizable; ⅄ on lower back; all original; circa late 1930s.

    UNUSUAL IDENTIFICATION FEATURE: Round pudgy face.

    MARKS: "Made in U.S.A.//Eugenia Doll Co. N.Y.// America's Finest Dolls" tag; none on doll.

    SEE: *Illustration 195.* (Color Section, page 94.) *Joyce Stock and Kathy Adams Collection.*

Saturday: 6in (15cm); composition with one-piece head and body; strung arms only; painted black shoes; painted blue eyes with light black long eyelashes; wavy auburn mohair wig; blue bodice, long pink skirt with a purple overnet, blue straw hat; white box decorated with brown and yellow circles; gold box label reads "A Touch of Paris//Copyright 1945//Eugenia//Saturday//Eugenia Goes to a Party." *Nancy Ann Storybook Doll* competitor; circa 1945.

    MARKS: None.

    SEE: *Illustration 196.*

Dolls Not Pictured

Johnnie and Janie: 10½in (27cm); composition; circa 1938-1938.

    These dolls resemble the *Patsy*-type composition babies of the period.

MARKS: "Johnnie and Janie//A creation by//Eugenia Doll Company//New York" paper tags; "Eugenia Doll Co.//World's Finest Dolls" tag.

European Doll Mfg. Inc.

During the 1920s and into the 1930s, European Doll Mfg. Inc., made an extensive line of composition dolls. The various types of dolls included *Mama* dolls from 11in (28cm) to 30in (76cm), black dolls and infant dolls.

In 1931 they took over the manufacturing of sets of *Famlee* dolls, originally made by the Berwick Company (see page 55). They often used "EDMA" to identify their company.

Famlee Doll: Came in many different sets over the years; this advertisement featured a set of seven character doll heads, two doll bodies and costumes to match each character (see also Berwick Doll Company, page 55).

SEE: *Illustration 197. Playthings,* April 1931.

Baby Boy Doll: Fur hair wig; dressed in silk rompers; embroidered bib; 1931.

The 1931 line included attractively dressed baby dolls with or without wigs. The company name in the advertisement was misspelled. It should be EDMA Doll Co.

UNUSUAL IDENTIFICATION FEATURE: Fur hair wig.

SEE: *Illustration 198. Playthings,* March 1931.

European Doll Mfg. Co., Inc.
Pictured here is one of the larger sets in a complete range of "Famlee" Dolls, covering a retail price range of from $1.00 to $10.00. The particular set pictured contains seven character doll heads, two doll bodies and costumes to match each character. The "Famlee" Dolls were prominently displayed among numerous numbers of the popular "Edma" Dolls, as well as a complete line of soft, cuddly, washable, fur-wig dolls.

Illustration 197.

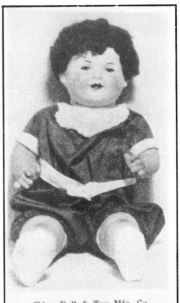

Edna Doll & Toy Mfg. Co.
This cuddly Baby Boy Doll, with a fur hair wig and dressed attractively in silk rompers and an embroidered bib, is typical of the line of Baby and Dressed Dolls shown both with and without wigs, that was on display in this exhibit.

Illustration 198.

Florentine Statuary Company (Canada)

From 1917 to about 1932, this Canadian company made composition dolls in Toronto. Most of their dolls had shoulder plate composition heads with molded hair. Sometimes a wig was added. The dolls were the typical *Mama* and baby dolls with cloth bodies and legs; composition arms or forearms. Some of the molded heads were unusual because one of the partners, Maxim Maggi, was a sculptor.

MARKS: "Florentine//Toronto" on shoulder plate on many dolls from this company.

International (Foreign) Composition Dolls

Germany, France and other European doll companies made composition bodies and dolls long before the United States began to perfect the "Can't Break 'Em" dolls. However, their china, bisque and cloth dolls sold well. When World War I cut the supply from Europe, the U.S. turned to their own composition. After the war, European manufacturers began to realize the composition doll potential and they, too, created their own type of composition dolls.

Foreign doll makers made both play dolls and large and small ethnic dolls. Many were spectacular. Here are only a few samples of some of the many made or dressed from countries around the world.

Illustration 199.

103

Illustration 202.

Illustration 203.

Argentina

Baby Dressed in Gaucho Clothes: 3in (8cm); all-composition; jointed at arms and shoulders; black leather over pants; white shirt and loose gaucho pants; silk scarf; black felt hat; leather boots; carefully painted face; all original; circa 1930s.

This tiny all original doll is a typical "candy store" type of doll. The face is expressive, and the costume is well-tailored.

MARKS: None.
SEE: *Illustration 199.*

Gaucho: 16in (41cm); composition head and ball-jointed body; sleep eyes; black wig; open mouth with four painted upper teeth; belt of medallions.

MARKS: "BEBILANDIA//(Picture of Crawling Baby)//MARCA REGISTRADA//INDUSTRIA ARGENTINA."
SEE: *Illustration 200.* (Color Section, page 94.) *Shirley Karaba Collection.*

Germany

Squeeze Doll: 6½in (17cm); composition head; bellows body; armature arms with wooden hands; no legs; well-sculptured character face; molded painted eyebrows; side-glancing eyes; ears; V-shaped mouth; unusual circle indicating chin; blue felt coat with red buttons; yellow felt scarf.

When the doll is pushed downward, the right arm moves and the bellows produce a squeaky sound.

MARKS: "Made in Germany" stamped on bottom of doll.
SEE: *Illustration 202.*

The registered trademarks, the trademarks and copyrights appearing in italics//bold within this chapter belong to El Gre Co.

Greece (El Gre Co.)

Dancer: 18in (46cm); all-composition; jointed in neck, shoulders and legs; walks when either arms or legs are moved; when arms are moved, makes a crying sound; sleep eyes with real lashes; open mouth; excellent quality composition; black and white spotted dress with white ruffle; white shawl with red fringe; circa late 1930s-1940s. Came with red and white striped trunk.

MARKS: "Hand-Made Toys//El//gre//Co//Made in Greece" heart-shaped tag.
"Fabrica de Articules de Vieje//Permiso N 1196//Facutra n//16395//Impuesto de lujo a metalica" marks on trunk.
SEE: *Illustration 203. Athena Crowley Collection.*

Cuba

Cuban Dancers: 10in (25cm); all-composition; molded and enameled with white paint; the man and the woman both wear white and red costumes; circa 1930s.

MARKS: None.
SEE: *Illustration 201.* (Color Section, page 94.)

104

Japan

Shirley Temple: 8in (20cm); all-composition; jointed at neck, shoulders and hips; molded, painted hair; smiling character face; open mouth with white paint in middle to simulate teeth; all original pink pleated dress; replaced shoes and socks; circa mid 1930s.

  MARKS: "S.T. Japan" back.
  SEE: *Illustration 204. Connie Lee Martin Collection.*

Lapland

Laplander Girl: 14in (36cm); composition head; cloth body; unusual sculptured character face; painted eyes; open mouth with teeth; dressed in bright blue felt with bright red trim felt and yarn trim; fur trim; pompon-type red cap; circa 1930s.

  The people of Lapland dressed in very bright clothing so they could be seen at a distance in the arctic fog and snow.

  MARKS: None.
  SEE: *Illustration 205. Sandra Strater Collection.*

Portugal

Girl with Glasses: 15in (38cm); excellent European-type composition; painted eyes with eyelashes above eyes; closed mouth; wig; red and blue plaid slacks; yellow blouse; straw hat and shoes; circa 1930s. Original owner had placed a tag on her marked: "Portugal."

  MARKS: "47/4" neck.
  SEE: *Illustration 206. Athena Crowley Collection.*

Sweden

Boy in Swedish Folkloric Costume: 12in (31cm); composition shoulder plate head with molded hair painted light yellow; painted eyes with eyelashes at corners of eyes; closed mouth; pink rayon cloth body; white shirt, yellow twill pants and blue felt stockings are incorporated as part of body structure; black felt shoes with buckles; black felt jacket with red trim; all original folkloric costume is carefully tailored.

  MARKS: None.
  SEE: *Illustration 207.* (Color Section, page 95.)

Illustration 204.   *Illustration 205.*   *Illustration 206.*

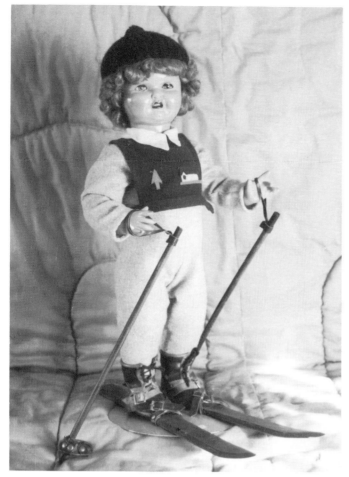

Illustration 208.

Spain

Gisela: 18in (46cm); all-composition; light blue glass eyes; real lashes; five top teeth; felt tongue; mohair wig; dimple in chin; well-formed unusual hands; wool ski pants; vest that buckles on side; stocking cap; leather ski boots; wood skis and poles with leather straps and bindings; all original; both doll and clothing of excellent quality; purchased in Spain; circa 1930s.

The original owner said that *Gisela* was a personality doll of the period with a variety of clothes.

    MARKS: "Gisela" signed on back of neck; "Gisela" cloth tag on outfit.

    SEE: *Illustration 208. Athena Crowley Collection.*

Canada
(FREEMAN TOY COMPANY)

Started during World War II, the Freeman Toy Company closed its doors after the war was over. During its short existence, the company made many composition dolls. Among their dolls were "Drink and Wet" babies, *Mama* dolls, baby dolls and an all-composition girl doll.

    MARKS: Most of the dolls were unmarked. Many had tags "A//Genuine//Freeman Doll (in script)// Made in Canada."

Taiwan

Fisherman: 10in (25cm); composition head, hands and feet; cloth body; brightly painted and enameled flesh tones; molded expressive face; painted mustache and beard; one hand molded with fingers shut to hold fishing pole; composition fish and water jar; blue peasant-type twill outfit; woven straw jacket and hat.

    MARKS: None.

    SEE: *Illustration 209.*

Illustration 209.

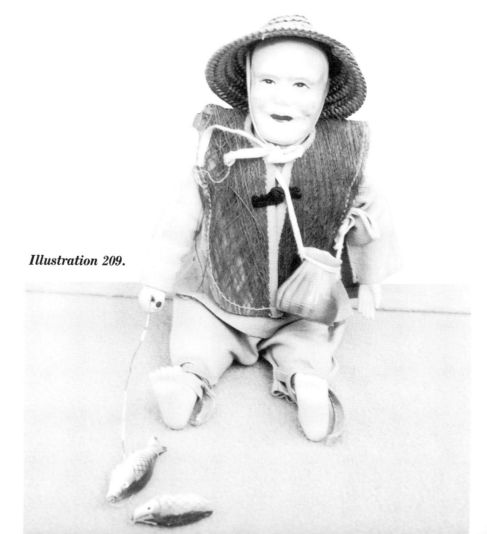

Freundlich, Inc., Ralph A.

Ralph Freundlich worked for the Jeanette Doll Company until he formed his own company in 1929 to produce inexpensive novelty type dolls. Many of these were sold by mail-order houses and "5 and 10 cent" stores. Some of the company's most interesting dolls were made during World War II.

Since most of these dolls were not marked, it has been difficult for researchers and collectors to identify them accurately. While the quality of the dolls is very uneven, they are becoming very collectible, and prices have risen accordingly.

Little Orphan Annie and Sandy: 12in (31cm); all-composition; molded blonde curly hair; large pupils in blue hues; closed mouth; original red and white dress; popular doll advertised in 1930s catalog.
Sandy: all-composition.
  MARKS: None
  SEE: *Illustration 210. Mary Merritt Museum.*

Feather Weight Doll: 28in (71cm); weight 24 ounces; composition head, hands and legs; assorted dresses, many with panties showing; shoes; socks; walking; talking (crier); cost $1.00 in 1930.
  SEE: *Illustration 211. Playthings,* February 1930.

Illustration 213.

Illustration 210.

FEATHER WEIGHT DOLL
"I only weigh 24 ounces"

Illustration 211.

Red Riding Hood, Grandmother, Wolf: 10in (25cm); all-composition; jointed at neck, shoulders and hips; *Patsy*-type body; *Grandmother* and *Wolf* have specially sculptured heads; the three dolls are dressed in original clothes; they were advertised in the 1934 Sears, Roebuck & Co. catalog; all three dolls were shown barefoot in the advertisement; they came in a lithographed schoolhouse box; 1934.
  MARKS: None on dolls.
  SEE: *Illustration 212.* (Color Section, page 95.)

Goo-Goo Eva: 15in (38cm); composition head; flesh-colored cloth body and limbs; "Goo-Goo" celluloid googly-type eyes; closed mouth; molded hair; square hands; dress not original; black version of this doll is called *Topsy*; circa 1937-1940s.

The 1938 Sears, Roebuck & Co. catalog listed this doll. Her original dress was printed percale with a poke bonnet. The original advertisement said, "The body could stand lots of hugging."

This particular doll was restuffed with a discarded percale adult apron. The print of the apron was very close to the print of the original doll dress.
  MARKS: None.
  SEE: *Illustration 213.*

Baby with Scale: 9½in (24cm); jointed at neck, shoulders and hips; dressed with diaper, bathrobe and socks tied with ribbons; blue and pink colors; 1934.
Scale: 4in (10cm) base; 5½in (14cm) high; weighs up to two pounds.
Basket on Scale: 11½in (32cm); 7in (18cm) wide.
Bedding: Pillow and mattress.
SEE: *Illustration 214. Playthings,* June 1934.

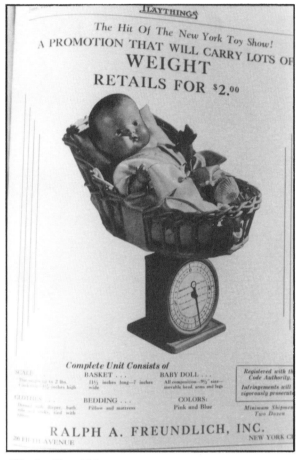

Illustration 214.

Illustration 217.

108

Quintuplets: 6¾in (17cm); all-composition (see *Quintuplets* Section, page 171.)
Quintuplets: Advertisement: all-composition (see *Quintuplets* Section, page 171).

Illustration 215.

Princess: 22in (56cm); all-composition; jointed at neck, shoulders and hips; sleep eyes with lashes; open mouth with teeth and tongue; dressed in white plush hat, coat and muff; fancy dress; rayon stockings; shoes; 1937.

This is a *Mama*-type doll which is slimmer than the ones in the 1920s.
SEE: *Illustration 215. Toys and Bicycles,* July 1937.

Baby Sandy: 19½in (50cm); all-composition; molded hair; metal sleep eyes; open mouth with two upper teeth and tongue; button with picture of *Baby Sandy*; all original; circa 1939-1940.

Baby Sandy Henville was featured by Universal in some movies in the late 1930s and the early 1940s. She was only four when her career was over. The dolls came in three sizes: (1) 7⅕in (19cm) (2) 11in (28cm) (3) 16½in (42cm). The larger size came with either molded hair or a wig. Some came with painted eyes. Other models had sleep eyes.
MARKS: "Baby Sandy" head; "Universal Star// Genuine Baby Sandy Doll" button.
SEE: *Illustration 216.* (Color Section, page 96.) *Sandy Strater Collection.*

Douglas MacArthur: 18in (46cm); composition; portrait doll of the general; 1940s.

General MacArthur was the distinguished leader of the Pacific Theatre of War during World War II. He had a unique personality and was always impeccably dressed, even in the midst of battle. Pictures of him showed a tilt to his guilt-edged cap which seemed to cheer the troops and boost the morale of everyone. Parents bought this composition doll for both boys and girls, and it helped give confidence to the home front during some of the dark and trying times.
MARKS: "General MacArthur//The Man of the Hour//manufactured by Freundlich Corp. New York, N.Y." tag.
SEE: *Illustration 217. Helen Krielow Collection.*

Illustration 218.

W.A.V.E., W.A.A.C., Soldier: 18in (46cm); composition; early 1940s.

W.A.A.C.: The biggest uniform change during World War II came with the design of clothes for women. The design for the W.A.A.C. (Women's Auxiliary Army Corps) caused much bickering among the men officers over the design, materials, colors and items to be issued. The basic masculine design did not enhance the W.A.A.C. image. The jackets were heavily padded and the skirts too narrow for women's hips because the uniforms were contracted to the suppliers of men's uniforms. The colors of the skirts and jackets rarely matched. There was also a controversy over the issuing of foundation garments, but it was generally agreed by the top generals that women should be required to wear them for a neat and military appearance.

W.A.V.E.: The Navy avoided the Army's uniform problems. They asked the well-known fashion designer, Mainbocher of New York, for an original design for their W.A.V.E.s. Then they contracted with the women's fashion industry to make the uniforms. They were a hit with recruits, and many volunteered to join the new naval service.

    MARKS: "Praise the Lord and Pass the Ammunition" tag.

    SEE: *Illustration 218. Marcia B. Creswell Collection.*

Dolls Not Pictured

1. *Dummy Dan:* the Ventriloquist Man.
2. *Two-faced Doll:* White doll called *Eva*; Black doll called *Topsy*.

Gem Doll Corporation

Illustration 219.

From 1913 to 1929 this company was known as the Gem Toy Co. In 1919 it changed its name to the Gem Doll Corporation. It made a variety of dolls each year in its line in several price ranges. Over the years, they made many baby and *Mama* dolls. They followed doll trends and imitated best-selling dolls. Often they sold through various mail-order companies including Butler Bros. Dolls were sold for premiums. They also made stuffed animals and other toys.

Topsy: 9½in (24cm); all-black composition; molded hair with three floss pigtails tied with red hair ribbons inserted in head; red and white checked rompers with red flowers printed in the cotton cloth; white booties with red ribbon ties; side-glancing eyes; closed mouth; circa late 1920s — early 1930s.
> MARKS: "Gem" back of doll; "Gem//Trade Mark Registered//Made in U.S.A.//Topsy" tag on dress.
> SEE: *Illustration 219. Sandy Strater Collection.*

Hug Me Dolls: A line of dolls featured in 1930. The dolls were made in a variety of price and size requirements. They advertised that the dolls had the latest developments in wigs, eyes, voices, costumes and other refining touches. This doll was typical of the "Hug Me" line of dolls featured that year. They were still being advertised in 1932.
> MARKS: "Gem" tag hung from neck of doll.
> SEE: *Illustration 220. Playthings,* March 1930.

Types of Dolls Made By Gem

1926 Advertised "A Doll for Every Occasion."
> *Babies:* With rubber panties and silk jackets.
> *Mama Doll:* Composition head, legs and arms; came with sailor suit, clown suit, maid costume, party dress, nightgown.
1927 *New Line of Mama Dolls:* Followed marketing trend with slimmer bodies.
1928 *New Smiling Baby Dolls: With dimples.*
> *Mama Dolls:* Continued the slimmer bodies.
1929 *Little Girl Dolls:* Short, knee-length dresses and bows in their hair.
1930 Introduced *Hug Me Doll.*
1931 *Patsy-type Doll:* Advertised in *Playthings.*

Illustration 220.

Gerling Toy Company

Illustration 223.

Illustration 221.

The Gerling Toy Company had offices in New York, London, Paris and Germany. They probably did not manufacture the actual dolls. They sold bisque, cloth and composition dolls in the 1920s and 1930s. Many of their dolls were very interesting novelty-types. In 1926 they sold a line of *Hotsy Totsy* boudoir dolls. In 1928 they advertised French Art and Novelty Dolls. In 1929 they advertised boudoir dolls including *Whoopee* and *Dancing Dollies*. They also made a *Mary Ann* which is a *Patsy* look-alike (see Identification Guide, page 188, Illustration 376).

Undressed Boudoir Dolls for Home Costuming: 28in (71cm); green sateen one-piece body; joints indicated by stitching only; composition head; face painted in 1920s manner with thick eyeliner lines and heavy eye shadow; red human hair wig; 1926 into early 1930s.

Many companies sold boudoir dolls in this wrapped position. They were either placed as a decoration in a room in the undressed condition, or they were dressed by the owner to match a particular style or color scheme. There were many patterns for clothes available.

MARKS: "Genuine//Human Hair Wig Flapper// Maker//Gerling Toy company//New York Paris" printed sticker on back of doll.

SEE: *Illustration 221.*

Dancing Dollies: Dancing couple imitated the Dean's Ragbook dancing dolls; cloth body; composition head; children could play with these dolls fastened together or separately; 1929.

SEE: *Illustration 222. Playthings,* February 1929.

Dancing-Dollies: 12in (31cm); composition head; molded hair; side-glancing eyes; cloth body and limbs; black cloth attached to body at ankles for shoes; closed mouth; not original clothes; circa 1929-1930.

These dolls are attributed to Gerling, but they may have been made by S. & H. Novelty Co. (see page 174, Illustration 336).

MARKS: None.

SEE: *Illustration 223.*

Mary Ann: *Patsy*-type (see Identification Guide, page 188, Illustration 376).

Illustration 222.

German Composition
(Often Attributed to Armand Marseille)

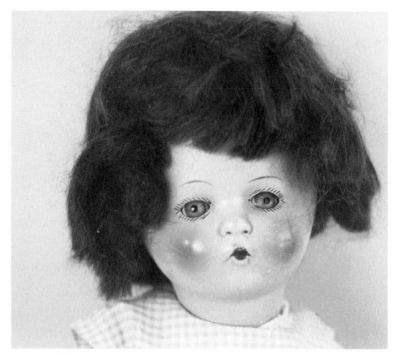

Illustration 224.

Girl with Red Hair: 13in (33cm); composition head and body; fully jointed; inset eyes; painted dark lashes around the eyes; *Just Me*-type of mouth; no ears; circa early 1930s.

This doll is often attributed to Armand Marseille because "971" is a known A.M. number.

Another doll with the same face mold was marked "Ϲ//971//Germany."

MARKS: "Germany 971" doll.
SEE: *Illustration 224. Ester Borgis Collection.*

The registered trademarks, the trademarks and copyrights appearing in italics//bold within this chapter belong to E. Goldberger.

Goldberger, E. (EEGEE)

The Goldberger company has made dolls since the early 1900s. In 1923 they began to use the trade name "EEGEE." They made composition dolls and after World War II, they changed to hard plastic and then vinyl.

For the most part, they followed the trends initiated by the other doll companies and made low-to-medium priced dolls. These were often offered by mail-order houses. As late as 1927 they were importing bisque heads from Armand Marseille.

They made a *Patsy* look-alike (see Identification Guide, page 188, Illustration 378).

Illustration 225.

Mama Doll: 24in (61cm); composition head, arms and legs; cloth body; sleep eyes with real lashes; walks and talks; open mouth with tongue and teeth; human hair wig with ringlets or long curls; also available in "French Bob;" shoes and socks; teddy; red polka dot dress with ruffle on yoke; matching hat.

Baby Doll: Composition head, arms and legs; cloth body; sleep eyes with real lashes; open mouth with teeth and tongue; leatherette booties; rubber pants; organdy dress with ruffles; ruffled bonnet; 1935.
SEE: *Illustration 225. Playthings*, September 1935.

Little Miss Charming: 13in (33cm); all-composition; jointed at neck, shoulders and hips; blonde mohair wig; green sleep eyes with real lashes; painted lashes above eyes; open mouth with six teeth; dimple in chin; felt tongue; second and third fingers molded together and slightly curved; slight mold line under knee; ⑁ on backside; circa 1936 to 1939.
MARKS: None on doll; "Everybody Loves Miss Charming" on box.
SEE: *Illustration 226.* (Color Section, page 129.)

Dolls Not Pictured

1. *Late Carnival (Cherub) Doll:* Dolls jointed only at arms.
2. *Mama Dolls:* Like the other manufacturers, Goldberger made these by the thousands; in the 1930s these were slimmer-type dolls.
3. *Baby Charming:* In competition with *Dionne Quintuplets.*

Miss Charming: Walking doll which turns her head with each step; comes in three sizes; 1936.
SEE: *Illustration 227. Toys and Novelties*, August 1936.

This Doll Can
Really Perform

A new walking doll called Miss Charming, which has just been brought out by E. Goldberger, 200 Fifth Avenue, New York, is offered as the only doll that positively walks and turns her head with each step. Miss Charming not only walks but she sits down. The doll comes in three sizes.

Illustration 227.

Hedwig (DE ANGELI)

Hannah: 15in (38cm); all-composition; jointed at neck, shoulders, and hips; metal sleep eyes with real eyelashes; short human hair wig; original clothes; red and dark yellow print dress; black shoes; black Quaker bonnet; circa early 1940s.
This doll represents Hannah in the book *Thee Hanna* by Marguerite de Angeli. As a Quaker child, she was not allowed to have long hair.
Other books and dolls include:
1. *Elin* in a Swedish costume from the book *Elin's Amerika.*

2. *Lydia* in a Pennsylvania Dutch costume from the book *Henner's Lydia.*
3. *Suzanne* in a French Canadian costume from the book *Petite Suzanne.*
These dolls are attributed to Arranbee.
MARKS: None on doll; "Hedwig Dolls//Registered authorized//From the Books//Marguerite de Angeli" wrist tag.
SEE: *Illustration 228.* (Color Section, page 129.) *Marianne Gardner Collection.*

Hera (NETHERLANDS)

Dutch Boy: 11in (28cm); excellent quality composition head, arms and legs; cloth body; black Dutch outfit; Dutch cap; wooden shoes; 1930s.

Dutch Girl: 11in (28cm); same general characteristics; matching black costume with multi-colored ruffle and yoke; black painted legs; unusual white Dutch hat; wooden shoes; 1930s.

> MARKS: "Hera" paper tag attached to clothes (both dolls); Rijks Waterstaat" button on boy.
> SEE: *Illustration 229.*

Illustration 229.

Hollywood Doll Manufacturing Co.

Cowboy and Cowgirl: 8in (20cm); all-composition; one-piece head and body with strung arms and legs; painted eyes, face and boots; *Nancy Ann Storybook Doll* competitor; the box is marked *Cowboy* only; circa 1948.

> MARKS: None on this doll; many Hollywood dolls of this same type are marked "Hollywood Doll."
> SEE: *Illustration 230.* (Color Section, page 96.)

May (left): 5in (13cm); all-composition with one-piece head and body; painted blue eyes; painted black shoes; white bodice with long, full blue skirt with a white floral pattern; white felt hat with blue felt ribbon; blonde wavy wig; in original box decorated with red stars; circa early 1940s.

Bride (right): 8in (20cm); all-composition with one-piece head and body; painted blue eyes; painted white shoes; light brown wavy mohair wig; white satin dress trimmed with white lace and net; blue garter; white net veil; circa early 1940s.

> MARKS: Left doll is unmarked; right doll "Hollywood//Doll."
> SEE: *Illustration 231.*

Illustration 231.

Illustration 232.

Pretty Kitty (doll on right): 5in (13cm); all-composition; one-piece head and body with strung arms and legs; painted eyes with five very long eyelashes; painted white shoes; wavy mohair wig; short version of middle doll with white dress with blue polka dots on skirt, blue ribbon for belt; bow on hair; tag on dress says "31."

Left Doll:: Same general characteristics; long gold satin dress with pipe cleaner flower on dress and hat.

Center Doll: Same general characteristics; long version of *Pretty Kitty* dress with red, white and blue ribbon trim on skirt, waist and hair bow.

Comparisons of this type of dolls (see Identification Guides, pages 185, Illustrations 365, 366).

  MARKS: "Hollywood" body of doll on left; other two dolls are unmarked.

  SEE: *Illustration 232.*

Horsman Co., Inc., E. I.

When Horsman first started to make their composition dolls, they were known for their extensive line. Most of the dolls had special head molds done by well-known doll artists. However, as the country plunged into a deep depression after the crash of 1929, Horsman turned to a smaller advertised line and changed the clothes rather than changing the molds. Often their dolls were made for ten or more years.

They had been a manufacturer of doll parts for many years, and during this depression period they also turned to supplying the smaller marketing companies with doll parts. They manufactured dolls of various qualities, but the one sold under the Horsman label usually was of high quality. This can clearly be seen in the mail-order catalogs of the period. They continued to mark their boxes with the "Art Doll" logo which featured a horse and rider. Boxes and tags can be seen in some of the illustrations in this book.

During the late 1920s and 1930s, they made many, many baby dolls, toddlers, and continued a type of slimmer *"Mama"* doll. They also imitated other companies with their *Bright Star* and *Babs* lines.

They did try to continue their wonderful character line with dolls such as *HEbee SHEbee* and *Whatsit*.

Like other major companies, they issued more extensive lines in 1938 and 1939, but by 1940 they were turning to war work. After the war was over, they hurried to put dolls from their older molds on the doll-starved market. However, they also started to experiment with the new hard plastic and by 1948, they had almost converted to these molds. Their *Campbell Soup Kids* in 1948 and 1949 were their farewell tribute to their wonderful, gentle, mischievous composition origins (see cover).

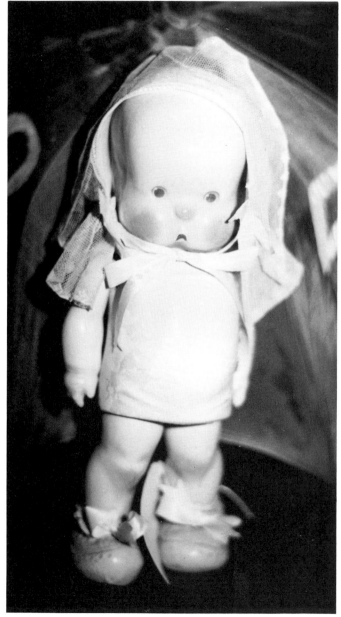

Illustration 233.

HEbee-SHEbee: 10in (25cm); all-composition; molded pink booties on legs; dressed as baby with net hat and original ribbons; unusual legs with cutout notch at the top; all original; 1925 into early 1930s.
    MARKS: "Trademark Charles Twelvetrees//Copyrighted 1925" label on foot.
    SEE: *Illustration 233. Joy Young Collection.*

Peterkins Family: 12in (31cm) — 13in (33cm); advertisement says, "The Peterkins family came trooping into the world for all those thousands of kiddies who can't wait for Christmas. Peterkins is an all year round seller."

The *Peterkins Family* was introduced into the Horsman Line in 1914 and stayed in the line until the early 1930s. This *Campbell Soup* look-alike is still popular and now beloved by many generations. Over the years it has had many changes in the form of the doll and in the costumes. However, it can always be identified by the mold of the hairline. The curl on the forehead is always on the left side. This can be seen in the older *Peterkins* doll in *Illustration 235*.

UNUSUAL IDENTIFICATION FEATURE:
　　Forehead curl on left side.
MARKS: "E.I. Horsman, Inc." head; some may not be marked.
SEE: *Illustration 234. Playthings,* May 1929.

Peterkins Head: *Campbell Soup Kid* look-alike; composition; molded, painted hair; point of combed hair is on left side; tiny arched eyebrows; painted eyes with large pupils; tiny watermelon mouth; dimple is in chin.

This doll has black hair because it was dressed as an Indian. The hair is usually a light shade of brown.

UNUSUAL IDENTIFICATION FEATURE:
　　The point of the hair is on the left side. The American Character *Petit Campbell Soup* doll is very similar. However, the point is in the middle of the head.
MARKS: "E.I. HORSMAN, INC." head.
SEE: *Illustration 235.*

Illustration 234.

Illustration 235.

Horsman and Amberg Connection

Illustration 237.

"It Dolls"

In 1928, a series of dolls was made by Amberg called "It." They were advertised as dolls with a "body twist" at the waist. There were at least three of these dolls. Each had a different hair mold. *Sue* had a side part. *Peter Pan* had a windswept style with short bangs. The third doll had heavier bangs (see *Illustration 72*).

While it was considered part of the "It" series, *Little Amby* did not have a twist waist. This model also had three different hair molds (see also *Illustration 72*).

In 1930 the Amberg Company was sold to E.I. Horsman, except for the Amfelt dolls which were sold to the Paul Cohen Company.

The "It" line and other dolls continued to be made in the Horsman factory. In 1930 Horsman advertised a *Peggy* doll which was not on a twist body. It had the same hair mold as the *Sue* doll. The body was marked "It" (see *Illustration 236*, Color Section, page 129.)

Both the Horsman and Amberg dolls were advertised with a toy dog with some models.

Peggy: 12in (31cm), 14in (36cm), 20in (51cm); all-composition; socket head like *Patsy*; jointed at neck, shoulders and hips; molded hair with left part; blue, yellow and black print on white cotton dress; organdy collar trimmed with lace; matching teddy; white socks; blue leatherette shoes with buckle; the nail which held her original large hair bow can be seen in the illustration; all original; 1930.

The Horsman advertisement in *Playthings* says, "She comes in a wide variety of dainty print dresses with a gay ribbon, and she is leading a little brown pup on a leather leash. Other dolls are dressed in soft shades of organdy. Some have pups and others do not. The small dolls have hair ribbons, but some of the larger sizes wear coats and berets or sunbonnets. The dolls with berets are outfitted in coats of French flannel or velvet in green, yellow or blue."

    MARKS: "IT" on back; "Horsman//Doll//Mfg in USA" tag on dress.
    SEE: *Illustration 236*. (Color Section, page 129.) *Illustration 236. Playthings*, November 1930; Horsman advertisement. (Color Section, page 129.)

Body Twist: 10in (25cm); jointed at neck, shoulders and waist; molded hair with part in middle; molded painted black shoes; painted eyes; closed mouth; came in both white and black versions; circa 1929-1930. A larger 24in (61cm) version has been seen. Quite often there is a crack in the bottom of the upper piece.
    MARKS: "Pat. Appld" back.
    SEE: *Illustration 237*.

Illustration 238.

Babs: *Patsy*-type (see Identification Guide, page 189, Illustration 379).

Babs: 12in (31cm); all-black composition; brown sleep eyes; open mouth with four teeth; black mohair wig; white and blue dotted, pleated dress; blue ruffle at neck; all original in box; early 1930s.

This is a rare black *Babs Shirley Temple* look-alike. *Babs* is seen more often with a *Patsy*-type molded head (see Identification Guide, page 189.)
    MARKS: "Horsman//BABS//Quality Doll" tag.
    SEE: *Illustration 238. Elliot Zirlin Collection.*

Toddler: 14½in (37cm); all-composition; jointed at neck, shoulders and hips; molded hair with three curls on forehead and curls at ends of hair in back of head; sleep eyes with real lashes; black eye shadow above eyes; dainty eyelashes below eyes; open mouth with two teeth and molded tongue; third and fourth fingers molded together; both arms gently curved; toddler legs; Υ on lower back; two dimples on each knee; excellent composition; unusually heavy doll for a toddler-type doll; mid-1930s.
    MARKS: None on doll; "A//Genuine//Horsman//Art Doll" paper tag sewn to dress.
    SEE: *Illustration 239.* (Color Section, page 96.)

WHATSIT Dolls Get Big Publicity Send-Off

Illustration 240.

Whatsit Dolls: 14in (36cm); all-composition; molded hair; painted eyes; right arm bent; left arm straighter; two different models with different faces; side-glancing eyes; both dolls have cotton print dresses; lace shoes; 1937.
Doll on Left: Molded hair has side buns.
Doll on Right: Molded hair has top knot tied with a ribbon.

The advertisement said, "WHATSIT DOLLS are truly different. There are two distinct models, each with different facial expressions. They are produced under a special license and will be featured in the 'Whatsit' — a newspaper by and for boys and girls, with a circulation of over three million copies."

This line of dolls was shown at the 1937 Toy Fair by Regal-Horsman. They are also known as *Roberta, Jeanne* and *Naughty Sue* (see *Illustration 241*).
    SEE: *Illustration 240. Toys and Bicycles*, June 1937.

Naughty Sue Whatsit Doll: 16in (41cm); all-composition; curved right arm, straight left arm; molded head with topknot for ribbon; large side glancing eyes; open mouth with molded tongue; not original clothes; 1937.
    MARKS: "Naughty Sue//c 1937" head.
    SEE: *Illustration 241. Patricia Snyder Collection.*

Illustration 241.

Snow White: 19in (48cm); all-composition; green sleep eyes; open mouth with four teeth and felt tongue; black mohair wig; typical *Snow White* beige and red velvet dress with rickrack trim; red velvet cape; tie shoes; all original even to the pins and ribbon in her hair; late 1930s.
   MARKS: None on doll; "Horsman Art Doll//No. 1917" box.
   SEE: *Illustration 242. Athena Crowley Collection.*

Girl in Patriotic Dress: 14½in (37cm); all-composition; sleep eyes with real lashes; delicate eyelashes surrounding the eye; eye shadow above the eye; jointed at neck, shoulders and hips; beautiful blonde wig with "flip" style; closed mouth; third and fourth fingers molded together; long slender legs; all original; excellent quality composition and clothing; circa late 1930s.
   This doll was in competition with a similar Alexander doll of the same period (see Color Section, page 36.)
   MARKS: None on doll; "Horsman 'Art' Doll//E.I. Horsman, Inc.//215/5054 1/2" box.
   SEE: *Illustration 243.* (Color Section, page 130.)

Illustration 244.

Doll in Pink Dress: 15in (38cm); all-composition; excellent color; jointed at neck, shoulders and hips; metal sleep eyes with coating; real lashes, mohair wig set in flip style; closed rosebud mouth; rosy cheeks and knees; long, slim legs; Y̊ on lower back; fingers molded together; pink and white dotted swiss dress; matching hat stapled to head; white socks and tie shoes; white muslin teddy; all original; late 1930s into the 1940s.
   The quality of the doll is excellent, but the material and factory-made clothes are inferior. This may have been made during World War II.
   MARKS: None on doll; "Horsman//Doll//Made in U.S.A." box; the original seal of the old Art Dolls is also on the box.
   SEE: *Illustration 244.*

Campbell Soup Kid: 12in (31cm); all-composition; molded painted hair; painted side-glancing eyes; watermelon mouth; dimples in knees; painted molded shoes and socks; blue cotton romper suit; white apron; chef's hat; pinned-on tag; all original; 1948-1949.
   MARKS: None on doll; "Campbell Kid//A Horsman Doll" tag.
   SEE: *Illustration 136.* (Color Section, page 85.) (See cover also.)

New Baby Dimples: Each year during the production of this doll, *Dimples* had new costumes; the body was often modified to meet the competition; in 1929 the company offered knit outfits as well as baby dresses.
   SEE: *Illustration 245. Playthings, June 1929.*

Illustration 242.

Baby Dimples: 18in (46cm); composition flange head, arms and legs; cloth body; molded hair; painted eyelashes above and below the sleep eyes; open mouth with two teeth and molded tongue; sucks thumb; a dimple on each side of the mouth; excellent quality composition; all original clothes; white baby dress with ruffles; matching bonnet; 1927 into early 1930s.

This very popular doll was competition for the Effanbee *Bubbles*. It came in several sizes with or without wigs. It also came in a toddler version.

SPECIAL IDENTIFICATION FEATURE: Dimple on each cheek.

MARKS: "E.I.H. Co, Inc." head; "(Embroidered seal of horse)//Horsman//Doll//M'F'D in U.S.A." cloth tag sewn in dress.

SEE: *Illustration 246. Joanne McIntosh Collection.*

Baby Dimples: Advertisement for the 1930 edition of the two dolls; "Radical changes have been made in the construction of the body. New expressions have been given to their faces. Different costumes have been designed adding an up-to-date wardrobe."

SEE: *Illustration 247. Playthings*, May 1930.

Rosebud (also called *Dolly Rosebud*): Several sizes; *Mama* doll; composition head and limbs; dimples in cheeks; sleep eyes after 1927; modifications of doll and clothes over the years; big sister to *Dimples*; 1914-1930s.

The *Mama* dolls became slimmer in the 1930s.

In 1928 the doll came dressed in marionette prints designed by Tony Sarg.

SEE: *Illustration 247. Playthings*, May 1930.

Illustration 245.

Illustration 246.

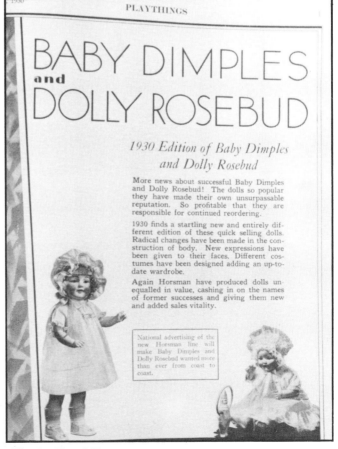

Illustration 247.

Illustration 248.

Babies: Various sizes from 15in (38cm) to 23in (58cm); advertised in the Sears, Roebuck & Co. Christmas catalog in 1947; composition heads; cloth bodies. This was one of the last years that Horsman made composition dolls. After World War II they used their familiar baby styles until they could retool and start the production of hard plastic dolls. Baby dolls were always an important part of the Horsman line.

SEE: *Illustration 248. Sears, Roebuck & Co. Christmas 1947 Catalog.*

Dolls Not Pictured

Shirley Little Colonel: *Shirley Temple* look-alike; sleep eyes; open mouth with teeth; dimples; blonde mohair wig; dress is lavender version of the "Little Colonel" outfit; 1930s.

Bright Star Line: Imitates Shirley Temple and other movie stars; most of them have an open mouth with teeth.

One Marked Bright Star Doll: all-composition; jointed at neck, shoulders and hips; mohair wig; blue tin sleep eyes; open mouth with four teeth.

MARKS: "Horsman's Bright Star//with eyes that shine and hair so fine" tag.

*Horsman Composition Dolls**
1928 to End of Composition Era

1920s Dolls which continued into the 1930s.
Baby Dimples (two dimples in cheeks).
Dolly Rosebud.
Gold Medal Baby.
Vanta Baby.

1929 **Peterkins Family** introduced.
HEbee-SHEbee 1925-1928.
Peggy 1929-30.
New Baby Dimples.
Body Twist Dolls: Merged with Amberg and produced their molds in Horsman factory.

1930s   **Bright Star** line of dolls (created to compete with *Shirley Temple* dolls).
Shirley (created to compete with *Shirley Temple* dolls).
Buttercup (created to compete with Effanbee *Lamkins*).
Dorothy: *Patsy* look-alike.
Skating Sue (a body twist doll): Wore roller skates.

1930   **Mary Mix-up:** slightly changed version of 1919 doll.
Little Tynie Tots: small all-composition dolls that came two to a box with extra clothes.

1931   **Babs** (*Patsy* look-alike): 12in (31cm); included both molded hair and wigged versions; included black versions.
Sue (same mold as *Babs*): 14in (36cm); *Patsy* look-alike.
Jane (same mold as *Babs*): 17in (43cm); *Patsy* look-alike.
Nan (same mold as *Babs*): 20in (51cm); *Patsy* look-alike.
Gold Medal Baby.
Grace: advertised in Sears, Roebuck & Co. catalog; 24in (61cm); beautiful long curls of real hair; sleep eyes with lashes; open mouth with teeth and tongue; voice box; flowered dimity dress with embroidered collar.
Joan: 22in (56cm); smaller version of *Grace*.

1932   **Buttercup** line of dolls: Continued into the 1930s.
Wee Buttercup.
Tiny Buttercup.
Little Buttercup.
Baby Buttercup.

1935   **Joyce** shoulder plate; tin eyes; open mouth with teeth.

1936   **Shirley:** *Shirley Temple* look-alike.

1937   **Naughty Sue:** 14½in (37cm); *Whatsit* Doll.
Whatsit Dolls: Some dolls marked: "Jeanne//Horsman;" some dolls marked "Roberta 1937 Horsman."
Brother: Similar to *Whatsit*.
Sister: Similar to *Whatsit*.
Snow White.
JoJo: 13in (33cm); marked: "JoJo" back; dimpled knees.

1939   **Sweetheart** 25in (64cm); slim teen doll.

1940s   **Bright Star Line:** Continued on into the early World War II period.

1945   **Baby Chubby:** Marked: "A/Horsman" on back.
Louisa: Shoulder plate and swivel neck.
Dolls dressed in patriotic outfits.

1946   Returned to pre-war composition lines.

1947   Extensive line of composition babies advertised in Montgomery Ward catalog.

1948-1949   **Campbell Soup Kids.**

* Partial list.

Mary Hoyer

In Reading, Pennsylvania, Mary Hoyer started her career as a designer of knit and crochet fashions for infants and children. She established a shop in Reading, Pennsylvania where her patterns, yarn and other handcraft items were for sale.

After she had made some clothes for her daughter's dolls in the 1930s, Mary Hoyer began to think about knit and crochet patterns for dolls. As a model she needed a slim, little girl doll that children could handle well. The Ideal Doll and Toy Company was making this type of doll, and she found a body twist doll that she thought was appropriate for her designs. She decided to add patterns and dolls to her mail-order line. There were two different dolls used during the composition era.

The first doll was a 13in (33cm) composition body twist called *Doll of Tomorrow* (see *Illustration 249 A* and *B*.) The earliest dolls had painted eyes. Later sleep eyes were used. According to the book *Mary Hoyer and her Dolls* by Mary

Hoyer, there were only approximately 2000 of these composition body twist dolls sold.

In 1937 when Ideal no longer would supply her with the expensive body twist dolls, Mary Hoyer asked Bernard Lipfert to design a second 14in (36cm) composition doll to her specifications, and the Fiberoid Doll Company produced the doll. The first 1500 were unmarked (see *Illustration 250*).

Soon Mary Hoyer decided to mark these dolls. Because of the difficulty in procuring steel eyes, some of these dolls also had painted eyes. They were marked: "The Mary//Hoyer//Doll" on the back. Later when sleep eyes were available, they were added to the same mold. These dolls with sleep eyes had the same marks on the back (see *Illustration 251*).

When hard plastic became available in 1946, the composition dolls were no longer made. According to Mary Hoyer, only about 6,500 composition were made totally.

Illustration 249A.

Body Twist Doll: 13⅛in (34cm); all-composition; blonde wavy mohair wig with metal hairpins on both sides; painted side-glancing eyes; painted eyelashes above eyes; light brown small eyebrows; fingers molded together with thumb separate; jointed at neck, shoulders, chest, waist and hips; strung with heavy rubber band; very slight molding to indicate toes; heavy mold line on bottom of left foot; right foot does not have the same mold line; costume has cotton batiste top and apron with white lace and red tape trim; attached red and white polka dot oil-cloth skirt with lace trim; white bias tape around bottom of skirt; white batiste pantalets; white socks; white leatherette shoes with Ideal-type cut-out shoes; circa 1937.

The clothes are thought to be original. However, the oilcloth skirt is very unusual for both Ideal and Mary Hoyer. The clothes are factory made.

MARKS: "U.S.A.//IDEAL DOLL//13" back.
SEE: *Illustration 249A.*

Ideal Early Doll with Sleep Eyes: 13½in; all-composition; mohair wig; sleep eyes; for other general characteristics, see *Illustration 249A.*

MARKS: "U.S.A.//IDEAL DOLL//13" back.
SEE: *Illustration 249B. Martha Foster Collection.*

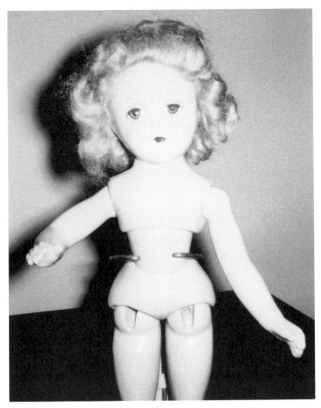

Illustration 249B.

Composition Doll with Painted Eyes: 14in (36cm); all-composition; jointed only at neck, shoulders and hips; painted side-glancing eyes; thin, widely-spaced eyelashes painted only above eyes; right arm slightly curved; straighter left arm; mohair wig; closed mouth; circa late 1930s.

The painted-eye dolls were featured in Volumes 5, 6, 9 and 10 of *Mary's Dollies.* This doll is wearing the skating costume shown on the cover of Volume 5 of *Mary's Dollies.* This is called the "Olga" skating costume. Another skating costume called "Lucretta" is also shown in Volume 6. Both outfits are trimmed in angora.

The costume for this doll was crocheted by the original owner when she was 13 years old.

SPECIAL IDENTIFICATION FEATURE: Head, body, arms and legs were made with two parts glued together. The seams were sanded over and painted, but they can be seen when inspected carefully.

MARKS: None.
SEE: *Illustration 250.* (Color Section, page 130.)

Composition Doll with Sleep Eyes: 14in (36cm); jointed only at neck, shoulders and hips; all-composition with slim arms, legs and body; sleep eyes with real lashes; painted lashes under eyes; closed mouth; circa mid 1940s.

The sleep-eyed dolls were featured in Volumes 11 and 12 of *Mary's Dollies.* The pattern for the ballerina dress was in Volume 12, page 9. It is turquoise net over bridal satin and decorated with sequins.

MARKS: "The//Mary Hoyer//Doll" back.
SEE: *Illustration 251.*

Illustration 251.

THE *Mary Hoyer* DOLL
and her very own
WARDROBE TRUNK

only $7.50 FOR BOTH!

Try to match this VALUE!

The Mary Hoyer Doll and Wardrobe Trunk will bring endless hours of enjoyment to your child. Both are the creation of Mary Hoyer, nationally-known designer of exclusive hand-knits for children.

This beautiful 14-inch doll is sturdily constructed of a hard durable composition with movable head, arms and legs. She not only has attractive movable eyes with eye-lashes, but a hair coiffure designed by Mary Hoyer of real hair that has been hand-curled. Four lovely shades: blonde, medium, dark brown and red. Undressed, but with shoes and stockings. You'll enjoy knitting or crocheting her beautiful outfits!

This big roomy Wardrobe Trunk is made of solid wood (no cardboard), cloth covered; and all hardware, including handle, lock and key is of brass. Doll fits snugly in left side and there is ample room for her clothes in right compartment, which is complete with hanger bar and drawer for accessories.

The Doll and the Trunk may be bought separately:

DOLL............$2.95
TRUNK...........$4.95
Both for Only......$7.50

Volume 11, newest instruction book of "Mary's Dollies" with every doll or doll-wardrobe combination.

UNDRESSED DOLL $2.95

DOLL'S WARDROBE TRUNK
as it appears when closed. 16" long, 7¼" wide, 6¾" deep.

JUVENILE STYLES KNITTING and CROCHETING BOOKS

Here is a modern library of Knitting and Crocheting for infants through 'teen age. Five big volumes of original creations designed by Mary Hoyer, beautifully illustrated with easy-to-follow instructions......................**30c** each

You'll surely want these other
FOUR ISSUES OF "MARY'S DOLLIES"

You'll not only love to knit and crochet the beautiful doll costumes in Volume 11, but also those in the four popular preceding issues, Volumes 5, 6, 9 and 10.........................**20c** each

YARN KITS AND ACCESSORIES

Yarn kits containing all the necessary materials, buttons, etc., to make the costumes for the Mary Hoyer Doll are available for a very nominal sum. We can also furnish such accessories as roller skating and ice skating shoes, skiies, etc.

Illustration 252.

Advertisement for Mary Hoyer Doll in a Trunk: 14in (36cm); all-composition; sleep eyes; solid wood trunk; 1948-1949.

The company advertised five different *Mary's Dollies.* Volumes 5, 6, 9, 10 and 11. They carried accessories such as yarn kits, buttons, roller and ice skates, shoes, trunks, and so forth.

SEE: *Illustration 252. McCall's Needlework,* Winter 1948-1949.

Icetime of 1948

Skater: 8in (28cm); one-piece composition doll with hard plastic arms; *Nancy Ann Storybook Doll* competitor; painted blue eyes; long painted black eyelashes; blonde mohair wig stapled to head; silver painted skates with attached silver blades; pink dress trimmed with white collar; blue felt hat trimmed with paper stars; pink ribbon banner reads "I'M FROM ICETIME OF 1948."
MARKS: None.
SEE: *Illustration 253.*

Illustration 253.

Ideal Novelty and Toy Co.

Ideal was started around 1906 by Mr. Morris Michtom and A. Cohn. By 1911 Mr. Cohn had left the company, and Mr. Michtom had begun an active, prosperous company which lasted until the 1980s.

Like other early large doll companies, Ideal had a large, varied line each year. Sometimes they advertised over 200 different numbers. They made dolls in many price ranges and often their dolls were used for premiums. They sold marked and unmarked dolls to mail-order companies.

They had a large doll manufacturing facility and made dolls for others as well as themselves. American Character, Arranbee, Eugenia, Gerzon and Mary Hoyer were among their customers. They made the traditional *Mama*, baby and character dolls and were proud of their "flirty eye" innovations in the 1930s.

Rather than imitate *Patsy*, they introduced in 1934 a *Shirley Temple* doll which started a trend toward movie star dolls. That assured their fortune during the dark years of the Depression. Each year they produced their *Shirley Temple* dolls with small changes in bodies and costumes, introduced a few new dolls and sold dolls and parts to other companies. They survived the Depression well.

By 1937 they started to expand their line, and their 1938-1940 dolls were some of the best ever made. Though war shortages hampered production during the World War II years, they continued to make a few dolls.

In 1946 they started to experiment with hard plastic, and soon the wonderful *Toni* and other hard plastic dolls began to take the place of *Shirley Temple*.

Peter Pan: 18in (46cm) composition head and gauntlet hands; cloth body and limbs; tin sleep eyes; closed mouth; dressed in red and yellow woodland suit; bright red jumper jacket laced down the front; red pointed shoes and pointed hat with a bell; cheeks painted bright red; sleep eyes; 1929.

This doll was a premium for sending four subscriptions of $.50 each to *Household Magazine*, Topeka, Kansas in 1929. The advertisement describes the doll, "This merry fellow is coming straight from fairyland to play with you." He also came in other sizes and costume colors.

MARKS: "Peter Pan//Ideal (in diamond)" head and tag.

SEE: *Illustration 254. Household Magazine*, 1929.

Advertisement for Ginger: "Body, arms and legs molded with absolute fidelity to the human body. New style ball and socket joints that enable arms and legs to assume natural and graceful poses. New double action glace eyes that flash, sparkle, sleep and flirt, and have real eyelashes. Dresses that are exact replicas of the smartest children's dresses in New York. Beautiful real hair wigs in all styles." They came in five sizes. Other dolls advertised in the 1934 included *Ducky, Honeysuckle, Tru-life Rubber Dolls, Snoozie, Kissable, Ideal Baby, Saucy Sue, Flossy Flirt and Tickletoes*; 1934.

SEE: *Illustration 255. Playthings*, July 1934.

Illustration 254.

Ideal advertised a new startling double-action glace eye with real long eyelashes at the Toy Fair in New York in 1934. The eyelashes were long and silky. They were supposed to "Flash, sparkle, flirt and sleep." The "flirty" eye was a feature of many Ideal dolls throughout the rest of the composition era.

Illustration 255.

BELOW: *HORSMAN* Peggy *(see page 118, Illustration 236)*.

ABOVE: *GOLDBERGER* Little Miss Charming *(see page 113, Illustration 226)*.

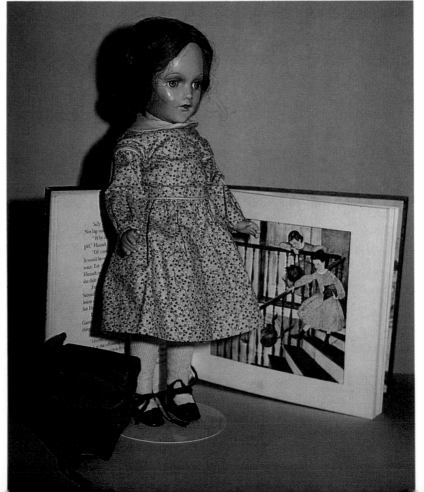

HEDWIG (De Angeli) Hannah *(see page 113, Illustration 228)*. Marianne Gardner Collection.

ABOVE: *HORSMAN* Patriotic
Girl *(see page 120, Illustration
243)*.

MARY HOYER Ice Skater *(see
page 125, Illustration 250)*.

IDEAL Little Bo Peep *(see page 148, Illustration 266).*

TOP LEFT: *IDEAL* Texas Ranger Shirley Temple *(see page 146, Illustration 262).*

IDEAL Shirley Temple *(see page 145, Illustration 258).* Mary Elizabeth Poole Collection.

IDEAL Shirley Temple Snow White *(see page 147, Illustration 264 A).*

IDEAL Large Ventriloquist Dopey *(see page 147, Illustration 264 B)*. Michele Teny Collection.

LEFT: *IDEAL* Deanna Durbin *(see page 148, Illustration 267).*

BELOW: *IDEAL Flexy* Fanny Brice and Mortimer Snerd *(see page 150, Illustration 274).*

IDEAL Judy Garland and Strawman *(see page 149, Illustration 270). William Stillman Collection. Photography by Tim McGowan Studios.*

LEFT: *UNKNOWN* Mama doll Girl in Yellow Dress *(see page 160, Illustration 295).*

KNICKERBOCKER Snow White *and* Dwarfs *(see page 159, Illustration 292).*

MARCIE Bride *(see page 161, Illustration 296).*

135

INSET: *RELIABLE* Royal Canadian Mounted Police *(see page 174, Illustration 333).*

MOLLYE Russian Girl *(see page 163, Illustration 301).*

ABOVE: MONICA in silver net dress *(see page 164, Illustration 305).*

ABOVE LEFT: *ALEXANDER* Quintuplets *(see page 169, Illustration 320).* Sandra Strater Collection.

LEFT: *RELIABLE* Joan *(see page 174, Illustration 335).* Jean Francis Collection.

UNKNOWN Quintuplets *(see pages 171-172, Illustration 330).*

FREUNDLICH Quintuplets *(see page 171, Illustration 327).* Connie Lee Martin Collection.

RIGHT: *ALEXANDER* Quintuplets *(see page 169, Illustration 321).* Sandra Strater Collection.

RIGHT: *SKOOKUM Apples* Indian *(see page 175, Illustration 337).* Madge Poole Copely Collection.

FAR RIGHT: *THREE-IN-ONE DOLL CORPORATION* Trudy *(see page 176, Illustration 340).*

BELOW: *S.F.B.J.* French Family *(see page 175, Illustration 339).*

ABOVE: *TOYCRAFT* Denny Dimwit *(see page 177, Illustration 343).* Felix A. Cappadona Collection.

RIGHT: *VOGUE* Military Group
(see page 180, Illustration 352).

ABOVE: *UNEEDA* Rita Hayworth *(see page 178, Illustration 346).*

LEFT: *VOGUE* Bo Peep *(see page 179, Illustration 349).*

LEFT: *VOGUE* Rosie the Waac-ette *(see page 181, Illustration 358).* Sandra Strater Collection.

BELOW: *VOGUE* Toddles Brother *and* Sister *(see page 180, Illustration 353).*

LEFT: *VOGUE* Victory Gardener Pair, Girl in Pink and Policeman *(see page 180, Illustration 354).*

BELOW: *ACME* Marilyn *(see page 7, Illustration 2).*

VOGUE Painted Eye Girl *(see page 181, Illustration 357).*

BELOW: *AMERICAN CHARACTER* Sally Petite Brother and Sister *(see page 186, Illustration 370).*

ABOVE: *VOGUE* Make-up *Doll (see page 183, Illustration 363), Joanne McIntosh Collection.*

RIGHT: German Patsy Look-alikes *(see page 188, Illustration 377)*.

Moravian Anna Nitschmann *(see page 190, Illustration 382)*.

Size, 13 inches high
ANNA NITSCHMANN DOLL

Named for Anna Nitschmann, born 1714, a distinguished worker among the women of the Moravian Church. The authentic costume of this doll is hand made by the Busy Workers of the Moravian Church. For information write to Mrs. Barry Jones, 439 High Street, Bethlehem, Pa.

MAXINE Mitzie and unknown Tootsie *(see pages 161, 177, 189, Illustration 380).*

Shirley Temple

In the depth of the Depression, a young movie star danced and sang her way into the hearts of Americans. After months of negotiation, Ideal won the rights to make a *Shirley Temple* doll. It was a stunning victory and in December 1934, the lovely blonde doll appeared on the market.

The doll's head mold went through many changes before it was presented to the public. The body was unique because it reflected a human child's rounded body. The doll was a "smashing" success almost immediately.

As usual in the doll business, *Shirley* look-alikes entered the lines of many companies. Although the original doll was rather expensive for the time, the "genuine" *Shirley Temple* was purchased by many doting parents who wished that their child could sing, dance and make as much money as Shirley.

Ideal's successful doll helped the company through the remaining depression years, and it led the way for both Ideal and other companies to make movie star dolls. The doll clothes industry designed wonderful costumes based on the roles that Shirley and other stars played in individual movies.

In the 1930s, people and their children needed a release from the grind of everyday life. The fairy tale quality of both the movies and the dolls can still be seen in the eagerly sought "star" dolls.

Shirley Temple: Picture of Shirley Temple and a *Shirley Temple* doll dressed in nautical dresses; middy collar with white trim; sail boat on front of dress.
  SEE: *Illustration 256. Playthings*, November 1934.

Shirley Temple: 20in (51cm); all-composition; jointed at neck and shoulders; for general characteristics, see below; all original; circa mid-1930s.
  Box end has 2020 printed on it.
  MARKS: "Shirley Temple//COP//N & T Co" head; "Genuine//Shirley Temple doll//Registered U.S. Pat. Off.//Ideal Nov. & Toy Co.//Made in U.S.A." tag on dress.
  SEE: *Illustration 257.* (Color Section, page 96.) *Athena Crowley Collection.*

Shirley Temple Shown With Her Shirley Temple Doll

Illustration 256.

Shirley Temple: 17in (43cm); all-composition; jointed at neck, shoulders and hips; rounded stomach; unusual curvaceous legs; second and third fingers molded together; curly blonde wig; sleep hazel eyes with real lashes; other eyelashes painted under eyes; open mouth with tongue and six teeth; beautiful flesh-colored composition; "Shirley Temple" dimples on either side of mouth; ⛛ on lower back; light pink paint on back of hands, elbows and knees; pink organdy dress with white embroidered collar; dress originally pleated; shoes and socks are not original; circa mid 1930s.
  The body was first used on the *Ginger* doll.
  This doll is shown in the color section with an Arranbee *Nancy* (see Color Section, page 46) also page 49. A comparison of the two dolls is found on page 49.
  MARKS: "Shirley Temple//Cop//N & T Co." head; none on body; "Genuine//Shirley Temple//doll//Red. U.S. Pat Office//Ideal Novelty and Toy Company" cloth tag on dress.
  SEE: *Illustration 89.*

Shirley Temple: 13in (33cm); all-composition; jointed neck, shoulders and hips; blonde curly mohair wig; sleep eyes; open mouth with teeth; dressed in early *Stand Up and Cheer* costume.
  MARKS: "Shirley Temple//13" body; "13//Shirley Temple//c Ideal" head; "Shirley Temple N.R.A.//Ideal Nov. and Toy Co. Code" dress tag.
  SEE: *Illustration 258.* (Color Section, page 131.) *Mary Elizabeth Poole Collection.*

Shirley Temple: 13in (33cm); the advertisement said, "This doll is the same as our higher priced *Shirley Temple* Dolls, except for the size 13in (33cm). The same charming face and winning smile and Shirley's cute dimples. The same hazel eyes, golden hair, the color and style of Shirley's. Dressed in exact copies of the beautiful dresses worn by Shirley in her hit pictures."
  This doll was priced at $1.98. Many mothers were happy to have the opportunity to buy a genuine *Shirley Temple* doll at a much lower price.
  SEE: *Illustration 258.* (Color Section, page 131.) *Playthings*, May 1935.

Illustration 259.

Illustration 261.

Shirley Temple: 13in (33cm); all-composition; open mouth with four teeth; for general characteristics, see page 145); all original except shoes; pink party dress and matching garden hat; 1935.

Ideal advertised the Shirley Temple trunk in *Playthings*, May 1935. It was a Children's Day Special. "The Trunks are exact replicas of regular wardrobe trunks, faithfully reproducing all authentic details." Sticker pictures of Shirley Temple are used on all sides of trunk instead of foreign labels; trunk came with wardrobe of doll clothes; trunk came in three sizes; 1935.
MARKS: "Shirley Temple" trunk.
SEE: *Illustration 259. Camille Brennan Collection.*

Illustration 260.

Four-Way Display Rack for Shirley Temple Dolls: Displayed a variety of doll sizes and costumes available for the *Shirley Temple* dolls.
SEE: *Illustration 260. Playthings,* June 1935.

Shirley Temple Baby Doll: Advertisement for new doll in 1935. "Shirley at 2! New double-action eyes with real eyelashes that flash, sparkle, sleep and flirt. Kapoc stuffed body; composition head, arms and legs; cry voice; six sizes."
SEE: *Illustration 261. Playthings,* September 1935.

Shirley Temple Texas Ranger Doll: Special souvenir of the Texas Centennial; 11in (28cm); all-composition; jointed at neck, shoulders and hips; blonde curly mohair wig; sleep eyes; open mouth with teeth; all original clothes; carrying a metal gun; 1936.
MARKS: "11 Shirley Temple" head.
SEE: *Illustration 262* (doll on left). (Color Section, page 131.)

Shirley Temple Texas Ranger Special Souvenir of the Texas Centennial: Advertised by Arnold-Fairyland; made in 11in (28cm); 17in (43cm); 27in (69cm); real Western metal ornaments; pistol and holster; ten gallon hat; 1936.
MARKS: "11 Shirley Temple" head.
SEE: *Illustration 262* (doll on right). *Toys and Bicycles,* October 1936. (Color Section, page 131).

Shirley Temple Texas Ranger Doll: Special souvenir of the Texas Centennial; 27in (69cm); dressed in red flannel shirt; brown leather chaps and vest decorated with studs; holster and gun; 1936.

SEE: *Illustration 263. Elizabeth Martz Collection.*

Dopey: 19½in (50cm); composition flange head; hinged mouth on drawstring; molded tongue; face painted to resemble dwarf in Walt Disney movie *Snow White and the Seven Dwarfs*; cloth body, arms and legs; composition hands with three fingers and a thumb; long trailing coat; cotton pants; felt shoes which are part of leg; cardboard in sole of shoes so the doll can stand alone; 1937.

This is a very large, rare *Dopey* character doll. It has the same picture box and tag as the smaller dwarfs. The mouth was hinged to let this model *Dopey* be used as a ventriloquist's dummy. Such "dummies" were very popular in 1937.

MARKS: "Snow White//-and the Seven Dwarfs//©
1937//W.D.ENT." paper tag hanging from belt;
"Ideal doll" molded on back of neck.
SEE: *Illustration 264B. (Color Section, page 133.)*
Michele Teny Collection.

Snow White: 18in (46cm); all-composition; *Shirley Temple* mold; jointed at neck, shoulders and hips; black mohair wig; flirty sleep eyes with real lashes; open mouth with four teeth; one dimple in chin; Ƴ on backside; Disney dwarf characters pictured around bottom of skirt; circa 1939.

Dwarf: *Snow White* is pictured with an all-cloth Ideal *Doc*, one of the seven dwarfs.

MARKS: "Shirley Temple//18" body; none on head.
SEE: *Illustration 264A. (Color Section, page 132.)*

Illustration 263.

Snow White: 16in (41cm); all-composition; black mohair wig; sleep eyes; closed mouth; eyelashes painted above eyes; red cotton bodice; white organdy skirt which has been printed with the Disney characters from the movie *Snow White and the Seven Dwarfs* in red; white organdy pantalets; all original; circa 1939.

This is an unusual Ideal version of *Snow White*.
MARKS: None
SEE: *Illustration 265.*

Illustration 265.

147

Little Bo Peep: 15½in (39cm); all-composition; jointed at neck and shoulders; second and third fingers molded together; sleep eyes with real lashes; open mouth with six teeth; eyelashes painted under eyes; slight eye blusher on upper lid; dimple on chin; third and fourth fingers molded together; shoes with openwork on toes; circa late 1930s.

MARKS: "U.S.A./16" back.

SEE: *Illustration 266.* (Color Section, page 131.)

Deanna Durbin: 21in (53cm); jointed at neck, shoulders and hips; human hair wig; open mouth with six teeth; felt tongue; eye shadow; sleep eyes with lashes; painted eyelashes under eyes; smiling portrait face that makes doll look like it is singing; second and third fingers molded together and curled; fingernail polish; clothes all original including unusual oxford shoes with flap and socks with tan stripe near the top; 1938-1939.

Deanna Durbin also came in a 14in (36cm) size.

MARKS: "Deanna Durbin//Ideal Doll" head; "Ideal Doll" body.

SEE: *Illustration 267.* (Color Section, page 134.)

Deanna Durbin as Gulliver: 21in (53cm); all-composition; jointed at neck, shoulders and hips; black mohair wig; open mouth with six teeth; painted eyes; white satin blouse; brown knit tights; pink overjacket; black suede boots; 1939.

SEE: *Illustration 268. Jackie O'Connor Collection.*

Gulliver's Travels Characters: composition.
1. *Gulliver:* 21in (53cm); *Deanna Durbin Doll.*
2. *Gabby:* 11in (28cm); clothing painted on doll.
3. *King Little:* 11in (28cm); clothing painted on doll.
4. *Princess Glory:* 11in (28cm); long organdy princess-style dress; crown.
5. *Prince David:* 11in (28cm); dark tights and tunic; cape; boots; hat.

SEE: *Illustration 269. Playthings,* December 1939.

Ideal Body Twist Dolls: jointed at shoulder plate and slightly below waist.
1. Some of the *Deanna Durbin* dolls were made with this type of body.
2. *Mayfair* Dolls: advertised in 1939 catalog but may never have been marketed.
3. *Mary Hoyer* Dolls: Ideal made about 2000 of these dolls (see page 124.)

Illustration 268.

148

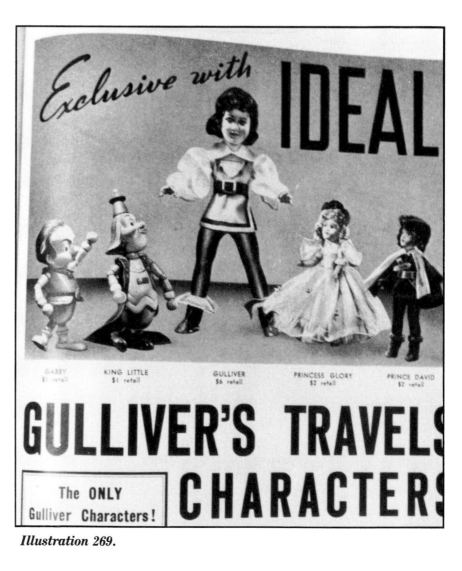

Illustration 269.

Judy Garland: 15½in (39cm); all-composition; sleep eyes; pigtails; all original costume of Dorothy in *Wizard of Oz;* 1939.

The following information is supplied by the well-known author and *Wizard of Oz* collector William Stillman.

"The doll was issued in three sizes: 13in (33cm), 15½in (39cm) and 18in (46cm). There seems to be a bit of a size discrepancy with the middle size as some dolls measure between 14in (36cm) and 15½in (39cm). This can be attributed to using various size body molds and attaching the same head. The *Shirley Temple* body mold was used. Also some of the middle-sized dolls have a heavier, chunkier face than others. It is rumored that Judy was unhappy with the pudgy appearance and requested the change; again, at this point, this is the stuff of legend and can't be confirmed.

"The doll was usually marked 'Ideal Doll' and 'Made in USA' on the back of the head (mine also has a small '15' above this as does another 15½in (39cm) size doll that I know of.) Some dolls **were not** marked on the head. This same marking was also on the doll's back with a number indicating the doll's size. They were never marked "Judy Garland" as some celebrity dolls were. The 15½in (39cm) doll is the most common size.

"The doll's shoes were usually a black suede oxford with flaps, but others wore black Mary Janes and red suede has been reported. There is nothing to suggest that Ideal ever considered attiring the doll in anything resembling the now-famous ruby slippers; at that time those slippers, which recently brought $165,000 at auction, had no significance.

"Hair ribbons were often a royal blue silk-like ribbon, in red for those dolls in the red checked dresses. At least one example I am aware of has white hair ribbons."

SEE: *Illustration 270.* (Color Section, page 134.) *William Stillman Collection.*

Strawman: 16in (41cm) all-cloth; pink sateen mask face; raised triangular eyebrows; raised button-type eyes; sculptured nose; yellow yarn hair; arms and legs sewn to white cloth body; back seam on head is machine sewn; back seam on body is hand-sewn; 1939.

SEE: *Illustration 270.* (Color Section, page 134.)

Illustration 271.

Illustration 272.

Charlie McCarthy, Inc.: Hand puppet; 4in (10cm) composition head; approximately 8in (20cm) overall; composition top hat molded onto head; face sculptured to look like the famous puppet of Edgar Bergen; body of puppet is black cloth with design of tuxedo printed on it; 1939.

MARKS: "Edgar Bergin's//© Charlie McCarthy, Inc.//Made in U.S.A."

SEE: *Illustration 271. Milly Myer Collection.*

Ideal Dolls in 1939: Advertisement in *Playthings,* April 1939; (from left to right).
Upper Row: *Deanna Durbin* — The Teen-Age Doll Hit
Shirley Temple — Box Office No. 1 Today
Princess Beatrix — America's Soft and Cuddly Baby
Lower Row: *Betsy-Wetsy* — The Ideal Nursing Doll
Ferdinand the Bull — Walt Disney Sensation
Charlie McCarthy — America's Newest Idol
The *Shirley Temple* doll was advertised as a more mature doll.

SEE: *Illustration 272. Playthings,* April 1939.

149

Illustration 273.

Illustration 275.

Pinocchio: 10½in (27cm); painted molded composition head; wide smiling mouth; large nose and ears; wood segmented body painted red and yellow; yellow felt cap; 1940.

Other wood segmented characters include:

King-Little: 14in (36cm).

Jiminy Cricket: 9in (23cm).

MARKS: "Ideal" bottom of right foot.

SEE: *Illustration 273. Jean Kelley Collection.*

Fannie Brice Flexy: 11½in (29cm); composition head, body and gauntlet hands; head mounted on ball to enable head to turn; smiling character face; open mouth with painted teeth; legs and arms made from flexible metal cable; yellow flowered print dress with wide beige cotton collar and belt; matching long pants; black shoes painted on molded feet; 1939.

Miss Brice was a star of stage, movies, radio and television.

MARKS: "Ideal Doll//Made in U.S.A." head; "The Doll of a Thousand//Poses//Made in U.S.A.//A Flexy Doll/Fanny Brice Baby Snooks" tag.

SEE: *Illustration 274* (doll on right). (Color Section, page 134.)

Mortimer Snerd: 12in (31cm); composition head, body, gauntlet hands and feet; head mounted on ball to enable head to turn; smiling character face; painted, long nose; "buck" teeth; legs and arms made from flexible metal cable; brown herringbone pants; brown felt jacket; white shirt; peach ribbon tie; 1939. *Mortimer Snerd* was a ventriloquist dummy used by Edgar Bergen on television.

MARKS: "Ideal Doll//Made in U.S.A." head.

SEE: *Illustration 274* (doll on left). (Color Section, page 134.)

Flexy Dolls: 12in (31cm); advertisement in *Playthings* says, "This doll can assume fifty-seven different positions. It comes in five different styles. Three of them retail at $1.00, while the Baby Snooks and Mortimer Snerd Flexy Dolls retail at $1.25."

Other Flexy dolls include *Sunny Sam, Sunny Sue, Soldier* and *Al Jolson.*

SEE: *Illustration 275.* Playthings, April 1939.

Soldier: 13in (33cm); jointed in head, shoulders and hips; molded hair; painted eyes with three eyelashes above the eyes on right side; watermelon-type mouth; khaki uniform with overseas cap; all original; late 1930s — early 1940s.

The soldier has *Flexy*-type head on an all-composition body. This type of head is usually found on a *Flexy* body with the coiled spring arms and legs.

MARKS: "13" head.
SEE: *Illustration 276. Sandy Strater Collection.*

Illustration 276.

Illustration 277.

Illustration 278.

Betty Jane: 16in (41cm); all-composition; beautiful blonde wig with pigtails; sleep eyes with real lashes; dressed in cotton print dress; organdy pinafore; straw hat; 1943.

Betty Jane also came in other sizes.
MARKS: "U.S.A//16" body; "Ideal Doll" tag.
SEE: *Illustration 277. Mary Lu Trowbridge Collection.*

Baby Smiles: 17in (43cm); composition head; cloth body; soft life-like rubber arms; dimpled knees; sleeping-winking eyes; cries, sucks her thumb, enjoys pacifier; clasps hands; wears pink organdy baby dress and matching bonnet; moccasins; stockings; rubber panties; circa 1931.

This is a coupon issued by the Ontario Biscuit Company of Buffalo, New York. Their offer said, "Send us 10 coupons and $2.00 cash or money order, and we will send you this doll immediately. Or give the coupons and money to your grocer who will get this doll for you."

MARKS: "Ideal" printed on lower left hand corner of the coupon.
SEE: *Illustration 278.*

Tickletoes the Wonder Doll: 14in (36cm); composition head; flirting sleep eyes; chubby soft rubber legs with a voice in each leg; rubber arms and hands; sucks thumb; she can wink her eyes and roll them; soft cloth body; organdy dress with matching bonnet trimmed with lace; petticoat; moccasins; knitted stockings; rubber panties; 1935.

This doll was given as a premium for *Needlecraft* magazine with five subscriptions at 50 cents each. *Tickletoes* was made for many years. In 1947, it was still being advertised in Christmas catalogs.

SEE: *Illustration 279. Needlecraft*, November 1935.

Walking Mama Doll: 19in (46cm); premium for selling subscriptions to *The Ladies' Home Journal*; composition head and arms; cloth body; curly brown wig with bangs and "flip" styling; 1931.

MARKS: "Ideal" tag pinned on both dresses.

SEE: *Illustration 280. The Ladies' Home Journal*, December 1931.

Precious: Premium for selling subscriptions to *The Ladies' Home Journal*; composition head; rubber arms and legs; feels as cuddly and soft as a real baby; doll cries when legs are pinched; December 1931.

Tag pinned on babies' dress says, "*Smiles*//Ideal Doll."

SEE: *Illustration 280. The Ladies' Home Journal*, December 1931.

Illustration 279.

I Sleep
I Wink
I use my Fingers

Tickletoes
"The Wonder Doll"
Soft Rubber Arms and Legs
that feel so real
Given for FIVE Subscriptions at 50 cents each
Make some little girl happy with this Doll

Illustration 280.

LADIES' HOME JOURNAL

My name is Precious. With my rubber arms and legs, I feel as cuddly and soft as a real baby. And if you pinch my knees, I cry for Mamma at once.

CAN'T you hear the joyous cries on Christmas morning? . . . The excited rapture as one of these gorgeous dolls is folded in some little mother's arms?

You'll think Santa Claus himself has been shopping for you when you see them. And you may have them . . . easily . . . *without spending any money.*

Shall we tell you how to make one . . . or both of them . . . *yours?* Just send a card with your name and address to:

MANAGER OF THE GIRLS' CLUB
Box 771, Independence Square, Phila., Pa.

I walk and talk too and have the prettiest, curly brown hair. But I want a Mamma of my own. Won't some little girl adopt me?

December, 1931

300 Happy Dolls for 300 Little Mothers!

The years between 1930 and 1935 were depression years. It was very common for magazines to urge boys and girls to solicit for subscriptions with the promise of free premiums. Often this premium was a doll. In 1933 *Needlecraft* magazine offered a 22in (56cm) Ideal baby doll for eight subscriptions. In 1934 times were no better and in many cases worse. The Needlecraft doll offer was a 14in (36cm) Ideal baby doll for only three subscriptions. The same picture was used for both offers. However, the doll's name was changed. No wonder collectors have trouble identifying their dolls.

Cuddles a Life-Size Baby Doll:
22in (56cm); composition head and legs; rubber arms and hands; crier; sleep eyes; open mouth with two upper and lower teeth; organdy baby dress and matching bonnet; 1933.

This doll was given with eight subscriptions at 50 cents each for *Needlecraft* magazine.

SEE: *Illustration 281. Needlecraft*, December 1933.

Sallykins is Growing Up:
14in (36cm); composition head and legs; soft kapok-filled body; molded rubber hands and fingers; winking and sleeping eyes; crier; organdy dress and matching bonnet; moccasin shoes; 1934.

SEE: *Illustration 281. Needlecraft*, December 1934.

Bathrobe Baby:
12in (31cm); composition head; all-rubber body; jointed at head, arms and hips; molded hair; came with flannel diaper and flannel bathrobe; 1933.

This doll was given as a premium for three subscriptions of *Needlecraft* at $.50 each.

SEE: *Illustration 282. Needlecraft*, December 1933.

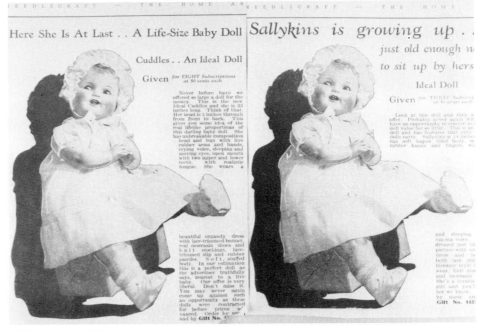

Illustration 281.

This new baby doll is too cute for words. Again we offer you an Ideal doll because in our opinion Ideal stands in the forefront of doll manufacturers. This Bathrobe Baby has an *all* rubber body with an unbreakable composition head. The hands and fingers are especially realistic in molded rubber. The head is jointed and moves in any direction. The doll is 12 inches long and comes with a flannel diaper and flannel bathrobe. We vouch for the thrill that any little girl will get with this extremely realistic baby doll. Order by name and by **Gift No. 4302.**

Illustration 282.

Magic Eye Dolls: In the latter part of the 1930s, Ideal made a line of Magic Eye dolls that was very popular. These dolls had eyes which moved to the left, moved to the right and closed for sleeping. It is difficult to tell them apart without the clothing, labels or boxes. The first lines included *Baby Beautiful* and *Cuddles*. The next year Ideal added the now-famous *Princess Beatrix* named for the daughter of Queen Wilhelmina of Holland.

•

Baby Beautiful: 16in (41cm), 18in (46cm), 20in (51cm), 22in (56cm), 27in (69cm); composition head, arms and legs; molded, dark brown hair; crier; Magic Eyes with real lashes; closed mouth; kapok-stuffed body; organdy dress and matching bonnet with elaborate trimmings.

Cuddles: 16in (41cm), 18in (46cm), 20in (51cm), 22in (56cm), 25in (64cm) and 27in (69cm); composition head, arms and legs; molded dark brown hair; crier; Magic Eyes with real lashes; closed mouth; kapok-stuffed body; organdy dress and matching bonnet.

Illustration 283.

Princess Beatrix: 14in (36cm), 16in (41cm), 22in (56cm); composition head, arms and legs; molded dark brown hair; crier; Magic Eyes with real lashes; closed mouth.

Ideal advertised this doll as "A popular new baby princess in doll form! Here is a doll that is truly a baby doll. It has the softest and cuddliest body that Ideal has ever produced — Beatrix's arms and legs are so jointed that they will fall backwards or forwards just as those of a real baby — her tiny fists are clenched like the fists of a newborn baby. Princess Beatrix can sit up or lie down just as a real baby would in any pose, with one foot in her mouth or with her hands beneath her head — or almost any other position a baby can take. Princess Beatrix is dressed in a fine organdy dress."

Princess Beatrix could be purchased in Master Craft Luggage which contained a layette and large pillow. This came in the 14in (36cm) and 22in (56cm) sizes.

Princess Beatrix also came dressed in printed pajamas only in the 14in (36cm), 16in (41cm) and 22in (56cm) sizes. The 14in (36cm) size only came with sleep eyes with lashes, not the Magic Eyes.

The same pajama doll could be obtained with an additional layette containing dress, hat, petticoat, slippers and stockings for an additional $.50 or $1.00.

Princess Beatrix also came in a regular baby dress with an additional hand-crocheted sweater and ornate cap to match. This came only in the 16in (41cm) and 22in (56cm) size.

SEE: *Illustration 283. Playthings*, July 1939.

Plassie: Composition arms and legs; early **plastic** head; purchased in 1943 by Mary Elizabeth Poole and given to her sister for Christmas; dress and bonnet made in 1944.

This is an example of the dolls which were made during World War II. The companies used whatever doll parts that could be obtained.

SEE: *Illustration 284. Mary Elizabeth Poole Collection.*

Pinafore Doll (doll on left): 18in (46cm); all-composition; sleep eyes with real lashes; mohair reddish wig; jointed at neck, shoulders and hips; open mouth with four teeth; eye shadow on upper eyes; Ÿ on lower back; pink organdy dress with ruffle around neck and skirt; all original outfit; 1947.

MARKS: "18" body.

SEE: *Illustration 285. Sandy Strator Collection.*

Pinafore Doll (doll on right): same general characteristics; advertised in Montgomery Ward catalog in 1947.

SEE: *Illustration 285.*

Illustration 284.

Illustration 285.

Ideal List of Composition Dolls*
1926 to End of Composition Era

1926   **Baby Mae.**
       Hush-a-Bye Baby.
       Vanity Fair: (1926-1929).
       Baby Smiles: Rubber arms; dimpled knees; sleeping-winking eyes; cries, sucks her thumb; enjoys her pacifier; clasps her hands; made for many years into the mid 1930s.

1927   **Kindergarten Baby.**
       Happy Flossy.
       Nightingale Baby.
       Twinkle Toes.
       Happie Flossie Baby doll.

1928 Most of the dolls had flirty eyes.
Peter Pan.
Cuddles: Rubber arms and legs that gave a crying sound when pinched; cloth body and legs; composition head and arms; flange neck; molded hair; 1928-1938. MARKS: "Ideal Doll//Made in U.S.A." head.
Standing **Mama**-type dolls: Rubber arms but not rubber legs.

1929 **Mama** Dolls: Now taller and slimmer.
Buster Brown.
Candy Kid (new model).
Buster Brown.
Tickletoes: One of most popular dolls; still advertised in Christmas catalogs in 1947.
Wendy: Mate to *Peter Pan*.
Winsome Winnie.
Vanity Flossie — Vanity Fair (1926-1929).

1930 **Baby Peggy (Pretty Peggy):** Composition head; straight legs; curved arms; open hand; flirty sleep eyes; open/closed mouth with molded tongue; four painted teeth. MARKS: "Ideal (in diamond)// U.S.A."

1931 **Honey Bunch.**
Precious *(Baby Smiles):* Premium doll.
Mama Dolls: Also offered for premiums.
Saucy Sue: Made for several years.

1932 Ideal used "Tru-flesh" rubber body parts.
Honeysuckle Line:
   Ducky.
   Snoozie: Cloth body; composition head, lower limbs; tin eyes; rubber arms; yawning mouth with molded tongue and teeth; cry voice; in line for several more years.
   Winnie.

1933 **Bathroom Baby:** Premium doll.

1934 **Ginger:** Advertised as a new type of doll with body, arms and legs molded with absolute fidelity to the human body. It had a new style of ball and socket joints that enabled arms and legs to assume natural and graceful poses. It also had new double action glace eyes that flash, sparkle, sleep and flirt.
Shirley Temple: First sold this year; *Playthings* announced that it was on the Ginger body. MARKED: "Cop.//Ideal//N.&T Co" head; no marks on body; original costume *Stand Up and Cheer.*
Shirley Temple Costumes Include: Nautical dress; plaid *Bright Eyes* dress.
Molded Hair Shirley Temple-type: 9in (23cm); painted molded hair. MARKS: "E//Ideal Doll."
Sallikins: Premium doll.
Kissable.

1935 **Hush-A-Bye Baby:** Composition head and arms; flange neck; cloth legs; tin sleep eyes; molded hair; open mouth; large dimples on each cheek; four upper teeth. MARKS: "Ideal (in Diamond)" head.
Shirley Temple: 13in (33cm); dress has NRA label. MARKS: "13" on body.
Shirley Temple: Costumes include *Curly Top, Our Little Girl* and *Littlest Rebel.*
Marilyn Knowlden Doll (movie star): 13in (33cm); all-composition; open mouth with four teeth; sleep eyes; black eye shadow; red mohair wig. MARKS: "U.S.A. 13" head; "Ideal Doll//Made in U.S.A." body.
Ticklette: 13½in (33cm); cry voice; cloth body; composition head (turns); rubber arms and legs; squeeze voice in each leg; open fingers; organdy dress and cap; rubber panties; socks, moccasins.
Shirley Temple Baby Doll: Composition head, arms and legs; kapok-stuffed body; cry voice.
Baby Smiles: Premium doll.

1936 **Sunbonnet Sue.**
Shirley Temple Texas Centennial Ranger costume.
Lifetime Doll.

1937 **Betsy Wetsy:** Composition head.
Flossie Flirt: Body limbs are slimmer.
Shirley Temple: *Heidi* costume.

1938 **Snow White:** Painted Disney dwarfs pictured around bottom of skirt.
Snow White: 18in (46cm); molded black hair with red painted bow in center front; composition shoulder plate; cloth body. MARKS: "Ideal" shoulder plate.
Shirley Temple: *Snow White* costume; flirty eyes. MARKS: "Shirley Temple//18."
Mary Jane: All-composition; flirty brown sleep eyes; blonde mohair wig. MARKS: "Ideal, 18."
Deanna Durbin: 21in (53cm); 25in (64cm).
Princess Beatrix.
Princess Sonja: All-composition; four teeth; dimple in chin.
Shirley Temple: *Heidi* Costume.

1939 **Judy Garland Wizard of Oz:** MARKS: "Ideal Doll//Made in U.S.A." head; "U.S.A." body.
Scarecrow.
Little Bo Peep: Open mouth; teeth.
Coquette (new mold): 9in (23cm) and 11in (28cm).
Toddling Sue.
Baby Beautiful.
Cinderella: 18in (46cm); made for Montgomery Ward 1939 Christmas catalog. MARKS: "Ideal" head; "Shirley Temple" body.
Mortimer Snerd and **Baby Snooks.**
Flexy, Sunny Sam and **Sunny Sue.**
Deanna Durbin: 14½in (37cm) and 19½in (45cm); added sizes.
Mature Shirley Temple.
Gulliver Series: *Gulliver (Deanna Durbin); Gabby; King Little; Princess Glory* and *Prince David.*
Charlie McCarthy: puppet.

1940 **Judy Garland Teen:** 21in (53cm). MARKS: "21" backward
Pinocchio.
Judy Garland: *Babes in Toyland* costume.
Jiminy Cricket.
Little Miss America.
Judy Garland: *Strike Up the Band* costume.
Deanna Durbin.

1941 **Gorgeous.**
Squeezums.
Deanna Durbin.
Shirley Temple: *Bluebird* costume; laced weskit and apron over dress. MARKS: "Shirley Temple" head; "U.S.A. Shirley Temple//18" body.

1942 **Flexy Characters:** Continued and included soldier.
Plassie: Composition heads, arms and legs; some came with hard plastic heads; composition arms and legs. This was one of first dolls to use hard plastic. It was made for several years.
Miss Deb.

1943 **Honey Baby:** Composition head and limbs; molded painted brown hair; sleep eyes; open mouth with molded tongue; two upper teeth. MARKS: "Ideal Doll//Made in U.S.A."
Betty Jane.
Baby Beautiful.
Queen of the Ice.
Lazy Bones.

1944 **Pin Up Girl.**

1945 **Bit of Heaven.**
Sleep Time Twins.
Continental.

1947 **Tickletoes:** Advertised in Montgomery Ward catalog.
Pinafore Doll: 17in (43cm); all-composition.

* Partial list.

157

Now being shown to millions of children in leading theatres throughout the country. These movies will create immediate demand for DARLING TODDLERS in your community—be sure to have a stock in your store to take advantage of this publicity.

Illustration 287.

Illustration 286.   **Illustration 288.**

Jolly Toys, Inc.

Girl in Blue Dress: 14in (36cm); all-composition; sleep eyes; eyelashes painted under eyes; open mouth with six upper teeth; both bangs and ends of wig are tightly curled; hair on top of head is straight; fingers molded together and all are slightly curved inward; toes are slightly molded; jointed at neck, shoulders and hips; *Shirley Temple* look-alike; clothes all original; blue marquisette dress with lace yoke and sleeves; embroidered braid trim; straw hat with pink ribbon trim; cotton slip attached to dress; separate teddy; circa 1935-1940.

UNUSUAL IDENTIFYING FEATURE: Two nails in back of neck.

MARKS: None on doll; "Jolly Toys, Inc//New York, U.S.A." cloth tag on dress.

SEE: *Illustration 289.*

Ideal (Mexico)

Mexican Lady: 18in (46cm); composition shoulder head and arms; straw-filled body and legs; dark flesh color on painted face; dark eyelashes and eye shadow; open/closed mouth with painted tongue; red flannel skirt trimmed with sequins; white blouse with red braid; red cloth shoes with gold buckle; red, white and yellow ribbon in hair; earrings and beads; all original; circa 1930s-1940s.

MARKS: "Ideal//Vida//Eterna" tag shaped like a doll.

SEE: *Illustration 286.*

Irwin

Irwin made "wind-up" walking boy and girl dolls and animals. There are 12 different characters.

Darling Toddlers (dolls): composition head; cardboard body with wind-up mechanism; wood legs and feet; stockings glued to top of leg; one-piece underwear is glued to the neck.

MARKS: "Doll Name" circular tag.

SEE: *Illustration 287. Toys and Novelties,* November 1932.

Jacobs & Kassler
(Succeeded Hitz, Jacobs & Kassler)

Begun in the early 1920s, this company specialized in baby dolls and *Mama* dolls both in composition and bisque. They were a distributing company, and at least some of their dolls were made in the Acme factory.

1928 *Baby Charming* and *Me Too* (young baby).

1930 *Kiddiejoy Dolls;* featured dolls whose composition was lighter than most of their competition; baby and *Mama* dolls.

Kiddiejoy Doll: Baby doll: 1930.

According to the advertisement in *Playthings,* "So soft and realistic, it is almost a real live Baby, and the price is truly remarkable."

SEE: *Illustration 288. Playthings,* June 1930.

Joy Doll Corporation

New York World's Fair, Inc., certified that the Joy Doll Corporation was licensed to produce and distribute dolls and stuffed toys incorporating its name, copyright and license.

Their *Miss World's Fairest* was 21in (56cm) and slender.

Another of their dolls was a *Shirley Temple* look-alike.

The Joy Doll Corporation also sold another group of popular dolls pictured in this book under the Dollcraft label (see page 64). These popular dolls were inexpensive, brightly-costumed dolls which were very popular in the 1930s and are extensively collected today.

World's Fair Dolls: Licensed by the World's Fair, 1939 Inc., to produce dolls and stuffed toys incorporating its name, copyright, and license.

The line also included *Miss 1939, Miss Terry Trylon, Miss Patty Perisphere, Miss World's Fair* and others; circa 1939.

SEE: *Illustration 290. Playthings,* February 1939.

World's Fair Dolls: Two in the Joy Doll Company's line of licensed New York World's Fair Dolls; 1939.

MARKS: "Officially Licensed//New York//World's Fair//1939 Inc." tag.

SEE: *Illustration 291. Playthings,* June 1939.

Illustration 289.

Illustration 291.

Illustration 290.

Knickerbocker Toy Company

Snow White: 14½in (37cm); all-composition; painted features; black molded hair with molded hair ribbon; 1938.

Dwarfs: 9in (23cm); all-composition; painted features; plush velvet clothes; character faces from the movie by Walt Disney; 1938. (From left to right) *Doc, Grumpy, Sneezy* and *Sleepy.*

MARKS: *Snow White:* "© Walt Disney" head; Knickerbocker Toy Co. New York" back.

Dwarfs: "© Walt Disney//Knickerbocker Toy Co." back.

SEE: *Illustration 292.* (Color Section, page 135.)

Dolls Not Pictured

Jiminy Cricket: 3¼in (8cm); composition head and limbs; stuffed cloth body.

MARKS: "Jiminy Cricket//W.D.PR. KN.T Co.// U.S.A." head.

Mickey Mouse: 9in (23cm); composition head; wooden body.

MARKS: "c//Walt Disney" back; "Knickerbocker// Toy Co. NYC" lower back.

Girl: 15in (38cm); all-composition; mohair wig; round sleep eyes; closed mouth.

MARKS: "Knickerbocker Toy Co.//New York" back.

Lee, H. D. Company

Buddy Lee: 12½in (32cm); composition; jointed at neck, shoulders and hips; molded painted face and head; smiling watermelon-type mouth; side-glancing eyes with painted eyelashes above eyes; dressed in red, black and yellow flannel shirt; jeans; leather belt with holster; 1922 through 1949. It was then made in hard plastic. The cowboy outfit was said to be the most popular.

The company said there were 17 different costumes. Others included Coca Cola; Phillips 66; Engineer (denim); Engineer (stripes); Union-all; Minute Man; Sinclair; Standard; John Deere; TWA; Highland Scotch Whiskey.

MARKS: None on doll; "Ride "Em Cowboy" pants.
SEE: *Illustration 293. Irene Trittschuh.*

Illustration 293.

Mama-Papa Dolls and Baby Dolls

Well Made Doll Co.

Illustration 294.

Girl in the Yellow Dress: 20in (51cm); composition shoulder plate, head and limbs; cloth body; mohair wig; sleep eyes with real lashes; feathered eyebrows; open mouth with two upper teeth; individual fingers; circa late 1920s to early 1930s.

This doll was one of the first that Pam and Polly purchased when they started collecting. Pam's grandmother made and smocked the yellow dotted swiss dress for Pam when she was about one year old. Today we have collected a wonderful wardrobe of period clothes for this doll which change with the seasons and occasions. She stands at the front door and greets our friends.

MARKS: None on doll.
SEE: *Illustration 295. (Color Section, page 135.)*

About 1915, there was a trend among dollmakers to add a crier box to composition dolls. These dolls now have become known as *Mama-Papa* dolls. They were an immediate hit and throughout the 1920s and into the 1930s, these dolls and baby dolls made up the great majority of all the dolls sold. Mothers and children loved both types of dolls which could often be dressed in the cast-off clothes of their owners (see *Illustration 295*). By the beginning of the 1930s, the stocky *Mama* doll had slimmed down considerably and by the late 1930s, many of the companies were selling dolls named after popular movie stars.

Today many collectors have been frustrated in their search for the names and makers of these largely unmarked dolls. Probably it will be impossible to accurately label each doll because they were made by almost every doll company, large and small.

In just one month, February 1929, *Playthings* showed six pictures of relatively unknown doll companies who showed *Mama* and baby dolls at the Toy Fair in New York. Many of these companies only produced dolls for a year or so, and then they went out of business. *Illustration 294* shows the Well Made Doll Co.'s 116 different dolls.

The magazine also showed pictures of Atlantic Toy Company's 31 dolls. Penn Stuffed Toy Co. showed 44 such dolls. Shaw Doll Company had 59 dolls in their line. Capital Toy Company presented 13. The Eureka Doll Company made 38. This is a total of 301 *Mama* and baby dolls which could be ordered from very small marketing firms. Hundreds more different *Mama* dolls could be ordered from the larger companies.

SEE: *Illustration 294.* Well Made Doll Company. *Playthings,* February 1929.

Marcie Dolls (A & H)

Bride: 7in (18cm); all-composition; one-piece head and body; jointed arms and legs; painted brown eyes with very long black painted eyelashes; unpainted molded socks with painted black shoes; *Nancy Ann Storybook Doll* competitor; mohair wig stapled to head; circa early 1940s.

The *Bride* was one of a doll series which was pictured in an accompanying brochure.

MARKS: None.

SEE: *Illustration 296.* (Color Section, page 135.)

Maxine Doll Co.

From 1926 until the late 1930s, the Maxine Doll Co. made dolls for the mass market. They followed current trends and their line included baby dolls and *Mama* dolls. In 1928 they made a doll with the general characteristics of *Patsy* (see Identification Guide, page 189). Effanbee sued and the Maxine Doll Company lost the case. *Mitzi* was quickly discontinued.

In 1929 they advertised a complete line of "*Pretty Pol*" dolls including *Gloria Lou, Baby Gloria, Gloriette and Kuddly Lou.*

In 1929 the Maxine Doll Company advertised their popular *Baby Gloria* in *Playthings.* They also had a line of other baby dolls and the ubiquitous *Mama* dolls. Their line of such dolls was called the "Maxine line."

The head of *Baby Gloria* was made in bisque and rubber as well as in composition. Later, one of their lines was called "Life-like."

Illustration 297.

Illustration 298.

In 1931 some of their dolls came complete with a wardrobe which was packed in an overnight case with a lock and handle. Some of their dolls were packed in a box that could be converted into a cradle.

SEE: *Illustration 297. Playthings,* January 1929.

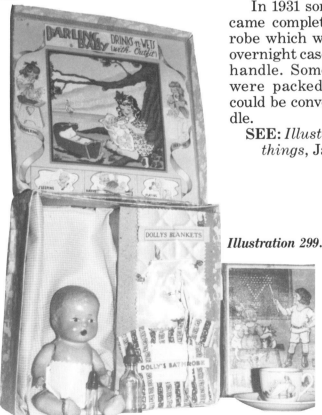

Illustration 299.

Minerva Doll Company

The Minerva Doll Company was a maker of inexpensive novelty dolls. They were competitive with the other doll manufacturers, and they kept up with the trends of the time.

Canadian companies often purchased the molds of the dolls made in the United States, and the Giltoy Company of Canada did use some of the Minerva molds and marks.

161

Snow White Look-alike: 14in (36cm); all-composition; jointed at neck, shoulders and hips; painted features; large eye pupils; closed mouth; clothes not original; original hair band stamped on head; also a *Patsy* look-alike; circa late 1930s.

This same doll, with the same marks, was also sold by the Giltoy Company of Canada.

MARKS: "W.O.L." head.

SEE: *Illustration 298.* (See also Identification Guide, page 189.) *Cobb's Auction Services.*

Darling Baby: 8in (20cm); all-composition; drinks and wets; jointed at shoulders and hips only; molded hair; open mouth with ring for bottle (see Identification Guide, page 194); came with layette; circa late 1930s.

MARKS: None on doll; "Minerva Doll Company" box.

SEE: *Illustration 299. Kerra Davis Collection.*

Dolls Not Pictured

Dorable Dolly: 11in (28cm); all-composition; jointed at shoulders and hips; bright yellow hair; painted side-glancing eyes; open mouth with ring for drinking; came with set of clothes to sew; also came in 8in (20cm) size.

MARKS: "W.O.L." head; "Dorable Dolly//Drinks and Wets" box.

The registered trademarks, the trademarks and copyrights appearing in italics//bold within this chapter belong to Molly-'Es.

Molly-'es (Mollye)

Mollye Goldman began her career with designs for clothes for the new *Shirley Temple* doll. She quickly established a cottage industry in her home in Philadelphia. Neighborhood women helped her sew the new designs. Soon she was designing clothes for many doll manufacturers such as Cameo, Effanbee, Goldberger, Horsman, Ideal, Madame Hendren and others. She also purchased dolls from companies, dressed them and marketed them under her own name. There were several variations of the Mollye logo.

To establish her business, Mollye advertised in trade magazines and showed her doll clothing and dolls at trade fairs. In April 1935, she announced a new line, "Hollywood Cinema Fashions for Dolls//the latest Styles of Famous Movie Stars reproduced in Doll Clothes." The advertisement also said that she made doll carriage sets, bed sets, layettes for *Dy-Dee Baby*, and dozens of fascinating novelties.

Along with her clothing line in 1935, she advertised *Raggedy Ann* and *Raggedy Andy* dolls and Educational Self-Help Stuffed Animals with Button on Legs. The name of her company at the time was "Molly-'es Doll Outfitters, Inc."

Mollye is reported to have purchased unmarked dolls from American Character, Hors-

Miss Glamour Girl   Miss Hollywood Irene

Illustration 302.

Illustration 300.   **Illustration 303.**

man, Ideal and Junel and dressed them under her own logo. Her dolls were variously priced. She continued designing doll clothes and selling dressed dolls after World War II.

Bridesmaid: 12in (31cm); all-composition; blonde wig; painted eyes; long, slender black eyelashes above eyes; tiny closed mouth; dressed in long green, gauze-type net dress which is flocked in a flowered pattern; pink felt hat with ribbons; late 1930s.

Mollye dressed many types of dolls in well-designed dresses. This is an example of a small, inexpensive doll which had the Mollye special "touch." She was one of the most important designers of doll clothes during this period.

MARKS: "Created by Mollye" tag; "Bridesmaid// International Doll Co.//Mollye" box. "International Doll Co.//Mfg. of dolls//Philadelphia Pa." box.

SEE: *Illustration 300. Treasures Collection.*

Russian Girl: 18in (46cm); all-composition; sleep eyes with lashes; eye shadow above eyes; human hair wig; closed mouth; Y on lower back; circa late 1930s. *Russian Costume* has elaborate head piece. This head piece is similar to the one worn by the *Russian* doll in the Mollye International Cloth Doll line.

Mollye dressed and sold a line of beautifully costumed composition international dolls.

MARKS: None
SEE: *Illustration 301.* (Color Section, page 136.)

Glamour Dolls of 1940: According to an advertisement in *Playthings* in 1940, "Molly-'es leads the style parade again! Glamour Girls of 1940 scores a new high in American made dolls. Each one is a collector's piece — at popular prices. They can sit or stand, are pliable, and have the finest clothes."

Shown in the advertisement on the left is *Miss Glamour Girl.* Shown on the right is *Miss Hollywood Irene.*

Other dolls in the Glamour Line included *Southern Belle, Modern Deb, Society Deb* and many others.

SEE: *Illustration 302.* (See page 162).

Modern Teen: 18in (46cm); all-composition; jointed at neck, shoulders and hips; human hair; sleep eyes with real lashes; closed mouth; dimity dress with lace trim; leatherette shoes with buckle; 1940s.

MARKS: "Lovely Gift//Molly-'es America's Finest Doll//Modern Teen//Molly-'es Leader in Doll's Clothing" tag.
SEE: *Illustration 303. Nancy L. Demory Collection.*

Baby: 17in (43cm); composition head, arms and legs; cloth body; molded hair; sleep eyes; two large teeth; pink organdy dress trimmed with lace; matching bonnet; hand-embroidered ends of the bonnet ties; moccasin-type baby shoes; all original.

MARKS: None on doll; "A Molly-'es Creation" box.
SEE: *Illustration 304. Nancy Chainey Collection.*

Dolls Not Pictured

1. **Sabu:** 15in (38cm); all-composition; fully-jointed; painted eyes with oriental slant; pink velvet vest, silk pants, turban with attached jewel; gold shoes; 1940.
   MARKS: None on doll; "Authentic//Dolls//Inspired by//Alexander Korda's//Thief//of//Bagdad//I am Sabu."
2. **Princess:** 15in (38cm) and 21in (52cm); all-composition; fully-jointed; Princess costume from "The Thief of Bagdad;" June Duprez was the actress; 1940.
3. **Toddlers:** Various sizes; all-composition; fully-jointed; mohair wigs; sleep eyes; well-made clothes.
4. **Ballerina Dolls.**
5. **Brides:** Various sizes; exceptional bride costumes. Mollye is well-known for her bridal finery. Many of the unmarked brides in both composition and hard plastic were dressed by Mollye.
   MARKS: Dolls usually not marked; some came originally with tags.
6. **Kutey:** Black babies and toddlers; made for "Hollywood Cinema Fashions;" various sizes; 1948.

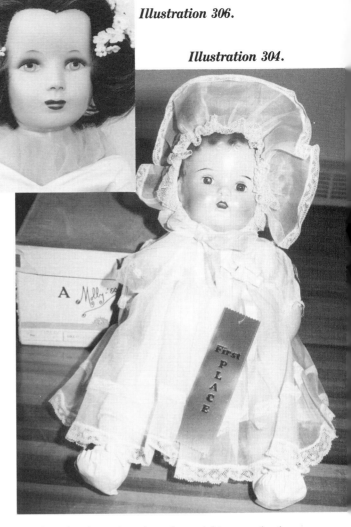

Illustration 306.

Illustration 304.

The registered trademarks, the trademarks and copyrights appearing in italics//bold within this chapter belong to Monica Studios.

Monica Studios

In 1941 Hansi Share created an unusual composition doll in Hollywood, California. The doll was unique because it had implanted human hair in a composition head. Another identification feature is a "widow's peak" in the center of the forehead. The heads and bodies were very beautiful, and the dolls were sold in expensive stores. The first two dolls were 20in (51cm) and 22in (56cm). From the beginning, the costumes were of the highest quality. The dolls were sold throughout the United States and Canada.

As can be seen in *Illustration 309,* the dolls were often given names. In 1942 they were called *Veronica, Rosalind* and *Joan,* and they were 17in (43cm) tall. Each year thereafter, new costumes and sizes of dolls were announced. In all, there were six different sizes, 11in (28cm), 15in (38cm), 17in (43cm), 20in (51cm), 22in (56cm) and 24in (61cm).

It has been reported that F.A.O. Schwarz put their label on some dolls as did Heirloom Doll Clothes.

Doll in Silver Net Dress: 20in (51cm); all-composition; jointed at neck, shoulders and hips; brown hair implanted in composition head; painted eyes with blue eye shadow; third and fourth fingers molded together; painted fingernails; blue flowers; taffeta slip; taffeta hooped skirt; white socks; black shoes with buckle; 1947.

An article in a March 1947 *Playthings* stated that the dolls wholesaled for $7.50 to $25. The silver net dress was the $25 model.

UNIQUE IDENTIFICATION FEATURES: Human hair implanted in composition head; widow's peak in middle of forehead.

MARKS: None on doll; "Monica//Doll//Hollywood" paper wrist tag.

SEE: *Illustration 305* (see Color Section, page 137). *Illustration 306*. Close-up of face, page 163.

Illustration 307.   *Illustration 308.*

Monica: 20in (51cm); all-composition; jointed at neck, shoulders and hips; reddish brown hair implanted in composition head; blue eye shadow; painted eyes; third and fourth fingers molded together; painted fingernails; long blue ruffled dress with pink flower attached to dress and in hair; 1947.

MARKS: None on doll; "Monica Doll//Hollywood" tag.

SEE: *Illustration 307. 1947 Montgomery Ward Christmas Catalog.*

Dorothy: 17in (43cm); all-composition; jointed at neck, shoulders and hips; brown hair implanted in composition head; blue eye shadow; painted eyes; third and fourth fingers molded together; painted fingernails; red coat and matching hat trimmed with looped braid; doll purchased and photographed in 1948 by the present owner.

UNIQUE IDENTIFICATION FEATURE: Hair implanted in composition.

MARKS: None.

SEE: *Illustration 308. Mary Elizabeth Poole Collection.*

According to the company brochure, Monica Studios created an expensive, unique doll in the 1940s. They implanted human hair in a composition head. This could be combed, curled and finger waved. The dolls were lifelike and came in 43 different styles and costumes. The two sizes were 17in (43cm) and 20in (51cm).

Each doll was named. The company brochure shows (clockwise) *Eleanor, First Schoolday, Dorothy* (see *Illustration 308*) and *Veronica*.

SEE: *Illustration 309. Mary Elizabeth Poole Collection.*

Doll Costumes*
Not Pictured Include:

1. Wave Uniform of navy rayon serge; brass buttons; anchor insignia on collar; white top attached to skirt; white piqué hat trimmed with navy blue.
2. Floor-length blue and white print dress trimmed with white organdy.
3. Negligee in light blue silk, blue satin trimmed with lace.
4. Two-piece suit of royal blue trimmed in red, white and blue, braid; white blouse; matching tam; star buttons.
5. Beach outfit; three pieces included bib top, shorts and light coat; red linen.
6. Peasant costume; white blouse with green trim; wine rayon skirt with green braid trim; embroidery on skirt.
7. Skating costume with hood; white with red buttons; blue and red rickrack trim.
8. Long dress: dotted swiss; ruffles at hem and neck; a ribbon sash.

*Partial list.

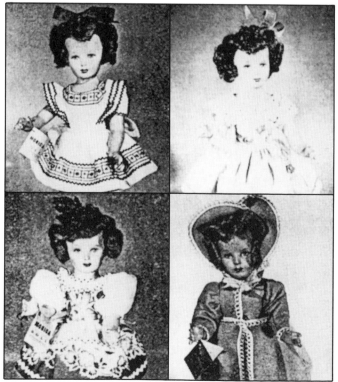

Illustration 309.

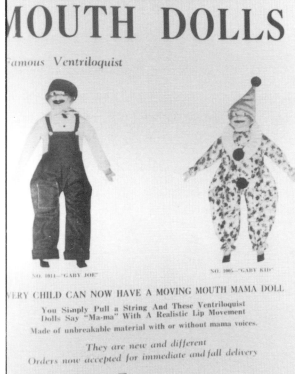

Illustration 310.

Moravian Dolls

Most of the dolls made by the Women's Circles of the Moravian churches of Bethlehem, Pennsylvania, were cloth dolls. For only one year in the late 1930s, the ladies purchased composition *Patsy*-type dolls and dressed them.

SEE: Identification Guide, page 190. (See also Color Section, page 143.)

PRICE: Most of the dolls are handed down from generation to generation. No sample prices available.

Munzer, Inc., Alfred

Gaby Moving Mouth Dolls:
1. #1016 *Gabby Buttons:* Dressed in sports coat, slacks, shirt.
2. #1012 *Gabby Kid:* Dressed in two-tone clown suit.
3. #1014 *Gabby Joe:* Dressed in overalls and cap.
4. #1005 *Gabby Kid:* Dressed in print clown suit.
   SEE: *Illustration 310. Playthings,* June 1929.

Natural Doll Co.

Brother Ritzie: This is one of the *Ritzie Family* of Dolls; fully jointed; composition head; soft or composition body; dressed in toddler's suit. He is one of the *Ritzie Family* of dolls. *Sister Ritzie* is a *Patsy* look-alike (see Identification Guide, page 190).

The Natural Doll Co. was another one of the many makers of baby and *Mama* dolls. They advertised regularly for many years and made medium-priced and inexpensive dolls. The line of dolls was called "Just-Lyke," which explains their attraction.

SEE: *Illustration 311. Playthings,* April 1931.

Ritzi: *Patsy*-type (see Identification Guide, page 190).

Illustration 311.

Dolls Not Pictured

Ritzy Chubby Baby: 13in (33cm); jointed hips and shoulders; 1940.
MARKS: "It's a Natural-Ritzy Chubby Baby Doll//Natural Doll Co., Inc.//Est. 1915//Made in U.S.A." paper tag.

Illustration 312.

P. & M. Doll Co.

Illustration 314.

Margit Nilsen Studios, Inc.

Thumbs Up Victory Doll: 7⅛in (19cm); flexible composition; one-piece jointed hips and shoulders; open crown under wig; came in several types of dresses; thumbs of hands are up for victory; 1941.
  MARKS: "Your $1.50 purchase of this doll helps in sending ambulances to Britain and her Allies and vitamins to undernourished children in England. An original creation of Margit Nilsen Studios, Inc." tag on doll.
  SEE: *Illustration 312. Lois Janner Collection.*

Noma Electric Corp.

Halo Angel: 8in (20cm); all-composition; strung arms; half doll with cardboard cone on lower body that could be attached to the top of a Christmas tree; painted blue eyes; painted long black eyelashes; white mohair wig; white satin dress trimmed with a silver belt and star; huge silver cardboard wings; silver headdress; an electric light was placed over the doll to produce the halo; *Nancy Ann Storybook Doll* competitor; 1940s.
  MARKS: None.
  SEE: *Illustration 313.*

When Effanbee sold their company to Noma right after World War II, they also had a division in Canada.

Doll Not Pictured

Kewpie: 12in (31cm); pink composition body with blue wings.

Illustration 313.

P. & M. Doll Co.

Baby Doll: Dressed in organdy dress with ruffle at hem; fur jacket and bonnet; 1930.
Patsy-type Doll: (see Identification Guide, page 190).
  SEE: *Illustration 314. Playthings,* March 1930.

Girl in Short Dress and Bonnet: *Patsy*-type (see Identification Guide, page 190).

Playmate Doll & Toys Co.

Bonnie Baby Doll: Composition head; soft body and hands; painted hair; inverted eyes to make it look more babylike; unusual face with pointed nose; copyrighted by Ethel R. Clays in 1934. According to the advertisement, she was "one of America's leading child portrait artists."

The doll was sold separately or in *Quintuplet* sets with a beautiful cradle.

SEE: *Illustration 315. Playthings*, November 1934.

Princess Anna Doll Co., Inc.

Daisy (doll on left): 7in (18cm); all-composition with one-piece head and body; painted brown eyes with painted black long eyelashes; very full red painted lips; molded unpainted socks; black painted shoes; white satin bodice with green organdy skirt trimmed with yellow braid; white lace hat; big daisy flower bouquet.

Bouquet (doll on right): Same general characteristics; long red satin dress trimmed with black braid and lace; blue felt hat.

Both dolls are *Nancy Ann Storybook Doll* competitors; circa early 1940s.

MARKS: "Princess Anna" back.
SEE: *Illustration 316.*

Girl Grouping: 7in (18cm); all-composition with one-piece head and body; painted brown eyes with long black eyelashes; *Nancy Ann Storybook Doll* competitor; full red lips.

Doll on Left: White organdy satin formal with red print and trim; white mohair wig.

Doll in Middle: Blue organdy dress trimmed with white ruffles; lace hat.

Doll on Right: Floral organdy skirt; black apron; blue satin bodice; red felt hat; black mohair wig; usually wide painted eyes; all dolls circa 1940s.

MARKS: "Princess//Ann" back.
SEE: *Illustration 317.*

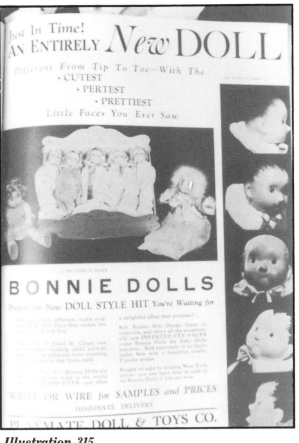

Illustration 315.

Illustration 317.

Illustration 316.

Pullan Company, Earl (Canada)

Illustration 318.

About 1947 the Earl Pullan Company, which had been established two years before, began to produce composition dolls. They made both the traditional dolls and character dolls. Their dolls were well-dressed with excellent detail. Mr. Pullan did not make as many composition dolls as some of the other Canadian doll companies because he started his business just as hard plastic and vinyl dolls were being introduced. He kept up with the competition, and for several years he was making all three types of dolls.

Eskimo: 16in (41cm); all-composition; black molded hair; open mouth with painted teeth; pinkish-gray flesh-color composition; snowsuit is black and white mock fur; 1930s.
   The Pullan *Eskimo* is very similar to the Reliable *Eskimo.*
   MARKS: "A Pullan Doll" body.
   SEE: *Illustration 318. Paul Applegate Collection.*

Dolls Not Pictured
1. **Miss Pullan:** 20in (51cm); composition toddler.
2. **Pixie:** Black baby doll.
3. **Baby Twinkle:** Knee-length blonde hair.
4. **Baby Beauty:** 22in (56cm); composition head; rubber arms and legs; cloth body.
5. **Brides:** Two elaborately dressed dolls.
6. *Skating Queen:* 18in (46cm); roller skating doll.

Quintuplet Dolls

In 1934, five special little girls were born. Emilie, Marie, Yvonne, Annette and Cecile were the small babies that managed to win the interest and hearts of the world, in spite of a massive depression which had rocked the economy. The Alexander company acquired the rights to produce *Dionne Quintuplet* dolls. In spite of published warnings by the Alexander company of copyright infringements, many other companies marketed sets of five babies under various names. People also purchased five of the same dolls and made their own sets of quintuplets. Some of these dolls are shown in this special section.

Alexander

Dionne Quintuplet Toddlers: 7½in (19cm); all-composition; jointed at neck, shoulders and hips; organdy dresses; *Marie* came in pink; *Annette* in blue; *Cecile* in yellow; *Emile* in lavender; *Yvonne* in green; each doll came with a locket with the *Quint's* name; price in 1936 was $.94 each.

The advertisement said that the *Quints* were walking now, and so the dolls stand alone. The dolls also came in an 11in (28cm) size for $1.88. All five babies came in rompers with a decorated rocking bench which could be purchased for $4.98.
   SEE: *Illustration 319. Toys and Novelties,* April 1936.

Illustration 319.

Illustration 322.

Dionne Quintuplet (doll on left): 8in (20cm); all-composition toddler; molded straight hair under mohair wig; painted eyes; short organdy dress; necklace with "Cecile" on it; all original except shoes and socks; circa 1936.
>   MARKS: "Dionne Alexander" head; "Alexander" body.
>   SEE: *Illustration 320.* (Color Section, page 137.) *Sandy Strater Collection.*

Dionne Quintuplet (doll in center): 21in (53cm); all-composition toddler; human hair wig; sleep eyes with lashes; open mouth with two teeth; individual fingers; "Yvonne" pin; original "pink" dress for Yvonne; all original; circa 1936.
    This is a rare doll with a composition body. Most of the larger dolls have a cloth body.
>   MARKS: "Madame//Alexander//N.Y." body.
>   SEE: *Illustration 320.* (Color Section, page 137.) *Sandy Strater Collection.*

Dionne Quintuplet (doll on right): 11in (28cm); all-composition; baby; sleep eyes with lashes; molded straight hair; pink flannel coat and bonnet dress; white organdy bib with blue "Marie" on it; all original including booklet which came with doll; circa 1936.
>   MARKS: "Dionne//Alexander" head; "Madame Alexander//New York" dress tag.
>   SEE: *Illustration 320.* (Color Section, page 137.) *Sandy Strater Collection.*

Dionne Quintuplets: 7½in (19cm); molded curly hair; all-composition; painted faces; closed mouths; piqué romper suits with matching bonnets; (from left to right with the colors assigned to each Quintuplet) *Cecile, Emily, Annette, Yvonne* and *Marie*; gold pins with matching names; all original except shoes; 1936.
>   MARKS: "Alexander" back; "Alexander" head.
>   SEE: *Illustration 321.* (Color Section, page 138.) *Sandy Strater Collection.*

Dr. Dafoe: 14in (36cm); all-composition; smiling painted face with dimple on chin; wide mouth; gray wig; doctor's uniform; all original including shoes; 1936.
>   MARKS: None on doll; "Madame//Alexander//New York" tag on uniform.
>   SEE: *Illustration 321.* (Color Section, page 138.) *Sandy Strater Collection.*

Dionne Quintuplets Nurse: 13in (33cm); Alexander doll; all-composition; *Betty*-face; brown sleep eyes; closed mouth; blonde mohair wig; came with set of *Quintuplets* and *Doctor Dafoe*; white cotton uniform; white socks and shoes; white hat with blue band; 1936.
>   MARKS: None
>   SEE: *Illustration 322. Shirley Sally Kille Collection.*

Dionne Quintuplets Toddlers: 14in (36cm); all-composition; sleep eyes; human hair wig; cotton dress with Swiss embroidered inset at yoke; dotted swiss sleeves; matching hats; all original; colors of outfits (left to right) blue, pink, turquoise, peach and yellow; circa 1935.
>   MARKS: "Alexander" body; "Genuine//Dionne Quintuplets//All Rights Reserves//Madame Alexander" cotton tag on dress.
>   SEE: *Illustration 323. John Poot Collection.*

Quintuplets Grow Up: The advertisement says, "The first *Dionne Quintuplet* dolls with hair are shown wearing costumes of blue bonnet blue silk crepe exactly like the new outfits which were presented to the Quints recently. The dresses have white silk crepe collars and sunbonnets piped in white."
>   SEE: *Illustration 324. Toys and Novelties,* August 1936.

Illustration 323.

FIRST SILK DRESSES FOR THE QUINTS

The first Dionne Quintuplet dolls with hair are shown wearing costumes of Blue-bonnet blue silk crepe exactly like new outfits which were presented to the Quints recently. The dresses have white silk crepe collars, and sunbonnets piped in white.

Illustration 324.

Chart of Alexander Composition Dolls

Composition Quintuplets: The **Dionne Quintuplet** dolls were very popular and widely imitated. They came in various sizes.

1. *7½in (19cm) Babies:* All-composition; molded hair; painted eyes.
2. *8in (20cm) Toddlers:* All-composition; molded hair; painted eyes.
3. *8in (20cm) Toddlers:* All-composition; wigs; painted eyes.
4. *11in (28cm) Babies:* All-composition; molded hair; sleep eyes.
5. *11in (28cm) Babies:* All-composition; wigs; painted eyes.
6. *11in (28cm) Toddlers:* All-composition; molded hair; sleep eyes.
7. *11in (28cm) Toddlers:* All-composition; wigs; sleep eyes.
8. *14in (36cm) Toddlers:* All-composition; wigs; sleep eyes.
9. *16in (41cm) Toddlers:* All-composition; cloth body.
10. *17in (43cm) Babies:* Composition head; cloth body.
11. *19in (48cm) Toddlers:* All-composition.
12. *21in (53cm) Toddlers:* All-composition.

Each of the Dionne Quintuplets was assigned a color:
1. Yellow for Annette.
2. Green for Cecile.
3. Lavender for Emily.
4. Blue for Marie.
5. Pink for Yvonne.

Arranbee

Arranbee Toddler Quintuplets: 7in (18cm); jointed at neck, shoulders and hips; curl in middle of forehead; redressed; mid-to-late 1930s. A *Debuteen* doll was used as a nurse in some sets.

Sunshine Baby Made by Arranbee but Dressed by Vogue: 7in (18cm); jointed at neck and hips; curl in middle of forehead; original silk coat; white organdy dress and slip; flannel diaper; booties replaced; late 1930s. The dolls dressed by Vogue had fancier clothes than those dressed by Arranbee.

MARKS: "R & B" on all six dolls.
SEE: *Illustration 325. Connie Lee Martin Collection.*

Illustration 325.

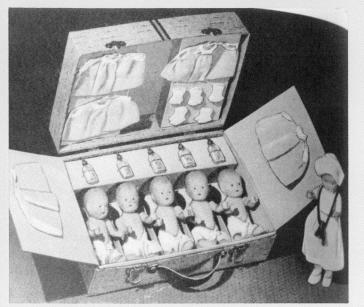

Illustration 326.

Freundlich

Quintuplets: 6¾in (17cm); all-composition; jointed at neck, shoulders and hips; inexpensive dolls with poorly painted faces; layette including five organdy dresses; five pairs of socks; five nursing bottles with animal figures on them.

Nurse: 9in (23cm); all-composition; *Patsy*-type head and body; dressed in white nurse's uniform; white shoes and stockings; wore a stethoscope.

The babies came with a sturdily built overnight case. Originally, the entire set retailed for $2.00 complete.

MARKS: None on dolls.

SEE: *Illustration 326. Playthings*, November, 1935. *Illustration 327.* (Color Section, page 138.) *Connie Lee Martin Collection.*

Japanese Quintuplets Made for Trucco of New York, N.Y.

Quintuplets: 7in (18cm); all bisque-like composition; jointed at neck, hips and shoulders; straight molded and painted hair; painted eyes and closed mouth; yellow rayon long dress; muslin slips and diapers; silk tie booties; all original; reproduction pins; early Japanese set; mid 1930s.

MARKS: "Japan" doll.

SEE: *Illustration 328. Connie Lee Martin.*

Illustration 328.

Unknown Quintuplets

Unmarked Composition Quintuplets: 7in (18cm); all-composition; jointed at hips and shoulders only; came with original stapled diaper and wooden animal rockers; hair and face detail is like the Effanbee *Tinyettes*, but more crudely painted; mid 1930s.

Rockers painted red and white.

MARKS: None on dolls.

SEE: *Illustration 329. Connie Lee Martin Collection.*

Quintuplets: 14in (36cm); all-composition; jointed at shoulders and hips, but not at neck; "chubby-type" toddler body; inexpensive "concrete-type" composition which has lasted well through the years; molded hair with Arranbee-type curl on forehead; *Baby Grumpy*-type face; open/closed mouth; dimples on either side of the mouth; mid 1930s.

These dolls were probably purchased separately and made into a *Quintuplet* set. The clothes are to-

Illustration 329.

tally sewn by hand. The seams are all finished with a tiny buttonhole stitch. The *Quints* are wearing matching dresses, coats and hats. Another set of cotton flowered print dresses came with the dolls. The dolls are each wearing a hand-sewn white cotton teddy. A slip also was made for each doll. Someone, long ago, made a clothesline for their clothes and a stand for each doll.

The whole world seemed excited by the birth of five little girls in Canada.

MARKS: None.
SEE: *Illustration 330.* (Color Section, page 138.)

Dolls Not Pictured

Other doll companies made babies which were sold in sets of five.
1. **Effanbee Baby Tinyette** (for picture of face, see page 79).
2. **Hollywood Dolls.**
3. **Playmate Bonnie Dolls** (for picture of the face, see page 167).

Illustration 331.

The registered trademarks, the trademarks and copyrights appearing in italics//bold within this chapter belong to Regal Doll Company.

Regal Doll Company

The Regal Doll Company took over the German-American doll company in 1918 and started making dolls. It continued to make dolls into the 1930s. Two of its famous lines were "*Kiddie Pal*" and "*Kiddiejoy.*" The company was a member of the American Doll Manufacturers' Association. They followed the general doll making trends of the period, and in the 1920s they made *Mama* and baby dolls. In the 1930s, their *Mama* dolls were the new slim type, and they imitated the popular *Patsy* and *Shirley Temple* dolls. Their two *Patsy*-type dolls were called *Maizie* and *Judy* (see Identification Guide, page 191).

Kiddie Pal Dolly: 16in (41cm); blonde, mohair *Shirley Temple*-type wig; tin sleep eyes with real lashes; jointed at neck, shoulders and hips; open mouth with six teeth; original pink organdy dress with blue hemstitching around a ruffled collar; white organdy teddy; circa mid 1930s.

MARKS: None on doll; "Kiddie//Pal//Dolly" tag.
SEE: *Illustration 331. Mary Lu Trowbridge Collection.*

Reliable Toy Company Limited (Canada)

Established in 1920 as the Canadian Statuary and Novelty Company, the present Reliable Toy Company Limited has a long and varied history of excellent doll making.

In the first years, they imported bisque heads from Germany and composition parts from the United States. In 1922 they began to produce their own composition *Mama* dolls, and by 1927 they had moved to larger quarters and were the first Canadian company to use the faster and more efficient hot process method of making composition dolls. Soon they were exporting dolls around the world.

Although they made typical Canadian dolls such as their famous Indian dolls and celebrity dolls, they purchased molds of well-known American dolls and produced the Canadian version. They also made tailor-made dolls for other countries around the world. Soon they were making hundreds of varieties each year.

As the materials of doll making changed, they kept up with the latest techniques, and their hard plastic and vinyl dolls became world famous also.

Illustration 332.

Hiawatha: 13in (33cm); all-composition; black mohair wig over molded hair; dark Indian skin tone; painted eyes; open mouth with hint of molded tongue; dimple in chin; jointed at shoulders and hips only; Y on backside; molded hands; gold flannel Indian suit with yellow, blue and red trim; leatherette moccasins; late 1930s into early 1940s.
> **MARKS:** "Reliable//Made in//Canada" head; "Hiawatha//Reliable//Made in Canada//Trademark;" paper tag.
> **SEE:** *Illustration 332.*

Indian Squaw: 12½in (32cm); all-composition; jointed at shoulders and hips only; dark Indian color composition; molded hair (same mold as *Hiawatha*); painted eyes; open/closed mouth with hint of molded tongue; fingers molded together; real leather Indian costume which is intricately beaded; real leather high moccasins; late 1930s into early 1940s.
> **MARKS:** "Reliable//Made in//Canada" head.
> **SEE:** *Illustration 332.*

Illustration 334.

173

Royal Canadian Mounted Police (Mountie): 17½in (45cm); composition head and arms; cloth body and legs; finely sculptured head that resembles Nelson Eddy; raised eyebrows; painted eyes; closed mouth; wears red-coated uniform of the mounted police; leather belt and strap; black pants with gold trim; leather high boots; epaulets are printed "R.P.M.;" early 1940s.

Although this doll is popularly known as "Nelson Eddy," it was not intended to be a portrait of the singing star. In fact, the mold was also used for other men dolls in the Reliable line.

MARKS: "Reliable//Made in//Canada" head.
SEE: *Illustration 333.* (Color Section, page 136.)

Barbara Ann Scott: 15in (38cm); all-composition; face sculptured to resemble the Canadian Olympic ice skater; sleep eyes with lashes; brown wig; open mouth with teeth; jointed at neck, shoulders and hips; straight legs; replaced ice skating costume; 1940s.

MARKS: "Reliable" head; none on body.
SEE: *Illustration 334. Jean Francis Collection.*

Baby Joan: 18in (46cm); composition toddler; curl in middle of forehead; sleep eyes with lashes; painted lashes under eyes; open mouth with two teeth; clothes all original; circa 1935.

MARKS: None on doll; tagged dress.
SEE: *Illustration 335.* (Color Section, page 137.) *Jean Francis Collection.*

Dolls Not Pictured

1. *Air Force Doll.*
2. *Baby Bubbles.*
3. *Baby Bunting.*
4. *Baby Jean.*
5. *Babykins.*
6. *Baby Marilyn.*
7. *Baby Precious.*
8. *Chuckles.*
9. *Cuddlekins.*
10. *Eskimo.*
11. *Gloria.*
12. *Hairbow Peggy.*
13. *Kenny-Tok.*
14. *Laddie.*
15. *Patsy*-type.
16. *Sally Ann.*
17. *Scottish Lassie.*
18. *Shirley Temple* (from Ideal mold).
19. *Shirley Temple* look-alikes.
20. *Snow White.*
21. *Soldier* and *Nurse.*
22. *Topsy.*
23. *Wettums.*

Most dolls are well marked with the Reliable name.
* Not all Reliable dolls listed.

The registered trademarks, the trademarks and copyrights appearing in italics//bold within this chapter belong to S. & H. Novelty Co.

S. & H. Novelty Dolls

Peppy Pals: 12in (31cm) dancing dolls manipulated by a string. They were advertised as "dolls that go through latest ballroom maneuvers." They came in a variety of costumes, color, fashions and wigs. In April 1930, the company announced that they had received a patent No. 1753032.

Amos 'n' Andy: Dancing dolls manipulated by a string; light weight; composition heads.

These dolls were in direct competition with Dean's Rag Book Company *Dancing Dolls.*

SEE: *Illustration 336. Playthings,* April 1930.

Illustration 336.

Illustration 337.

Skookum Apples

Once upon a time, and all good doll stories start this way, in the mid 1930s in North Carolina, several children were tallying the sizes of apples inside a refrigerator railroad car. They saw a wonderful product label from a Skookum apples box that someone had pasted in the car. It had come from Wenatchee, Washington, and the children thought it was cute. One little girl, Madge Poole, wrote to the company and asked them to send her one of these labels.

Not only did she get labels, but the company also sent a coloring book and information about a wonderful doll. Madge still wonders where her family got the money to send for the doll because they did not have any money "hanging" around. However, she did send for the wonderful *Skookum Apple Indian Doll*.

Over 50 years later she and her sister, Mary Elizabeth Poole, found the wonderful composition Indian in its original box, and sent this picture to the authors so its smile could be shared with doll lovers everywhere.

Skookum Apple Indian Doll: 14in (36cm) tall and dressed in a blue felt Indian jacket, red felt pants with black fringe, and a print shirt. A red feather and earrings complete the costume. A copy of the original label on the box is also shown. (*Illustration 338*, page 174).

    MARKS: None on doll.
    SEE: *Illustration 337.* (Color Section, page 139.)
        Madge Poole Copely Collection.
        Illustration 338. Madge Poole Copely Collection.

Société Français Fabrication Bébés et Jouets (S.F.B.J.)

Organized in 1899, S.F.B.J. was a French attempt to organize doll and toy companies and form a syndicate to meet the growing competition in Europe. Although the French made quality dolls, they needed a more inexpensive product to meet this competition. The syndicate lasted almost 50 years.

By 1910, the new composition doll industry was growing in the United States, and S.F.B.J. turned their attention to unbreakable heads which they called carton-pate. Another name used was incassable.

The three dolls pictured in *Illustration 339* all have the same mold number 301. This mold was one of the most popular, and it was used for various dolls, from expensive bisque dolls to dolls for the mass market. Each of the dolls pictured has a different type of composition. The Unis number 60 usually has the same characteristics.

There are a few characteristics that most the 301 (Unis 60) dolls have in common regardless of the material, size or price:
1. They have an open mouth with four upper teeth.
2. They have either set or sleep eyes.
3. Their eyebrows are usually feathered and/or molded.
4. The head has an open pate.

The model number 301 seemed to be reserved for the more expensive dolls. Model number 60 was sometimes given to the cheaper dolls of the same mold, but not always.

French Provincial Man (301): 13½in (34cm); inferior quality composition (might be called papier-mâché in the United States); articulated at neck, shoulders, elbows, wrists and hips; knees not movable; socket head; open pate; coarse red mohair wig; feathered eyebrows; metal eyes; open mouth with four teeth; all original; 1920s-1930s.

    MARKS: "Unis//France//301" head.
    SEE: *Illustration 339.* (Color Section, page 139.)

French Provincial Lady (301): 12in (31cm); excellent quality smooth composition head; excellent flesh tone; articulated at neck, shoulders, elbows, wrists, hips and knees; socket head; open pate; mohair wig; feathered eyebrows; glass sleep eyes with real eyelashes; open mouth with four teeth; dimple in chin; clothes all original; 1920s-1930s.

    MARKS: "S.F.B.J.//Paris/3" head; "3" back.
    SEE: *Illustration 339.* (Color Section, page 139.)

Bleuette-type Flapper (301): 10in (25cm); medium quality composition; molded eyebrows; sleep eyes; delicate painted eyelashes around eyes; open/closed mouth with paint indicating teeth; dimple in chin; jointed at neck, shoulders and hips only; all-composition; all original; 1920s-1930s.

    UNUSUAL IDENTIFICATION FEATURE: The mark "S.F.B.J. is high on the head under the wig.
    MARKS: "S.F.B.J.//Paris//5/0" head; "Ma Tete//Et Incassable//et Peut Se Laver//Fabrication France" tag; "Unis//France//71 149" in corner of tag.
    SEE: *Illustration 339.* (Color Section, page 139.)

Three-In-One Doll Corporation

Illustration 341.

Trudy: 15in (38cm); for general characteristics, see *Illustration 340* green and gold *Easter Bunny* costume; circa 1946-1947.

MARKS: None
SEE: *Illustration 341. Betty Shriver Collection.*

Tipica Munica Mexicana

Mexican Boy and Girl: 8in (20cm); all-composition; jointed at shoulders and hips only; molded painted hair; painted face; mustache for boy; floss wig with pigtails for girl.

Boy: White shirt with embroidery; heavy blue cotton pants; multi-colored serape; Mexican felt sombrero; 1930s and later.

Girl: White blouse with embroidery; red and green skirt; sequins on skirt; Mexico embroidered on skirt. Multi-colored ribbon on hair. Excellent quality composition Mexican tourist dolls. According to a sticker on the box, they were purchased in Tijuana, Mexico.

    MARKS: None on doll; "TIPICA//MUNECA MEXICANA//IRROMPIBLE//HECHO EN MEXICA//AUTENTICOS VESTIDOS REGIONALES" box.

    SEE: *Illustration 342.*

Trudy: 15in (38cm); composition head and arms; cloth body and legs; three faces (smiling, sleeping and crying); turns with a knob on the top of her head; shiny composition; floss hair attached which does not turn with head; also came in 20in (51cm) size called *Big Sister*; made by Ideal and listed in their catalogs.

    Doll came in several costumes including *Easter Bunny*, flannel pram suit, party dress and daytime dress.

    MARKS: None.
    SEE: *Illustration 340.* (Color Section, page 139.) (*Playthings*, March 1947.)

Illustration 342.

Tootse

In 1928, an advertisement in the Butler catalog said, "New! New! 'Tootse'//Champion of 1928 Dolldom." This *Patsy* look-alike came in three different outfits with a matching bonnet or hair ribbon; all-composition; jointed at neck, shoulders and hips; molded hair with part in the middle of head and hair pulled back at both sides.

    This doll is very different from the *Tootsie* advertised in the Sears, Roebuck & Co. catalog in 1929.

    MARKS: "Tootse" back.
    SEE: Identification Guide, page 191.

Girl in Short Pink Dress: *Patsy*-type (see Identification Guide, page 191, *Illustration 387*).

Tootsie

In 1929, Sears, Roebuck & Co. advertised a "Tootsie" doll in their catalog in a lawn dress, matching teddy and hair ribbon. The doll on the left in *Illustration 380* has the same dress tagged "Tootsie" as in the picture in the catalog. She is shown with a Maxine *Mitzi* which has the same body characteristics. The Averill body twist *Dimmie* also has the same composition head. All three dolls are *Patsy* look-alikes and were probably made by the same company.

MARKS: "Tootsie" cloth label on dress.
SEE: Identification Guide, page 189. (See also Color Section, page 144.)

The registered trademarks, the trademarks and copyrights appearing in italics//bold within this chapter belong to Toycraft, Inc.

Toycraft, Inc.

Denny Dimwit: 11½in (29cm); all-composition; hollow body mounted on stick fastened to top of leg and attached to body with metal rod; entire doll painted; oversized ears; same construction as *Swing and Sway Girl*; 1948.

The box said, "Denny Dimwit from Winnie Winkle, the Breadwinner, by Branner."

The box was decorated with copies of the comic strip.

Illustration 344.

MARKS: "Denny Dimwit, He wiggles — He waggles — He's Smart — He's Friendly. By Permission of the Famous Artists Syndicate, c 1948, the Chicago Tribute."
SEE: *Illustration 343.* (Color Section, page 139.) *Felix A. Cappadona Collection.*

Illustration 345.

The registered trademarks, the trademarks and copyrights appearing in italics//bold within this chapter belong to Toy Products Manufacturing Company.

Toy Products Manufacturing Company

The company was formed in the mid 1920s, and became a member of the doll Parts Manufacturing Association. The members made dolls for jobbers and quantity buyers. Toy Products' own line was usually marked. However, they did sell their dolls unmarked to other companies. About 1930, they established the "We" line of dolls.

Their *Patsy* look-alike was called *Little Sis*.

Lil Sis: 15in (38cm); all-composition; unusual pale flesh color; spring jointed; painted features; first, second and third fingers molded together; long, slim arms and legs; clothes not original; unusually heavy doll that stands without support; *Patsy* look-alike, circa 1930.

This composition has held up every well. There is no visible crazing even though this is a well-played with doll with two broken fingers. For a better picture of the molded hair (see Identification Guide, page 191).

MARKS: "Toy Products Mfg. Co. Inc." embossed on back.
SEE: *Illustration 344.*

"We" Line of Dolls: "Dolls that are made right, priced right, and sell on sight. This big new line includes dolls for every class of trade, from popular price to deluxe quality."

The trade mark was a round circle with a *Mama* doll and baby doll pictured. "We" was written at the top in script.

UNUSUAL IDENTIFICATION FEATURE: Most of the dolls were spring strung.
MARKS: "Toy Product Manufacturing Co." body of most of the dolls.
SEE: *Illustration 345. (Playthings, January 1930.)*

George Washington Dolls: 1932 Bicentennial of George Washington's Birth doll (see page 82).

The registered trademarks, the trademarks and copyrights appearing in italics//bold within this chapter belong to Uneeda Doll Company.

Uneeda Doll Company

For most of the 20th century, the Uneeda Doll Company made popular priced dolls. Starting in 1917, the company made a good quality composition doll. By 1927, they were making dolls for jobbers, mail-order houses, and stores. Most of the dolls were *Mama* and baby dolls.

They did not advertise very much in the trade publications, and most of their dolls were not marked. They stayed in business because their quality was excellent for the price.

Rita Hayworth: 14in (36cm); all-composition; jointed at neck, shoulders and hips; red mohair wig; sleep eyes with real long lashes; eye shadow above eyes; painted long eyelashes below eyes; gold shoes; clothes all original; 1939.
MARKS: "The Carmen Doll//© W.I. Gould & Co., Inc. Mfrd by Uneeda Doll Co.//Inspired by//Rita Hayworth's//Portrayal of Carmen//in//the Loves of Carmen" tag; none on doll.
SEE: *Illustration 346. (Color Section, page 140.)*

Doll Not Pictured

Baby Sweetheart: 17in (43cm); all-composition; jointed at neck, shoulders and hips; deeply molded curly hair; open mouth with metal tongue; two upper teeth; 1930s.
MARKS: "Everybody Loves Baby Sweetheart// Product of Uneeda Doll Co." tag.

Illustration 347.

The registered trademarks, the trademarks and copyrights appearing in italics//bold within this chapter belong to Alberani Vecchiotti.

Alberani Vecchiotti (Italy)

Girl in Organdy Dress and Girl in Regional Costume: 8in (20cm); head is cross between composition and celluloid; cloth bodies; stockinette arms tied at wrists; mitt hands with thumb separate; Lenci lookalike faces.
Girl on Left: White organdy long dress with ruffles; felt flowers on skirt.
Liguria Girl on Right: Provincial costume; dark blue skirt; pink felt apron with colored stripes; green and orange dirndl; white blouse with red felt cuffs; white regional headdress; circa 1930s.
MARKS: "Alberani Vecchiotti" tag on dress.
SEE: *Illustration 347. Diane Domroe Collection.*

Illustration 348.

Vogue Doll Company

Just Me: 8in (20cm); BISQUE head; five-piece jointed body; sleep eyes; open crown; wig; silk-lined trunk in several sizes; costumes include beach pajamas, dress sets and other ensembles, 1931.

As early as 1931, and possibly before, Jennie Graves had imported the *Just Me* doll from Germany and dressed it for sale in her shop. These dolls were the forerunners of the famous *Toddles* dolls in composition and the *Ginny* dolls in hard plastic. When World War II began in Europe, Mrs. Graves changed from bisque to composition.

MARKS: "Just Me/A. 310/11/O.M." back.
SEE: *Illustration 348. Playthings*, March 1931.

VOGUE 7in (18cm) — 8in (20cm); All-Composition Dolls (TODDLES):

When the bisque *Just Me* doll could no longer be obtained from Germany, Vogue needed another source of small dolls that could be dressed. During the late 1930s, they purchased a small all-composition doll from the Arranbee Doll Company.

They continued to use small composition dolls until the late 1940s when they changed to hard plastic. Throughout this decade, there have been several changes in the dolls themselves. In the following section, these dolls have been grouped to show these changes.

Four Types of Composition Vogue Dolls Known As "Toddles"

Doll #1: 7¾in (20cm); molded hair with curl in forehead; may be under a wig; painted eyes slightly slitted; no eyelashes above or below eyes; closed mouth; jointed at neck, shoulders and hips; both arms almost straight; all four fingers molded together and slightly curled; chubby body and face; 1937 to early 1940s.
MARKS: "R & B" middle of back.

Doll #2: 7½in (19cm); wigged head over slightly molded hair; medium-sized painted eyes; delicate eyelashes with light brown line above eye; closed mouth; second and third fingers molded together and slightly curled; jointed at neck, shoulders and hips; right arm bent at almost a right angle; left arm only slightly bent; early 1940s.
MARKS: "Vogue" head; "Doll Co." middle of back.

Doll #3: 7¼in (18.5cm) very slim body; jointed at neck, shoulders and hips; deeply molded hair with curls around face; medium-sized painted eyes; delicate eyelashes with light brown line above eye; right arm bent at almost a right angle; left arm only slightly bent; early 1940s.
MARKS: "Vogue" head only.

Illustration 350.

Doll #4: 8in (20cm); chubby bodies and faces; large rounded painted eyes; thicker eyelashes with lash nearest the eye painted longer; fingers molded together and slightly curled; both arms almost straight; middle to end of 1940s.
MARKS: "Vogue" head; "Vogue" upper back.

The Toddles group of dolls was begun when the supply of small bisque dolls from Germany was curtailed due to World War II. The early dolls had molded hair, and they usually have "R & B" faintly marked on their head. The tiny dolls were very popular during the later 1939s and 1940s. They included:

1. Children in pretty clothes (see *Illustration 353*).
2. A military group (see *Illustration 352*).
3. American worker's group (see *Illustration 354*).
4. Patriotic group (see *Illustration 354*).
5. Nursery rhyme group (see *Illustrations 349* and *350*).
6. Fairy tale group.
7. Foreign costume group (see *Illustration 355*).
8. Historical group (see *Illustration 350*).
9. Brother and sister sets (see *Illustration 353*).
10. Babies (see *Illustration 356*).

Bo-Peep: 7¾in (19cm); for general characteristics, see Doll 1, page 179; circa 1937-1940s. There were variations of this costume through the decade.
MARKS: "R. & B." in middle of back; "Bo Peep" printed on left shoe.
SEE: *Illustration 349.* (Color Section, see page 140.)

Pilgrim John Alden: 7¾in (19cm); for general characteristics, see Doll 1, page 179; one of the earliest composition dolls; light cotton Pilgrim outfit with white organdy collar; beige felt hat; leather belt with buckles at waist and on hat; late 1930s.

A later *John Alden* using a later body type was made during World War II and was dressed in a heavier cotton costume with a white felt collar and cuffs and black hat.

MARKS: "R. & B." in middle of back; "Vogue in script" gold tag on pants; "John Alden" printed on left shoe.

SEE: *Illustration 350.*

Illustration 351.

Illustration 355.

Twin Dolls in Nautical Hamper Basket: All-composition; painted eyes; closed mouth; jointed at neck, shoulders and hips; white sailor suits with red and blue piping; other outfits include capes and berets in blue and red; knitted swimsuits; organdy frocks and bonnets with sashes of red and blue; accessories; 1937.

The advertisement said that the Hamper Dolls were available at the Vogue Doll Shoppe, 152 Willow Ave., West Somerville, Massachusetts.

SEE: *Illustration 351. Toys and Bicycles,* July 1937.

Military Dolls: 7½in (19cm); for general characteristics, see Doll #2, page 179.
FROM LEFT TO RIGHT:
Naval Officer.
MARKS: "Vogue" head; "Doll Co." back.
Civilian Defense Worker.
MARKS: "Vogue" head; "Doll Co." back. "Air Raid Warden" printed on shoe; "C.D. band sewn on arm.
Soldier.
MARKS: "Vogue" head; "Doll Co." back; "Draf-tee" printed on shoe.

Red Cross Nurse.
MARKS: "Vogue" head; "Doll Co." back; "Nurse" printed on bottom of shoe.
Aviator.
MARKS: "Vogue" head; "Doll Co." back.
Air Force Officer.
Other dolls dressed in military uniforms include a *Sailor* and a *Royal Air Force Aviator.*

SEE: *Illustration 352.* (Color Section, page 140.)

Toddles Brother and Sister: 7¼in (18.5cm); for general characteristics, see Doll #3, page 179. Dressed in matching outfits; delicate hand-embroidery on side panels of each outfit; matching caps; leatherette shoes. Doll and clothes are of unusually fine quality.

The entire group of small Vogue composition dolls have been given the name *Toddles.* This *Toddles* name seems to have been derived from these two specific dolls.

MARKS: "Vogue" head only; "Toddles" printed on right shoe; "Vogue in script" gold seal on clothes.

SEE: *Illustration 353.* (Color Section, page 141.)

Wee Willie Winkie: 8in (20cm); for general characteristics, see Doll # 4, page 179; two-piece white pajamas with colorful print including candy canes, horses, elephants, seals and clowns; pink leatherette bedroom slippers with yarn pompon on toes; knitted white stockinette cap.

The difference in the size of the eyes can be seen in this illustration. This is from the *Nursery Rhyme Series.*

MARKS: "Vogue" on head; "Vogue" on upper back.

SEE: *Illustration 350.*

Toddles Victory Gardeners (dolls on extreme left and right): 8in (20cm); for general characteristics, see Doll #4, page 179; carrying hoe; all original; 1940s.

Hoes and rakes were among the accessories which could be purchased separately.

MARKS: "Vogue" head; "Vogue" upper back.

SEE: *Illustration 354.* (Color Section, page 141.)

Toddles Girl (second from left): 8in (20cm); for general characteristics, see Doll #4, page 179; all original; 1940s.

MARKS: "Vogue" head; "Vogue" upper back.

SEE: *Illustration 354.* (Color Section, page 141.)

Toddles Policeman (second from right): 8in (20cm); for general characteristics, see Doll #2, page 179; all original; 1940s. Other dolls in this series include a *Fire Chief, Jockey, Pirate* and *Cowboy.*

MARKS: "Vogue" head; "Doll Co." middle of back.

SEE: *Illustration 354.* (Color Section, page 141.)

Russian Boy: 8in (20cm); for general characteristics, see Doll #4, page 179; dressed in a white suit with fringed pants and sleeves; purple ribbon sash; ruby-colored bolero; tall cossack hat; leather shoes with uppers to simulate boot.

MARKS: "Vogue" head; "Vogue" upper back; "Vogue in script" seal on pants.

SEE: *Illustration 355. Betty Lo Serro Collection.*

Baby: 8in (20cm); all-composition; molded hair; jointed at neck, shoulders and hips; no eyeliner above eyes; delicate painted eyelashes above eyes; fingers molded together; curved baby legs; organdy dress; early 1940s.

Vogue had a Sunshine line of babies (see page 170). Some dolls were marked "Vogue" on head; "Doll Co." on back.

MARKS: None on doll; tagged dress.

SEE: *Illustration 356. Betty Lo Serro Collection.*

Painted-Eye Doll with Blonde Hair: 14in (36cm); all-composition; jointed at neck, shoulders and hips; slightly curved right arm; straighter left arm; long slender legs; painted eyes with liner over eyes; delicate eyelashes painted above eyes; ⅄ on backside; excellent composition with good color; mohair wig with deep waves and curls; closed small mouth; original clothes; circa mid-1940s. This doll was probably made by Ideal and dressed by Vogue. The smaller *Toddles* dolls issued during World War II have similar characteristics.

MARKS: None on doll; "Vogue" in script seal on bottom of dress.

SEE: *Illustration 357.* (Color Section, page 142.)

Rosie the Waac-ette: 14in (36cm); all-composition; jointed at neck, shoulders and hips; sleep eyes with real lashes; long painted lashes under the eyes; eyeliner above eyes; no molded hair under mohair wig; right arm curved like a *Patsy* doll; left arm straight; fingers on right hand molded together; third and fourth fingers on left hand molded together and slightly curved; ⅄ on backside; slender long legs; brown khaki military uniform; brown leatherette tie oxfords with two eyelets on each side; brown socks; same brown leatherette used for military pocketbook; brass button with eagle on hat; dark brown buttons with eagle on hat; dark brown buttons with eagle on them down front of the uniform and on pockets; teddy attached to uniform; 1944.

MARKS: "Waac Vera Abigglin, Chattanooga, Tenn., 1944" on paper glued to the outside of pocketbook; no marks on doll; "Vogue" in script on gold seal on uniform; "Waac-ette" printed on left foot; "Rosie" on right foot.

SEE: *Illustration 358.* (Color Section, page 141.) *Sandy Strater Collection.*

The same doll was also dressed as a W.A.V.E. "Wave-ette" is printed on the bottom of a shoe.

Pantalette Doll: 13in (33cm); all-composition; jointed at neck, shoulders and legs; glassene sleep eyes with real lashes; mohair wig; pink organdy skirt over lace-trimmed pantalettes and petticoat; pink felt jacket and poke bonnet; hand-worked details; 1947.

SEE: *Illustration 359. Montgomery Ward catalog, 1947.*

Illustration 356.

Illustration 359.

181

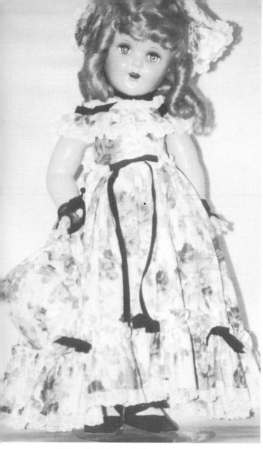

Illustration 360.

Girl in Southern Costume: 19½in (50cm); all-composition jointed at neck, shoulders and hips; Y on backside; sleep eyes with lashes; eye shadow above eyes; open mouth with indications of teeth; white, pink, rose and tan flowered print dress with white eyelet ruffles at neck, shoulders and hem of skirt; large ruffle at bottom of dress; matching bonnet and purse; black velvet ribbon trim; black leatherette tie shoes; probably made in the late 1940s. A similar doll from the Montgomery Ward 1947 catalog is shown in *Illustration 359.*

The doll is attributed to Ideal and dressed by Vogue.

MARKS: None on doll; "Vogue Dolls, Inc.//Medford, Mass." tag on dress.

SEE: *Illustration 360. Mary Lu Trowbridge Collection.*

Girl in Dress and Coat: 19½in (50cm); all-composition; jointed at neck, shoulders and hips; Y on backside; sleep eyes with lashes; eye shadow above eyes; open mouth with indications of teeth; red and white princess-style dress with rickrack trim between gores; mock fur coat, hat and muff; red leatherette tie shoes; probably made in the late 1940s.

The doll is attributed to Ideal and dressed by Vogue.

MARKS: None on doll; "Vogue Dolls, Inc.//Medford, Mass." tag on clothes.

SEE: *Illustration 361. Mary Lu Trowbridge Collection.*

Two Make-up Dolls: 13in (33cm); all-composition; sleep eyes with lashes; eye shadow above eyes; jointed at neck, shoulders and hips; long slender legs; open mouth with teeth; all original clothes; blue leatherette tie shoes; matching pocketbooks with make-up inside; mirror, can of powder and powder puff; late 1940s. Dolls are attributed to Ideal and dressed by Vogue.

Doll on Left: Blue cotton play dress with white trim; matching bonnet and bolero and pocketbook.

Doll on Right: White ruffled Sunday dress; matching bonnet; pocketbook.

MARKS: "13" body of doll on left; none on doll on right.

SEE: *Illustration 362. Mary Lu Trowbridge Collection.*

Illustration 361.

Illustration 362.

Make-up Doll: 13in (33cm); all-composition; sleep eyes with lashes; jointed at neck, shoulders and hips; long slender legs; closed mouth; all original clothes; tiny pocketbook contains mirror and powder puff; white leatherette shoes with yellow ties; late 1940s.

The matching pocketbook was used with many Vogue outfits for a doll of this size.

MARKS: "Vogue Doll, Inc. Medford, Mass" tag on dress.

SEE: *Illustration 363.* (Color Section, page 142.) *Joanne McIntosh Collection.*

The registered trademarks, the trademarks and copyrights appearing in italics//bold within this chapter belong to Wondercraft.

Wondercraft

Swing and Sway with Sammy Kaye: 11½in (29cm); all-composition; hollow body mounted on stick fastened to top of leg and attached to body with metal rod; entire doll painted; dress is pink with blue collar, buttons and bow; 1940s.

When this doll is touched, she sways. It is named after the famous bandleader of the 1930s whose radio program started with "Swing and Sway with Sammy Kaye." The doll's dress was painted a variety of colors on other dolls. This doll is sometimes called *Bobbi-Mae.*

MARKS: "Pat. Pending" inside of dress.
SEE: *Illustration 364.*

Illustration 364.

Identification Guide
Table of Contents

Identification: Marks and Names on Composition Dolls

1. A.	Ideal Novelty and Toy Co.	44. Jedco	Jeannette Doll Co.
2. A.C.; A.D.C.	American Character Doll Co.	45. Just-Lyke	Natural.
3. A.D.	Alexander Doll Co. (seen on some Quintuplets).	46. K. & K.	Fiberoid; Domec.
		47. Kewty	Arranbee.
4. A.D.C.	Acorn Doll Co.; Horsman Doll Company.	48. Kiddiejoy	Hitz, Jacobs, Kastler; also Jacobs, Kastler.
5. A.D.T.	Atlas Doll and Toy Co.	49. Kiddie Pal	Regal.
6. A.M.	Armand Marseille.	50. L.A. & S.	Amberg.
7. A.P.	Les Artas du Papier.	51. Lifelike	Maxine.
8. Acme or Toyshop	Acme Doll Co.	52. Lil Sis	Toy Products.
9. Alex.	Alexander Doll Co.	53. M//16	Amberg; George Borgfeldt.
10. Amer. Char.	American Character Doll Co.	54. M.B.C.	Beehler Arts.
11. Am. Char.	American Character Doll Co.	55. M.D.C.	Modern Doll Co.
12. Amfelt	Amberg; George Borgfeldt; Paul Cohen.	56. M.V.D.	Moo-V-Doll Mfg. Co.
		57. M.Y.C.	Modern Toy Co.
13. B & B	Baker and Bennett Co.	58. N.D.	Natural Doll Co.; National Doll Co.
14. Baby Sandy	Ralph A. Freundlich, Inc.		
15. C.D.	Century Doll Co.	59. N.T.I.	Nottingham Doll Mfg. Co.
16. C.P.M.	Charles Perls Mfg. Co. (London).	60. Nenco	New Era Novelty Co.
		61. Nutoi	New Toy Mfg. Co.
17. Campbell Kids	Horsman, E.I.Co.; American Character Doll Co.	62. Pat. Appld.	Horsman Body Twist Doll.
		63. Petite	American Character.
18. D.P.	Dora Petzold.	64. Phyllis	Bouton Woolf.
19. D.& C.	DeeanCee Company (Canada).	65. Playmate	George Borgfeldt.
		66. R-B Dolls	Reisman, Barron.
20. D.T.C. and D.T.M.C.	Dominion Toy Mfg. Co. Ltd. (Canada).	67. R & B	Arranbee Doll Company
		68. R. B. & L.	Roth, Baitz & Ripsitz; also Roth, Josephy.
21. D.V.	Davis & Voetsch Doll Company.		
		69. Ritzi	Natural Doll Co.
22. Dapper Dancing Dolls	S. & H. Novelty Co.	70. S & Co.	Davis & Voetsch.
		71. S.K. Novelty	S. Kirsch & Co.; also S.K. Novelty Co.
23. DEEanCee	DeeanCee Toy Company Limited (Canada).		
		72. S.T.	Shirley Temple (Japanese doll).
24. Dee Vee	Davis & Voetsch.		
25. Domec	Century; Doll Corp. of America.	73. Sally	American Character.
		74. Sayco	Schoen & Yondorf.
26. E.D.M.A.	European Doll Mfg. Co., Inc.	75. Steha	Herman Steiner.
27. E.G.	Goldberger (Eegee).	76. Sunshine Line	Vogue; Sears Roebuck.
28. E.I.H.	Horsman, E.I. Co.	77. T.S.	Toy Shop.
29. E.I.H.//A.D.C.	Horsman, E.I. Co.	78. T-23	Ideal.
30. E T & N Co.	Elektra.	79. Toddles	Atlas; Vogue.
31. Ellar	Ellar Novelty Company.	80. Toy Company	Acme.
32. F.A.D.F.	First American Doll Factory.	81. U.S.A.	Effanbee; Ideal; Averill.
33. F.O.P. Co.	Federal Doll Mfg. Co.	82. Unis	S.F.B.J. (France).
34. Famlee	Berwick Doll Co; European Doll Mfg. Co.	83. W.D.	Walt Disney.
		84. W.M.D.C.	Well Made Doll Co.
35. G.B.	George Borgfeldt.	85. W.O.L.	Minerva (U.S.); Giltoy (Canada).
36. GTC	Giltoy Company (Canada).		
37. Gisela	Personality doll from Spain.	86. "We" Dolls	Toy Products.
38. H.B. or H.B.C.	Hudson Bay Company (Canada).	87. X	Arranbee; Sayco; maybe others.
39. Hotsy Totsy	Gerling Toy Co.		
40. Hug Me or Hug-Me	Gem; Regal Doll Mfg. Co.	**NUMBERS**	
		1. 13, 15, 16, 17, 18	Ideal Novelty & Toy Co.
41. ISCO	Indestructible Specialties Co.	2. 16	Amberg; George Borgfeldt
42. Gisela	Personality doll from Spain.	3. 971	Armand Marseille in bisque and attributed to Armand Marseille in composition.
43. J. & K.	Hitz, Jacobs, Kastler; also Jacobs, Kastler.		

Advertising Dolls*

1. **American Character:** *Campbell Soup Kids.*
2. **Cameo:** *Bandy* for General Electric Radios; composition head; wood segmented body; jointed at knees, wrists, elbows, ankles, wrists; wears drum major-type uniform; carries a baton.*
3. **Cameo:** *Radiotron;* 15½in (39cm); composition head; wood segmented and jointed body; MARKED: "RCA//Radiotron" head; Mfg.//Cameo Doll Co., N.Y." foot.*
4. **Dee and Cee** (Canada): *Campbell Soup Kids.*
5. **H.D. Lee:** *Buddy Lee;* Coca Cola; Phillip 66; Union-all; Sinclair; Standard Oil; T.W.A.; Highland Whiskey.*
6. **Horsman:** *Campbell Soup Kids.*
7. **Ice Follies:** *Ice Skater.*
8. **Ideal:** Baby *Smiles* Coupon for doll by bakery.
9. **Phillip Morris, Inc.:** 15in (38cm) *Bellhop;* composition head; wide open/closed mouth; cloth body; felt hands; bellhop uniform; removable pill box hat.*
10. **Phillip Morris, Inc.:** *Bellhop;* 11in (28cm); composition head; closed mouth; red bellhop uniform formed part of cloth body; molded pill box hat.*
11. **Skookum Packers Association**, Wenatchee, Washington: *Indian.*

* Not pictured in book.

Cartoon Dolls From 1920s*

1. **Cameo:** *Popeye.*
2. **Cameo:** *Betty Boop.**
3. **Effanbee:** *Skippy.*
4. **Freundlich:** *Little Orphan Annie and Sandy.*
5. **Horsman:** *Little Mary Mixup.**
6. **King Features:** *Wimpy**
7. **Knickerbocker:** *Seven Dwarfs; Mickey Mouse*; Jiminy Cricket*.*
8. **Toycraft:** *Denny Dimwit* from "Winnie Winkle the Breadwinner".

* Not pictured in book.

Competitors of Nancy Ann Storybook Dolls

1. **Beehler Arts**
2. **Confetti**
3. **Eugenia**
4. **Hollywood**
5. **Ice Follies**
6. **Marcie**
7. **Noma Electric**
8. **Princess Anna**

Nancy Ann Storybook Doll Competitor Faces: The painting of the eyes, lips and eyelashes vary from company to company and can help identify an unmarked small composition doll. For a picture and description of the doll, see the individual company.
TOP ROW:
Eugenia Doll Company (doll on left).
Hollywood Doll Mfg. Co. (doll in center).
Marcie (doll on right).
BOTTOM ROW:
Beehler Arts Co. (doll on left).
Confetti Dolls, Inc. (doll in center).
Princess Anna (doll on right).
SEE: *Illustration 365.*

Nancy Ann Storybook Doll (doll on left): Pictured for comparison and not found in other sections of this book.

Nancy Ann dolls were not made in composition. They were made only in bisque and hard plastic.
Hollywood Doll (doll on right).
SEE: *Illustration 366.*

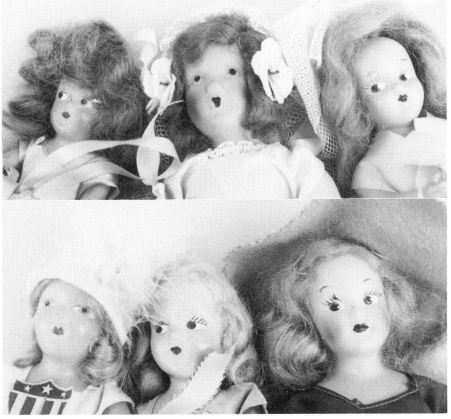

Illustration 365.

Illustration 366.

Illustration 368.

Illustration 367.

Competitors of Patsy Dolls

Children loved the gentle all-composition *Patsy* doll. They soon learned to collect the look-alike dolls from the other companies. They had tea parties for *Sally, Nancy, Phyllis, Babs, Marilyn, Mitzi* and other "friends" of *Patsy*.

Because of patent infringement suits, other companies made different molds for heads and bodies and designed new costumes. There were several lawsuits, but gradually the suits stopped and the dolls continued to be made. They remain today in collections, in antique stores, in booths at doll shows and in our hearts along with *Patsy*.

Collectors long to know exactly who these *Patsy* look-alikes are and where they came from. The search is long and on-going. Even as this book goes to press, the authors have identified another doll. However, they have also found another unidentified doll.

In this section, there are 27 identified dolls and six unidentified ones. The search continues, and it is fun to share our findings with you. When we go to doll shows or to visit the collections of our friends, we always hope to find an unidentified *Patsy* look-alike in a marked box or tagged. At a Columbus auction recently, we found the *Minerva*. Gigi Williams and Sherry Balloun found the Acme *Marilyn* in Chicago. Irene Gulick had a marked Goldberger in Cleveland. Pat Butikofer had the *Tootse* in Erie, Pennsylvania. If you can help, please contact us through Hobby House Press, Inc.

We hope there are many more of these cute dolls out there — somewhere. It has been fun.

Nancy Ann Storybook Competitor Legs: Most of the small composition dolls had painted shoes, and others also had molded socks. The painting and style of the shoes and socks can help identify unmarked dolls. For further information about a doll, see the individual company listed below.

Eugenia Doll Company (doll on left): Painted black shoe only.

Beehler Arts (doll in left center): Mary Jane shoe painted black; molded socks and shoe strap are unpainted.

Hollywood Doll (doll in right center): Painted white slipper.

Hollywood Doll (doll on left): Larger size has unpainted white slipper strap.

SEE: *Illustration 367.*

Nancy Ann Storybook Doll Competitor Legs:

Princess Anna (doll on left): Black shoes; unpainted molded socks with ridges.

Marcie Doll (doll in center): Black shoes; unpainted molded socks with ridges.

Confetti Doll (doll on right): Black painted shoes; no molded socks.

SEE: *Illustration 368.*

Acme Toy Mfg. Co.

Marilyn: 18in (46cm); all-composition; excellent skin tone; brown sleep eyes with real lashes; painted eyelashes below eyes; molded hair with wave in center of forehead; closed mouth; jointed at neck, shoulders and hips; second and third fingers molded together; homemade (of period) costume; matching *Patsy*-type hat with cut-out on top; circa early 1930s.

The composition on this doll is still excellent, in spite of its age and obvious played-with condition.

MARKS: "Acme Toy Company" head.
SEE: *Illustration 369.* (Color Section, page 142.)

American Character

Sally Petite Brother and Sister: 12½in (32cm); all original including shoes; circa 1930-1935.

MARKS: "Sally//A//Petite Doll" back; "A Washable Petite Doll//drawing of doll//Sally" tag on clothes.
SEE: *Illustration 370.* (Color Section, page 142.)

Arranbee

Nancy: 12in (31cm); all-composition; jointed at neck, shoulders and hips; painted eyes with tiny painted eyelashes above eyes; closed mouth; molded hair with side part; hair has wave as it goes across the forehead; pincurls across bottom of back hair; third and fourth fingers curled and molded together; right arm bent; left arm straight; slender legs; red and white checked original dress; shoes and socks not original.

The *Nancy* doll is not as "stocky" as some of the *Patsy*-type dolls.

The Arranbee *Kewty* has similar molded hair.

MARKS: "Arranbee//Doll Co." back.

SEE: *Illustration 371.*

Averill

Peaches: Various sizes; all-composition; *Patsy* look-alike; *Big Peaches, Little Peaches, Blossom Peaches*; circa 1931.

MARKS: "A. Co. Inc"; "A.D."; none.

SEE: *Illustration 372. Playthings*, March 1931.

Peaches: Various sizes; all-composition; *Patsy* look-alike; 1931. Advertisement introduces other dolls in the Averill line for 1931 including *Bud, Blossom, Polly* and *Dolly Peaches*.

MARKS: "A.Co.Inc."; "A.D.;" none.

SEE: *Illustration 373. Playthings*, April 1931.

Illustration 371.

Illustration 372.

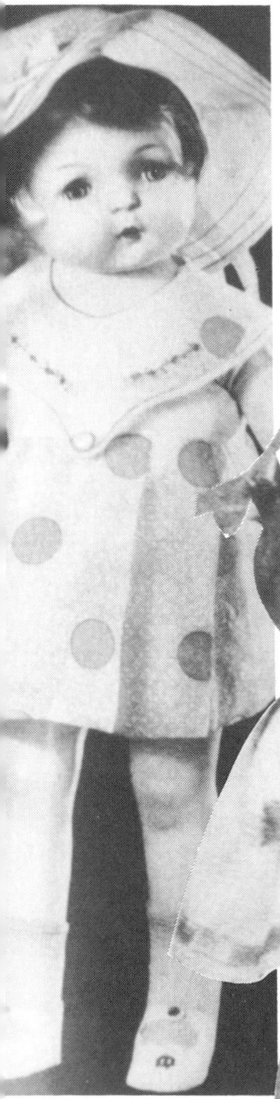

Bouton Woolf

Phyllis: 11½in (29cm); all-composition; jointed at neck, shoulders and hips; bow in hair; costumed in organdies, dimities and broadcloth; both black and white dolls made in their own factory.

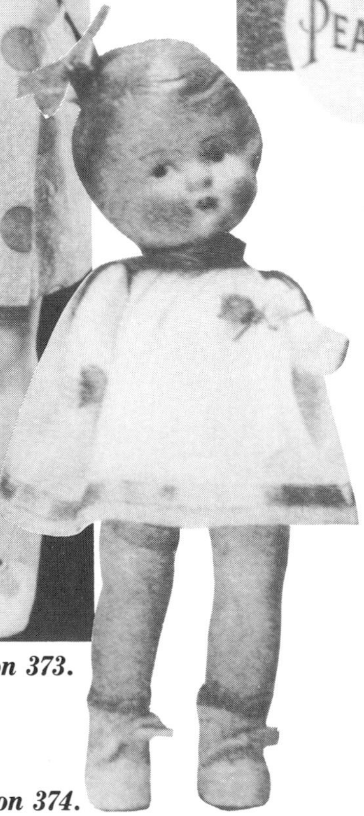

Other dolls with "Phyllis" on their backs are from a different mold. One has bangs with a center part.

MARKS: "Phyllis" back; all dolls may not be marked.

SEE: *Illustration 374. Playthings*, April 1931.

Doll Craft or Joy Doll Company

Miss Italy (dolls on left): 9in (23cm) and 13in (33cm); all-composition; painted side-glancing eyes; large dark eyelashes painted above eyes; molded hair under wig; tiny closed mouth; left arms curved more than right arms; large dolls wear shoes; small dolls have unpainted molded shoes and socks; large doll has Italian provincial costume of yellow print skirt; blue apron with ribbon trim; red top trimmed in lace; leather dirndl fastened with laces; small doll has same costume with the same colors but with different material; both have same style embroidered lace headpiece; late 1930s.

MARKS: "Miss Italy" yellow tag on large doll.

SEE: *Illustration 375.*

Illustration 373.

Illustration 374.

Illustration 376.

Mary
Ann

Illustration 375.

Illustration 378.

188

Jeannine of Alsace-Lorraine: 9in (23cm) and 13in (33cm); same general characteristics as *Miss Italy* dolls; the larger doll has a much better grade composition; both dolls have unusual wig with tight curls; both dolls have same costume with different materials; large doll has striped white, green and red striped skirt with rickrack trim; yellow apron with orange bias trim; green blouse and peplum combination; white "mob" cap; small doll has blue, green, white and red print skirt; all other costume parts are the same colors and materials.

MARKS: "I am//Jeannine//of//Alsace-Lorraine" yellow octagonal tag on small doll.

SEE: *Illustration 375.*

For more information about these dolls, see pages 64 and 65.

Gerling

Mary Ann: 13in (33cm); all-composition; jointed at neck, shoulders and hips; can stand alone; various costumes (some with matching hats); molded hair; fingers molded together with separate thumb; 1932.

This doll was given as a premium with two subscriptions at $.50 each.

SEE: *Illustration 376. Needlecraft,* October 1932.

German Patsy Look-Alike

German Patsy Look-alike (doll on left): 10½in (27cm); all-composition; jointed at neck, shoulders and hips; molded hair with part on left side and wind-swept bangs; painted side-glancing eyes; delicate eyelashes above eyes with heavy black line under eyelashes; both arms curved; quality of composition of the smaller dolls is slightly inferior; all original; 1930s. This doll came in the box pictured. It had a felt coat, matching hat and a white dress in the box.

MARKS: "Germany"//"(cannot decipher letter)" neck; "Doll//MC243// Made in German" box.

SEE: *Illustration 377.* (Color Section, page 143.)

German Patsy Look-alike (doll on right): 13in (33cm); all-composition; jointed at neck, shoulders and hips; molded hair with part on left side and wind-swept bangs; painted side-glancing eyes; delicate eyelashes above eyes with black line under eyelashes; both arms curved; "stocky" body with rather short legs; fingers molded together; circa 1930s.

MARKS: "Germany//A/M" head.

SEE: *Illustration 377.* (Color Section, page 143).

The "Germany" mark on both dolls is the same. The second lines of the marks on both dolls are very difficult to read, but they are NOT the same.

The type of composition of both dolls is different from the American composition, but it is beautiful in its own right.

They are attributed to Armand Marseille.

Goldberger

Patsy Look-alike: 15in (38cm); composition shoulder head and arms; molded hair with hole for bow; molded band on front of head; painted eyes; painted open mouth with white paint in center to represent teeth; fingers molded together; cloth body and legs; legs seamed at ankle with black cloth for shoes or socks; clothes not original; circa early 1930s.

    MARKS: "E. Goldberger" head.

    SEE: *Illustration 378. Irene Gulick Collection.*

Horsman

    The Horsman Line for 1931: Included *Patsy* look-alikes in four sizes.

1. *Babs* 12in (31cm).   3. *Jane* 17in (43cm).
2. *Sue* 14in (36cm).   4. *Nan* 20in (51cm).

    All-composition; jointed at neck, shoulders and hips; *Patsy*-type dresses; some had matching hats; molded hair with a tuft in the middle of the forehead; one arm bent; circa 1931.

    Some of these dolls had wigs.

    SEE: *Illustration 379. Playthings,* April 1931.

Maxine

Mitzie (doll on left): 13½in (34cm); all-composition; jointed at neck, shoulders and hips; curved right arm only; molded hair with slight bangs; painted brown eyes with large pupils; long eyelashes; open mouth with molded tongue; stocky body and legs; no line on backside; third and fourth fingers molded together; all original dress and matching hair ribbon with elastic in back; circa 1929. This doll has the same mold as *Tootsie,* and the Averill *Dimmie* is very similar.

    MARKS: "Mitzi//Maxine" back.

    SEE: *Illustration 380.* (Color Section, page 144.)

Illustration 379.

Unknown

Tootsie (doll on right): 13½in (34cm); all-composition; jointed at neck, shoulders and hips; curved right arm only; molded hair with slight bangs; painted eyes with large pupils; delicate eyelashes above eyes with black line under lashes; open mouth with molded tongue; stocky body and legs; no line on backside; third and fourth fingers molded together; all original dress and matching teddy; in Sears, Roebuck & Co. catalog in 1929. Her characteristics are the same as the Maxine *Mitzi* and the Averill body-twist *Dimmie.*

    This is not the same doll as *Tootse.*

    MARKS: "Tootsie" cloth tag on dress.

    SEE: *Illustration 380.* (Color Section, page 144.)

Minerva

Patsy and Snow White Look-alike (doll on left): 13½ in (33cm); all-composition; jointed shoulders and hips; molded hair with molded unpainted hair bow in front; right arm curved; left arm straight; brown hair; painted side-glancing eyes; closed mouth; slender long legs; pink organdy pleated dress; well-made slip and teddy combination; all original except shoes; circa late 1930s.

    The Giltoy Doll Company (Canada) sold a doll from this same mold marked "W.O.L."

    MARKS: None.

    SEE: *Illustration 381.*

Illustration 381.

Snow White Look-alike (doll on right): 12in (31cm); all composition; jointed at shoulders and hips only; molded hair; *Snow White* blue hair ribbon in front; heavy roll of curls around head which are quite different from the other doll in the picture; large painted eyes looking straight ahead; heavy eyelashes above eyes; heavy black line around eye; open mouth with white paint indicating teeth; circa late 1930s.

Ideal made a *Snow White* doll with a similar mold.
MARKS: None.
SEE: *Illustration 381.*

Moravian Dolls

Anna Nitschmann Doll (*Patsy* Look-alike): 13in (33cm); all-composition jointed at neck, shoulders and hips; molded hair with left part and curled around ears; side-glancing eyes with large pupils; closed mouth; fingers molded together; dimples on sides of kneecap; line under knee; all original and handmade clothes; circa 1938-1939.

For many, many years it has been the custom of the Women's Circles of the Moravian Churches of Bethlehem, Pennsylvania, to make cloth dolls of the early pioneers of their church. These dolls have been sold to raise funds for the work of the church women.

In the late 1930s, the Busy Workers of the Moravian Church in Bethlehem decided to dress a composition doll. A group of these dolls were purchased and dressed authentically. Only a few were made during this time, and then the workers returned to the customary cloth dolls.

This doll honors Anna Nitschmann, born 1714. She was a distinguished worker in the Moravian Church. The sewers worked hard to authenticate the early attire. The clothes are completely hand-sewn, and all the seams are overcast. The tiny eyelets for the lacing in the jacket have almost invisible buttonhole stitches. The petticoat and long pants are also completely hand-sewn.

All of the Moravian dolls are treasured and handed down from generation to generation. There is a display of them in the Moravian Museum in Bethlehem, Pennsylvania.
MARKS: None on doll.
SEE: *Illustration 382.* (Color Section, page 143.)

Natural Doll Co., Inc.

Ritzi Girl and Boy: 12in (31cm) to 20in (51cm); part of the "Just-Lyk" line of Natural Dolls. They advertised that this face appealed to young and old.

In February 1931, they advertised that they had a new line of baby and *Mama* dolls. They also made doll parts for other companies.
MARKS: "Ritzi" has been found on some dolls.
SEE: *Illustration 383. Playthings,* June 1931.

190

"The Hit of the Chicago Fair"

Illustration 383.

Illustration 384.

P. & M. Doll Co., Inc.

Patsy-type Doll: During the Toy Fair of 1934, P. & M. displayed their line of dressed dolls and stuffed animals; one of the dolls was a *Patsy* competitor.
SEE: *Illustration 384. Playthings,* March 1934.

Regal Doll Mfg. Company Inc.

Maizie: All-composition; jointed at neck, shoulders and hips; right arm curved more than the other; molded hair with bangs almost all across the forehead; older sister of *Baby Hug-Me*; 1931.

The advertisement said, "Meet the Little Princess."

SEE: *Illustration 385. Playthings, April 1931.*

Judy: All-composition; jointed at neck, shoulders and hips; molded hair with slight bangs; member of the *Kiddie Pal Family*; 1931.

This doll has a head mold similar to the *Maxine Mitzi*.

MARKS: "Judy" tag.

SEE: *Illustration 386. Playthings, April 1931.*

Tootse

Tootse: 13½in (34cm); all-composition; jointed at neck, shoulders and hips; molded hair with center part; bent right arm; third and fourth fingers molded together; clothes not original but appropriate to period; coral sleeveless dress and matching hair ribbon; circa early 1930s.

This is not the same doll as *Tootsie*.

MARKS: "Tootse" back.

SEE: *Illustration 387. Pat Butikofer Collection.*

Toy Products

"Lil Sis" Boy: 12½in (32cm); spring jointed at neck, shoulders and hips; molded hair with side part; painted blue side-glancing eyes; closed mouth; clothes may not be original; white shirt with red tie; embroidered Bavarian short pants and suspenders; circa 1930-1932.

UNUSUAL IDENTIFICATION FEATURE: Spring jointed.

MARKS: "Lil Sis//A//Toy Product" back.

SEE: *Illustration 388. Barbara Comienski Collection.*

Uneeda

Patsy Look-alikes: 14in (36cm); all-composition: spit-type curl in middle of forehead; hair parted on right side of doll: puckered mouth; painted eyes with large black pupils and small amount of blue around pupils, rest of eye white; curved left arm; single stroke eyebrows; jointed at shoulders and hips (not at neck); each doll is all original in separate boxes; dresses with matching bonnets; rickrack trim at neckline; front scalloped shoes; doll on left is in red and white; doll on right is in blue and white; dolls originally belonged to twin sisters; early to mid 1930s.

MARKS: "Beauty Quality, A Uneeda Doll//Uneeda Doll Co., Inc. N.Y.C.//Made in U.S.A." paper tag; "Beauty, Quality, A Uneeda Doll Since 1917" end of box.

SEE: *Illustration 392. McMasters Productions*, picture on page 193.

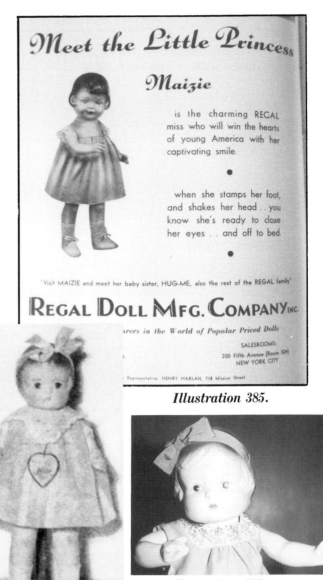

Illustration 385.

Illustration 387.

Illustration 386.

Illustration 388.

Unknown

Black Patsy Look-alike: 12in (31cm); all-composition; molded wavy hair; red ribbon on left side part of mold; painted eyes; closed mouth; both arms not curved; fingers molded together; jointed at neck, shoulders and hips; clothes not original; late 1920s to early 1930s.

Although unmarked, this doll has the same molded hair as a marked 9in (23cm) Effanbee doll.

MARKS: None.
SEE: *Illustration 390.*

Girl with Slitted Eyelashes: 13in (33cm); all-composition; jointed at neck, shoulders and hips; molded hair with unusual part; painted side-glancing eyes with cut-out slit for inserting eyelashes; closed mouth; both arms curved; slim legs with dimple on each side of knee; pink dotted swiss original dress with white organdy collar and bonnet; pink teddy; white shoes and socks; came with travel trunk; extra clothes; circa early 1930s. Slit can be seen in the illustration above left eye.

UNUSUAL IDENTIFICATION FEATURE: Slit above the eyes so the lashes can be inserted.
MARKS: None.
SEE: *Illustration 390.*

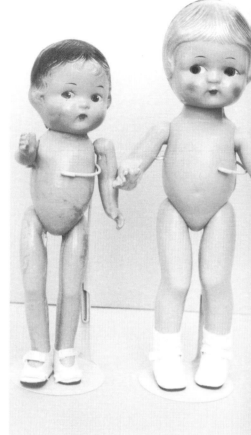

Illustration 391.

Patsy Look-alike (doll on right): 11⅕in (29cm); all-composition; jointed at neck, shoulders and hips; molded hair with center part; painted side-glancing eyes; closed mouth; right arm curved; left arm straight; fingers molded together; slender long legs; circa early 1930s.

This doll has a similar hair mold and characteristics of the American Character *Sally Petite.* While it is a very nice doll, it does not quite have the quality of *Sally.*

MARKS: None.
SEE: *Illustration 391.*

Patsy Look-alike (doll on left): 10in (25cm); all-composition; jointed at neck, shoulders and hips; both arms are straight; deeply molded wavy hair with center part and two pin curls facing each other in front; painted eyes with painted lashes above eyes; black line above side-glancing eyes; closed mouth; fingers molded together; not original clothes circa early 1930s.

MARKS: None.
SEE: *Illustration 391.*

Illustration 389.   *Illustration 390.*

192

Other Patsy Doll Competitors
Pictured in Main Section of Book
1. **Alexander:** *Betty* (page 10).
2. **American Character:** *Twosome Carol Ann Berry* (page 29).
3. **Effanbee** *Button Nose* (page 69).
4. **Freundlich:** *Little Red Riding Hood* (Color Section, page 95).

Not Pictured
1. **Arranbee:** *Kewty*; molded hair similar to Arranbee *Nancy*.
2. **Bouton Woolf:** *Phyllis* (both black and white); molded hair with straight bangs across the front of head.
3. **Eugenia:** *Johnie* and *Janie*.
4. **Regal:** *Kiddie Pal Dolly*.
5. **Reliable:** 12in (30cm); all-composition; jointed at shoulders and hips only; closed mouth; molded hair with wavy strands in center of forehead.
   MARKS: "Reliable Doll//Made in Canada" head.

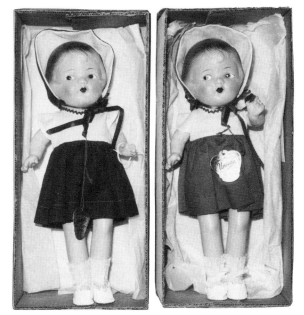

Illustration 392.

Competitors of Shirley Temple Dolls*
1. **Alexander:** *Little Colonel.*
2. **American Character:** *Sally Star*; dolls with dimples on their cheeks made during World War II.
3. **Arranbee:** *Nancy* (with wig).
4. **Germany:** *Shirley Temple* look-alike.*
5. **Goldberger:** *Little Miss Charming.*
6. **Horsman:** *Bright Star* Line; *Babs* (with wig).
7. **Ideal:** *Ginger.*
8. **Ideal:** *Betty Jane*; Ideal number on back; Y on lower back.
9. **Japanese:** *Shirley Temple.*
10. **Jolly:** *Shirley Temple* look a-like.
11. **Joy Doll Corp.:** *Miss World's Fairest.*
12. **Regal:** *Kiddie Pal* Line.
13. **Regal Horsman:** *Little Colonel*-type.*
14. **Reliable:** Licensed in 1934 to make the *Shirley Temple* doll in Canada; a few *Shirley Temple* heads were imported with the Ideal marks, but most had both "Shirley Temple" and "Reliable/made in Canada" on the doll.*

*Dolls not pictured in this book.

Competing Snow White Dolls
1. **Alexander:** Black hair; traditional dress.
2. **Ideal:** *Shirley Temple* Snow White.
3. **Ideal:** Black hair; MARKS: None.
4. **Giltoy:** MARKS: "W.O.L." head.*
5. **Knickerbocker:** MARKS: "© Walt Disney" head; "Knickerbocker Toy Co." back.
6. **Minerva:** MARKS: "W.O.L." head; none on some dolls.*
7. **Reliable:** 15in (38cm); composition shoulderhead; lower arms; black line over eye; molded bow in hair. MARKS: "A Reliable Doll//Made in Canada."

Dimples on Composition Dolls
Dimple on Each Cheek
1. **Alexander:** *Little Betty.*
2. **Alexander:** *Sonja Henie.*
3. **American Character:** Petite dolls; example-*Wave.*
4. **Averill:** *Baby Hendron.*
5. **Ideal:** *Shirley Temple.*
6. **Horsman:** *Baby Dimples.*
7. **Reliable:** *Baby Joan.*
8. **Unknown:** *Quintuplets.*

Dimples on Chin
1. **Alexander:** *Dr. Dafoe.*
2. **Amberg:** Some *Amfelt* (imported dolls)
3. **Effanbee:** *Lovums, Sweetie Pie, Touslehead, Baby Bright Eyes, Tommy Tucker.*
4. **Goldberger:** *Little Miss Charming.*
5. **Horsman::** *Peterkins.*
6. **S.F.B.J.:** #301 face and Unis 60 face.

Dimple Above Mouth
1. **American Character:** *Sally Joy.*

Illustration 393.

Minerva

Minerva Darling Baby: Head of baby doll showing apparatus for feeding composition doll; red metal ring in open mouth; tube runs through body cavity; circa mid 1930s.

Several large companies and other smaller novelty companies sold this type of doll. This one marked: "Darling" on the back of the head may have been one of the novelties promoted by Jean Darling, a movie star. Another novelty item promoted by her was a sewing kit. The same, or a similar mouth ring, is on a Pullan doll from Canada.

MARKS: "Darling" head.
SEE: *Illustration 393.*

Drink and Wet Dolls*

1. **American Character:** *Wee Wee.*
2. **Arranbee:** *Drink 'N Babe.*
3. **Effanbee:** *Dy-Dee Baby.*
4. **Ellar Noverlty by Berk-Winn:** *Tweedy.**
5. **Freeman Toy Company (Canada):** *Didy Wet*; circa 1945.*
6. **Ideal:** *Betsy Wetsy.*
7. **Minerva:** *Darling Baby.*
8. **Minerva:** *Dorable Dolly.**
9. **Pullan:** *Dinky Drinky.**
10. **Reliable:** *Wetums.**
* Not pictured in book.

Eyes (Unusual)

Companies Which Used Eye Shadow on Some of Their Composition Dolls

1. **Alexander:** *Margaret O'Brien; Baby McGuffey;* Large Portrait Dolls.
2. **Amberg:** *Amfelt* imported dolls.
3. **Arranbee:** Most of their dolls.
4. **Averill:** *Dimmie* and *Jimmie.*
5. Bed dolls.
6. **Burgarella:** French court dolls.
7. **Horsman:** Large Toddler; *Bright Star*-type.
8. **Hoyer:** Last composition doll.
9. **Ideal:** *Deanna Durbin;* other later dolls.
10. **Mollye:** Teen dolls.
11. **Monica Studios:** *Monica.*
12. **Uneeda:** *Rita Hayworth.*
"FLIRTY-TYPE" EYES
1. **American Character:** A few of their babies.
2. **Butler Bros. Catalog:** *Toddler Sue.*
3. **Effanbee:** *Baby Bright Eyes; Tommy Tucker.*
4. **Ideal:** Many of their dolls.

Unusual Eyes

1. **American Character:** Petite Line (advertised "...their sleep eyes do not merely "plunk" shut. They go to sleep only when you WANT them to.") Dolls included *Toddle-Tot, Sally, Sally Joy, Toddles.*
2. **Freundlich:** *Goo-Goo* (large eyes which move under celluloid frame).

Unusual Eyelashes

1. **Alexander:** Added long eyelashes to Portrait Dolls.
2. **Ideal:** Double-action "glace" eyes that "flash, sparkle, flirt, sleep;" advertised for *Ginger* and *Shirley Temple* dolls.
3. **Mollye:** Black long, widely spaced on inexpensive *Dream World*-type doll with nice clothes.
4. **Patsy Look-alike:** Slits cut in composition for insertion of eyelashes.

Hair (Unusual)

Molded Hair with Curl or Curls in Middle of Forehead

1. **Acme:** *Marilyn.*
2. **American Character:** Many of their babies.
3. **Arranbee:** Many of their babies, especially the small *Dionne Quintuplet-type.*
4. **Effanbee:** Several models.
5. **Ideal:** *Betsy Wetsy.*
6. **Freundlich:** *Baby Sandy.*
7. **Gem:** Topsy; *Hug Me* doll.
8. **Horsman:** Toddler; *Campbell Soup Kid* (1946); *Baby Dimples.*
9. **Reliable:** *Baby Joan;* Indians.

FLOSS OR YARN HAIR WIG
(SUBSTITUTED DURING WORLD WAR II)
1. **Averill:** *Harriet Flanders.*
2. **Effanbee:** *Little Lady.*
3. **Effanbee:** *Brother* and *Sister.*
4. **Ideal:** *Betsy Wetsy.*
*Not a complete list.

Unusual Molded Hair

Campbell Soup Kids: Molded Hair

1. **American Character Petite:** Curl in center of forehead.
2. **Dee and Cee (Canada):** Curl in center for forehead; same mold as Horsman 1946 doll.
3. **Horsman:** Curl on left side.
4. **Horsman 1946:** Curl in middle of forehead.

Tight Ringlets on Bottom Edge of Back Hair

1. **Averill:** *Whistler.*
2. **Horsman:** Some babies and toddlers.
3. **W.A.A.C.**

Center Part with Bangs

1. **American Character:** *Sally Petite.*
2. **Bouton Woolf:** *Phyllis.*
3. **Effanbee:** *Patsy;* other *Patsy* family members.
4. **Freundlich:** *Little Red Riding Hood* and others.

No Part with Short Bangs Swept Slightly to Right

1. **Averill:** *Dimmie* and *Jimmie.*
2. **Maxine:** *Mitzi.*
3. **Regal:** *Judy.*
4. **Tootsie:** *Tootsie.*

No Part with Very Short Hair

1. **Alexander:** Quintuplets.

Side Part

1. **Arranbee:** *Nancy* (left side).
2. **Averill:** *Peaches* (slightly to right side; straight hair swept to left side.
3. **Bouton Woolf:** (right side; straight hair swept to left side).
4. **German Patsy-type:** (left part with semi-bangs).
5. **Moravian doll:** (left part).
6. **P. & M.:** (right part).
7. **Patsy-type with Slitted Eyes:** (right part).
8. **Regal:** *Maizie* (right part).
9. **Toy Products:** *Lil Sis* (part on right).

Hole in Head for Bow

1. **Bouton Woolf:** *Phyllis.*
2. **Goldberger:** *Patsy* look-alike.
3. **Cameo:** *Joy.*
4. **Horsman:** *Peggy.*
5. Many dolls have one or more nail holes in their heads for hair bows.

Topknot

1. **Horsman:** *Whatsit;* also called *Naughty Sue.*
Irregular (jagged) Hairline
1. **Playmate:** *Bonnie* Doll.

Very Curly Hair

1. Black Patsy Look-alike.
2. **Freundlich:** *Orphan Annie.*
3. **Japanese:** *Shirley Temple.*

Lambskin Wigs

1. **Effanbee:** *Patsy Baby; Patsy Babyette; Baby Brite; Mary Lee; Touslehead; Sugar Baby; Sweetie Pie; Dy-Dee Baby* and *Lovums.*

Fur Wig

1. **European Doll Co.** (EDMA): Baby doll.

Hair Inserted in Composition Head

1. **Monica:** *Monica.*

Hands (Unusual)

Hands (Magnetic)

Magnetic Hands: Magnets were implanted by the toy company, F.A.O. Schwarz, in palm of doll's hand so doll could hold accessories. These accessories included dishes, household utensils such as brooms, pans, and so forth. Since this was a patriotic time, flags were also magnetized and placed in the dolls' hands.
1. **Effanbee** *Little Lady.*
2. **Effanbee** *Patsy.*
3. **Effanbee** *Suzanne.*
4. **Effanbee** *Suzette.*

Arm and Hand of Effanbee *Little Lady* Doll.
   MARKS: "Effanbee//U.S.A." on head and back.
   SEE: *Illustration 394.*

Illustration 394.

Celluloid Fingernails
   1. **Effanbee.**

Starfish Hands
   1. **Cameo** *Scootles.*
   2. **Cameo** *Kewpies.*

Cloth Mitt Hands
   1. **Vecchiotti:** 8in (20cm).

Hole in Clenched Fist
   1. **Alexander:** *Miss America.*

Ideal Dolls Used by Other Companies

Identification of all dolls is difficult because companies buy or exchange molds, body parts and whole dolls. Ideal was a toy company and made products other than completed dolls. Molds were even sold to companies in other countries. For instance, Ideal sold the mold franchises for the *Shirley Temple* doll to Reliable of Canada. Other companies known to have purchased dolls or molds from Ideal include:
1. **American Character.**
2. **Arranbee.**
3. **Eugenia.**
4. **Hoyer, Mary.**
5. **Gerson.**
6. **Vogue.**

Unusual Joints on Dolls

Jointed at Waist
(called "Body Twist" dolls).
   1. **Alexander:** *Wendy Ann.*
   2. **Amberg:** *It* dolls; *Peter Pan; Amby.*
   3. **Averill:** *Dimmie* and *Jimmie.*
   4. **Horsman:** Twist dolls.
   5. **Hoyer, Mary:** First composition doll.
   6. **Ideal:** First composition Mary Hoyer doll.
   7. **Ideal:** Some *Deanna Durbin* dolls.
   8. **Twistum:** *Parboy.*

Jointed at Wrists

1. *Composition Novelty Co.*
2. *Cameo: Joy; Margie.*

Jointed at Knees

1. *Cameo: Joy; Margie.*

Jointed at Ankles

1. *Cameo: Joy; Margie.*

New Style Ball and Socket Joints

1. *Ideal Ginger; Shirley Temple.*

Little Colonel-Type Dolls

1. *Alexander.*
2. *Ideal.*
3. *Horsman.*
4. *Regal-Horsman.*
5. *Vogue.*

Makers of Composition Dolls After 1927 Not Listed in Book*

1. ABC Toy Company.
2. American Wholesale Corp: Distributor.
3. Adoree Berry.
4. American Tot.
5. Art Metal Works.
6. Bradley, Milton.
7. Bruckner.
8. Century Doll Co.
9. Domec.
10. Doll Corporation of America (also Domec and Century).
11. Dominion Toy Manufacturing Company Limited (Canada).
12. Eagle Doll & Toy Co.
13. Fiberoid Doll Supply Co.
14. Freeman Toy Company (Canada).
15. Frisch Doll Supply Co.
16. Furga (Italy).
17. Globe Doll Works.
18. Gold Doll Co.
19. Goldstein, Joseph.
20. Hitz, Jacobs, Kessler.
21. Howard Pottery Co. Ltd.
22. Imperial (Hungary).
23. Jutta (Germany).
24. Kago.
25. Kaufman, Levenson & Co. (also known as Paramount).
26. King Innovations.
27. Lenci (Italy).
28. Libby Doll & Novelty Co.
29. Love Doll Co.
30. Majestic Doll & Toy Co.
31. Marga (Hungary).
32. Marti, Anna.
33. Markon Mfg. Co.
34. Metropolitan Doll Company.
35. Morin, L. (Paris, France).
36. Mutual Novelty Co.
37. Newly Born.
38. Nibur Novelty Co.
39. Novelty Doll & Toy Co.
40. Ohlhaver, Gebrüder.
41. Paramount (also known as Kaufman, Levenson & Co.).
42. Penn Stuffed Toy Co.
43. Perfect Doll Company.
44. Primrose Doll Co.
45. Prisard, Mme. E. (Paris).
46. Reisman, Barron & Co.
47. Roma Doll Co.
48. Roullet & Decamps.
49. Roxy Doll & Toy Co.
50. S & H Novelty Co.
51. S & S Doll Co.
52. Saxon Doll Co.
53. Scherzer & Fisher (Germany).
54. Schilling (Germany).
55. Schmidt, Franz & Co. (Germany).
56. Sibyl Fortune Telling Co. (Los Angeles).
57. Simon & Halbig (Germany).
58. Société Nouvelle des Bébés Réclames (France).
59. Steiner, Herman (Germany).
60. Twistum Co.
61. Yagonda, Bros & Afrik.
* Partial list.

Military and Patriotic Dolls

Military Dolls

1. **Alexander:** *W.A.A.C.; W.A.V.E.; Marine.*
2. **American Character:** *W.A.A.C.; W.A.V.E.*
3. **Arranbee:** *W.A.A.C.; W.A.V.E.*
4. **Averill:** *Soldier; sailor.*
5. **Berick:** *Famlee sailor.*
6. **Effanbee:** *Baby Grumpykins soldier.*
7. **Freundlich:** *General McArthur;* soldier; sailor, *W.A.A.C.; W.A.V.E.*
8. **Ideal:** *Soldier (all-composition).*
9. **Ideal:** *Soldier (Flexy)*
10. **Monica:** *W.A.A.C.; W.A.V.E.*
11. **Vogue** *Toddles:* Soldier, sailor, aviator, Naval officer; Air Force officer; nurse.
12. **Vogue:** *Waac-ette; Wave-ette.*

Patriotic Dolls

1. **Alexander:** *Miss America.*
2. **Horsman:** Girl in patriotic costume.
3. **Margit Nilson:** *Victory* Doll.
4. **Vogue:** *Air Raid Warden.*
5. **Vogue:** *Victory Gardeners.*

Movie Star and Personality Dolls

Although there have been personality and theatrical dolls for many years, dolls modeled or named for famous people were unusually popular in the 1930s and early 1940s.

1. **Alexander:** *Queen Elizabeth.*
2. **Alexander:** *Sonja Henie.*
3. **Alexander:** Shirley Temple as *Little Colonel.*
4. **Alexander:** Juanite Quigley as *Baby Jane.*
5. **Alexander:** *Jane Withers.*
6. **Alexander:** *Margaret O'Brien.*
7. **Alexander:** Vivien Leigh as *Scarlett.*
8. **American Character:** Shirley Jean Rickerts as *Sally Star.*
9. **American Character:** Carol Ann Berry as *Twosome Doll.*
10. **Amberg:** Peggy Jean Montgomery as *Baby Peggy.*
11. **Effanbee:** *Anne Shirley.*
12. **Effanbee:** Jackie Cooper as *Skippy.*
13. **Freundlich:** Baby Sandy Henville as *Baby Sandy.*
14. **Freundlich:** *General Douglas MacArthur.*
15. **Ideal:** *Deanna Durbin.*
16. **Ideal:** Fanny Brice as *Baby Snooks.*
17. **Ideal:** *Judy Garland.*
18. **Ideal:** *Marilyn Knowlden.*
19. **Ideal:** *Princess Beatrix.*
20. **Ideal:** *Shirley Temple.*
21. **Ideal:** Sonja Henie; *Princess Sonja.*
22. **Goldberger:** *Little Miss Charming,* Shirley Temple look-alike.
23. **Moo-V-Doll Mfg. Co.**
24. **Horsman:** *Little Colonel;* Shirley Temple look-alike.
25. **Reliable:** *Barbara Ann Scott.*
26. **Reliable:** *Maggie Muggins,* radio star.
27. **Reliable:** Nelson Eddy as Royal Canadian Mountie (not advertised as Nelson Eddy; same mold used for other dolls).

Movie Influence on Doll Clothes

In the 1930s, the movies influenced American life. In the middle of a depression, movies were inexpensive and entertaining. They were also glamorous and trend setting. Although Paris was still a center of world fashion, more and more Americans turned their fashion eyes toward Hollywood. The stars and their clothes became models.

Dolls have always followed the fashion trends of the time. With the advent of the *Shirley Temple,* doll companies and doll clothing designers turned to the movies for inspiration. Soon there was a dramatic drop in *Mama* dolls and baby dolls, and Hollywood glamour dolls and clothes changed the doll market.

The following companies, designers and stars influenced the clothes of composition dolls, children and adults:

1. **Alexander:** *Jane Withers.*
2. **Alexander:** *Little Colonel* line of dolls.
3. **Alexander:** *Margaret O'Brien.*
4. **American Character:** *Sally Star.*
5. **Freundlich:** *Baby Sandy* line of dolls.
6. **Horsman:** *Bright Star* line of dolls.
7. **Ideal:** *Deanna Durbin.*
8. **Ideal:** *Judy Garland.*
9. **Ideal:** *Marily Knowlden.*
10. **Ideal:** *Princess Sonja* (Competing with Alexander *Sonja Henie*).
11. **Ideal:** *Shirley Temple.*
12. **Mollye:** *Glamour Dolls.*
13. **Mollye:** Hollywood Cinema Fashions.
14. **Reliable:** *Barbara Ann Scott.*

Illustration 395.

Shoes

Arranbee (shoe on left): Snap slipper with open work on side of shoe; often color matched clothing. Arranbee also used another style on less expensive dolls. These shoes had a scalloped front over the arch of the foot.

Amberg Felt Dolls (shoe on right): Felt with distinctive white stitching and pompons. Other companies which imported these dolls were Paul Cohen and George Borgfeldt.

   SEE: *Illustration 395.*

Sonja Henie Skates: Open toe; tongue sewn in at vamp; slim boots to fit leg, ankle and small foot; metal eyelets; felt-like material; laces match color of boot; metal eyelets; blades made of dull pot metal and curved for figure skating; blade attached to boot with two small brass rivets.

   These are the original *Sonja Henie* skates found on the dolls during the war years.

   SEE: *Illustration 396.*

Illustration 396.

Multi-Heads and/or Faces

1. **Alexander:** *Topsy Turvey.*
2. **Berwick:** *Famlee.*
3. **Three-in-One Corporation:** *Trudy* (*Trudy* was made by Ideal).

Rubber Parts on Composition Dolls

Rubber Arms and/or Legs

1. **Horsman:** *Sweetheart Doll.*
2. **Ideal:** *Baby Smiles.*
3. **Ideal:** *Bathroom Baby.*
4. **Ideal:** *Cuddles.*
5. **Ideal:** *Precious.*
6. **Ideal:** *Sallykins.*
7. **Ideal:** *Tickletoes.*

Teen Dolls

1. **Arranbee:** *Debuteen.*
2. **Horsman:** *Sweetheart*; 25in (63cm); composition head, body and legs; hard rubber arms; glass sleep eyes; hair parted in middle.
3. **Ideal:** *Deanna Durbin.*
4. **Ideal:** Mature *Shirley Temple.*
5. **Joy Doll Co.:** *Miss World's Fairest.*
6. **Mollye:** *Modern Teen.*
7. **Monica:** *Monica.*

Υ on Lower Back of Dolls

When Ideal designed the *Shirley Temple* doll, they were proud of her unique lifelike body. The two dimples above the Υ on the lower back appeared on Ideal dolls about that time. This is an identification feature for both composition and hard plastic Ideal dolls. The following companies have used composition dolls with this feature.

1. **American Character.**
2. **Arranbee.**
3. **Eugenia.**
4. **Ideal.**
5. **Horsman.**
6. **Vogue.**

Price Guide

ACME TOY MFG. CO.

Marilyn (Illustration 2) $80-175 depending on size

ALEXANDER DOLL CO., INC.

Alice in Wonderland (Illustration on Title Page) $400-425

Alice in Wonderland (Illustration 40) $400-450

Antoinette (Marie Antoinette) (Illustration 70) $1700 plus (very few sample prices available)

Baby Genius (Illustration 56) $175-200

Baby McGuffey (Illustration 57) $150-200

Baking on Saturday (Illustration 7) $250-275

Ballerina (Degas) (Illustration 63) $1700 plus (very few sample prices available)

Betty (Illustration 11) $325-375

Bitsey (Illustration 60) $200-225

Butch (Illustration 60) $225-275

Carmen (Illustration 26) $350-400

Carmen (Illustration 62) $1700 plus (very few sample prices available)

David Copperfield (Illustration 5) $250-275

Dopey (Illustration 20) $325-375

Egypt (Illustration 10) $260-280

Fairy Princess (Illustration 4) $250-275

Fairy Queen (Illustration 28) $375-425

Flavia (Illustration 64) $1700 plus (very few sample prices available)

Jane Withers (Illustration 46) $750-800 (13in [33cm], closed mouth)

$850-900 (15in [38cm] — 16in [41cm], open mouth)

$1000-1100 (21in [53cm], open mouth)

Jeannie Walker (Illustration 51) $400-450

Jeannie Walker Comparison (Illustration 52) right $550-600; left $400-450

Lady Windermere (Illustrations 65 and 66) $1700 plus (very few sample prices available)

Little Colonel (Illustration 16) $500-550 (all original)

Little Women (Illustration 6) $250-275 (each)

Madeleine de Baine (Illustration 29) $525-575

Margaret O'Brien (Illustration 38) $650-725

Margaret O'Brien (Illustration 39) $500-550

McGuffey Ana (Illustrations 8 and 9) $260-280

McGuffey Ana (Illustration 22) $400-450

McGuffey Ana (Illustration 23) $425-475

Melaine (Illustration 67) $1700 plus (very few sample prices available)

Miss America (Illustration 34) $550-600

Mistress Mary (Illustration 3) $250-275

Mother and Me (Illustration 53) $325-350

Orchard Princess (Illustrations 68 and 69) $1700 plus (very few sample prices available)

Pinky (Illustration 58) $175-200

Precious (Illustration 59) $125-150

Princess Elizabeth (Illustration 14) $500-550 (with wardrobe)

Princess Elizabeth (Illustration 17) $400-425

Princess Elizabeth (Illustration 18) $400-425

Princess Elizabeth (Illustration 19) $450-500

Scarlett (Illustration 33) $550-600

Scarlett O'Hara (Illustration 32) $375-425

Scarlett O'Hara (Illustrations 30 and 31) $375-450

Snow White (Illustration 20) $375-425

Snow White Marionette (Illustration 47) $275-350

Sonja Henie (Illustration 49) $550-600

Sonja Henie (Illustration 50) $550-600 plus

Southern Girl (Illustration 27) $400-450

Special Girl Doll (Illustration 54) $475-550

Topsy Turvy (Illustration 44) $150-200

W.A.V.E. (Illustration 35) $500-550

Wendy (Illustration 36) $525-575

Wendy Ann (Illustration 24) $325-375

Wendy Ann (Illustration 25) $350-400

ALLIED-GRAND DOLL MANUFACTURING INC.

Jackie Robinson (Illustration 71) $500-600

AMBERG, LOUIS, & SON

Amfelt Art Dolls (Illustration 73, left) $150-300 (depending on size, style, type of composition)

Amfelt Art Doll (Illustration 73, right) $150-300 (depending on size, style, type of composition)

AMERICAN CHARACTER DOLL COMPANY, INC.

Campbell Kid Dolls (Illustration 75) $300-400

Carol Ann Berry, The Hollywood Twosome Doll (Illustration 81B) $150-200 plus

Chuckles (Illustration 83) $175-200 (each)

Mama Doll (Illustration 85) $25-50 (as is)

Petite W.A.V.E. (Illustration 80) $250-300

Sally (Illustration 76) $150-175

Sally Joy (Illustration 78) $250-300 plus

ARRANBEE DOLL CO.

Debuteen (Illustration 96) $250-300

Dutch Twins (Illustration 93) $300-325

Girl from Southern Series (Illustration 90) $275-325

Girl from Southern Series (Illustration 91) $275-325

Ink-U-Bator Baby (Illustration 99) $275-300 (very few sample prices available)

Little Bo-Peep (Illustration 94) $225-250

Mary Had a Little Lamb (Illustration 95) $225-250

Nancy (Illustration 87) $250-275

Nancy (Illustration 89) $275-325

Nancy in a Trunk (Illustration 88) $400-450 plus (very few sample prices available)

Pirate (Illustration 92) $135-165

Toddler Boy (Illustration 100) $125-175

W.A.A.C. (Illustration 97) $125-150

AVERILL MFG. CORP., GEORGENE NOVELTIES, INC., MME. HENDREN, GEORGENE AVERILL, BROPHY DOLL COMPANY (CANADA)

Dimmie (Illustration 104) $400-425

Harriet Flander (Illustration 108, right) $150-200 12in (31cm)

Kewpie Lamp (Illustration 108, left) $200-235 16in (41cm)

Val-encia (Illustration 105) $350-400

Whistling Cowboy (Illustration 102) $200-250

Yawning Baby (Illustration 109) $375-450

BEEHLER ARTS CO. (VIRGA DOLL)

Girl (Illustration 110) $15-20

BERWICK DOLL COMPANY

Famlee Doll (Illustration 111) $600-1000 plus (depending on the number of heads and costumes)

BICENTENNIAL OF GEORGE WASHINGTON'S BIRTH

AMERICAN CHARACTER DOLL COMPANY, INC.

George Washington (Illustration 112) $250-275

George Washington Bicentennial Doll (Illustration 113) $65-125

Martha Washington (Illustration 113) $100-125

EFFANBEE DOLL CORPORATION

Bicentennial George and Martha Washington Patsyette (Illustration 116) $650-700 (pair)

Suzette Martha and George Washington (Illustration 115) $650-700 plus (pair)

TOY PRODUCTS

George Washington Dolls (Illustration 117) $100-110

BORGFELDT, GEORGE

My Playmates $75-200 (depending on size, costuming and condition of doll)

BOUTON WOOLF CO., INC.

Phyllis (Illustration 118) $125-175

BURGARELLA

Woman and Man Dressed in 18th Century Clothes (Illustration 119) $900-1000 (pair)

CAMEO DOLL COMPANY

Giggles (Illustration 128) $425-450

Joy (Illustration 120) $275-325

Kewpies (Illustration 127) $150-200 (each)

Margie (Illustration 121) $225-275

Scootles (Illustration 124) $375-400 (each)

Scootles (Illustration 125) $400-500 (very few sample prices available)

CIRCLE X

Girl in Green Dress (Illustration 132) $150-175

COHEN, HERMAN AND THE HOUSE OF PUZZY

Puzzy (Illustration 130) $300-350

Sizzy (Illustration 131) $250-300

CONFETTI DOLLS, INC.

Alpine (Illustration 133) $40-50 (in box)

CROWN TOY MFG. CO., INC.

Dopey Puppet (Illustration 135) $40-60

Pinocchio (Illustration 134) $250-300

DEE AND CEE COMPANY LTD. (CANADA)

Dee and Cee Soup Kid (Illustration 136) $375-450 (each)

DOLL CRAFT

Edith the Nurse (Illustration 138) $95-125

Emine of Turkey (Illustration 138) $95-125

Girl of the Golden West (Illustration 138) $95-125

Scarlet (Illustration 137) $95-125

DREAM WORLD DOLLS

Bride (Illustration 141) $140-175

Carmen Miranda Look-alike (Illustration 139) $110-140

Chinese Doll (Illustration 140) $110-140

Spanish Doll (Illustration 140) $110-140

EFFANBEE DOLL CORPORATION

1492 Primitive Indian (Illustration 147) $400-450

1620 Plymouth Colony (Illustration 147) $400-450

1720 Pioneering American Spirit (Illustration 149) $400-450

1840 Covered Wagon (Illustration 148) $400-450

1896 Unity of Nation Established (Illustration 148) $400-450

1946 Patsy (Illustration 181) $185-250

1946 Patsy Joan (Illustration 187) $375-400

Amish Boy (Illustration 144) $85-100

Amish Father (Illustration 144) $200-250

Amish Girl (Illustration 144) $85-100

Amish Mother (Illustration 144) $200-250

Anne Shirley in Original Box (Illustration 166) $450-500

Aviator Skippy (Illustration 193) $450-500 (in aviator costume)

Baby Tinyette as a Dutch Boy (Illustration 174) $225-250

Black Grumpykins (Illustration 145) $250-275

Button Nose (Dutch Boy and Girl) (Illustration 146) $150-200

Candy Kid (Illustration 162) $400-450 (rare doll dressed in this outfit)

$275-450 (dressed in other outfits)

Early Patsy (Illustration 170, left) $300-325

Carolee of Covered Wagon Set (Illustration 150) $400-500

Gaye of Unity of Nation Established Set (Illustration 150) $400-450

Girl in Long Blue Dress (Illustration 168) $325-375

Girl in Raincoat (Illustration 168) $325-375

Gloria Ann of the American Children Series (Illustration 143) $1100-1200

Honey (Illustration 154) $300-350

Little Lady (Illustration 164, left) $325-350

Little Lady (Illustration 164, right) $300-350

Lovums (Illustration 155) $250-275

Lovums (Illustration 156) $250-275 (in original clothes)

Lovums Heartbeat Baby (Illustration 157) $275-300

Majorette (Illustration 167) $300-350

Mary Ann (Illustration 142, right) $240-265

Mary Lee (Illustration 142, left) $200-225

Patricia (Illustration 184) $600-700 plus (doll in this costume)

$350 up (doll in playclothes)

Patricia as Anne Shirley (Illustration 183) $600-700 plus (doll in costume)

$350 up (doll in playclothes)

Patsy (Illustration 170, right) $300-325

Patsy (Illustration 170, left) $300-325

Patsy (Illustration 179, left) $250-325

Patsy (Illustration 179, right) $285-325

1946 Patsy (Illustration 181) $85-250 depending on condition of doll

Patsy and Friends (Illustration 180) $250-275

Patsy Ann (Illustration 189) $400-450

Patsy Ann with Molded Hair (Illustration 188) $400-450

Patsy Ann with Wig (Illustration 188 and 189) $450-550

Patsy Baby (Illustration 175) $225-250

Patsy Joan (Illustration 185) $375-400

Patsy Joan (Illustration 186) $375-400

1946 Patsy Joan (Illustration 187) $375-400

Patsy Lou (Illustration 190) $425-475

Patsy Mae (Illustration 191, right) $650-700

Patsy Ruth (Illustration 191, left) $650-700

Patsy Tinyette Doctor (Illustration 173) $450-500 (rare)

Patsyette (Illustration 176) $225-250

Patsyette Hawaiian Twins (Illustration 177) rare, not enough sample prices

Patsyette (Illustration 179) $225-275

Patsykins (Patsy Jr.) (Illustration 178) $300-325

Portrait Doll (Illustration 151) $175-225

Scottish Costume (Illustration 167) $325-375

Sister (Illustration 163) $100 (as is); $175-200 (in original clothes)

Skippy (Illustration 192) $500-550 (very few sample prices available)

Sleeping Babyette (Illustration 160) $275-350

Suzanne (Illustration 152) $225-275 (in original clothes)

Suzanne Nurse (Illustration 153) $350-400 plus

Sweetie Pie (Illustration 159) $250-275

Tommy Tucker (Illustration 161) $225-275

Wee Patsy Durable Doll (Illustration 172) $350-400 (in excellent condition)

Wee Patsy Twins (Illustration 171) $300-325 (each)

EUGENIA DOLL COMPANY
Girl in Pink Dress (Illustration 195) $175-225
Saturday (Illustration 196) $35-45

EUROPEAN DOLL MFG. INC.
Famlee Doll (Illustration 197) $600-1000 plus (depending on number of heads)

ARGENTINA
Baby Dressed in Gaucho Clothes (Illustration 199) $50-75
Gaucho (Illustration 200) $250-275

CUBA
Cuban Dancers (Illustration 201) $70-100 (pair)

GERMANY
Squeeze Doll (Illustration 202) $35-50

GREECE (EL GRE CO.)
Dancer (Illustration 203) $125-175

JAPAN
Shirley Temple (Illustration 204) $225-250

LAPLAND
Laplander Girl (Illustration 205) $125-175

PORTUGAL
Girl with Glasses (Illustration 206) $125-175

SWEDEN
Boy in Swedish Folkloric Costume (Illustration 207) $85-110

SPAIN
Gisela (Illustration 208) $150-200

TAIWAN
Fisherman (Illustration 209) $85-120

FREUNDLICH, INC., RALPH A.
Baby Sandy (Illustration 216) $150-175 7½in (19cm)
$185-200 11in (28cm)
$300-350 16in (42cm)
$375-425 19½in (50cm)
Douglas MacArthur (Illustration 217) $250-275
Goo-Goo Eva (Illustration 213) $75-100
Little Orphan Annie and Sandy (Illustration 210) $200-250
Red Riding Hood, Grandmother, Wolf (Illustration 212) $400-500 (complete set)
W.A.V.E., W.A.A.C., Soldier (Illustration 218) $145-165 (each)

GEM DOLL CORPORATION
Topsy (Illustration 219) $100-135

GERLING TOY COMPANY
Dancing-Dollies (Illustration 223) $50-75 as is

Undressed Boudoir Dolls for Home Costuming (Illustration 221) $65-85

GERMAN COMPOSITION
Girl with Red Hair (Illustration 224) $125-150

GOLDBERGER, E. (EEGEE)
Little Miss Charming (Illustration 226) $225-275

HEDWIG (DE ANGELI)
Hannah (Illustration 228) $300-350

HERA (NETHERLANDS)
Dutch Boy and Dutch Girl (Illustration 229) $175 (pair)

HOLLYWOOD DOLL MANUFACTURING CO.
Bride (Illustration 231, right) $50
Cowboy and Cowgirl (Illustration 230) $60 (pair)
Doll (Illustration 232, center) $20-30
Doll (Illustration 232, left) $20-30
May (Illustration 231, left) $30 (right) $50
Pretty Kitty (Illustration 232, right) $20-30

HORSMAN CO., INC., E. I.
Babs (Illustration 238) $400-500
Baby Dimples (Illustration 246) $250-300
Body Twist (Illustration 237) $200-250
Campbell Soup Kid (Illustration 136) $400-450 plus
Doll in Pink Dress (Illustration 244) $125-150 (in the box)
Girl in Patriotic Dress (Illustration 243) $275-325 plus (very few sample prices available)
HEbee-SHEbee (Illustration 233) $450-500
Naughty Sue Whatsit Doll (Illustration 241) $200-225 (all original)
Peggy (Illustration 236) $200-250
Peterkins (Illustration 235) $275-300 (depending on outfit)
Snow White (Illustration 242) $375-425 plus (very few sample prices available)
Toddler (Illustration 239) $125-150
Whatsit Dolls (Illustration 240) $200-225

MARY HOYER
Body Twist Doll (Illustration 249A) $400-450 plus, very few samples prices
Composition Doll with Painted Eyes (Illustration 250) $350-400 plus (prices of dolls in marked Mary Hoyer clothes may be higher)
Composition Doll with Sleep Eyes (Illustration 251) $350-400 plus (prices of dolls in marked Mary Hoyer clothes may be higher)

Ideal Early Doll with Sleep Eyes (Illustration 249B) $350-400 plus

ICE TIME OF 1948
Skater (Illustration 253) $20-30

IDEAL NOVELTY AND TOY CO.
Baby Smiles (Illustration 278) $125-175

Bathrobe Baby (Illustration 282) $85-135

Betty Jane (Illustration 277) $275-325

Charlie McCarthy (Illustration 271) $50-75

Cuddles a Life-Size Baby Doll (Illustration 281) $150-200

Deanna Durbin (Illustration 267) $450-500 14in (36cm)

$475-525 17in (43cm)

$600-625 21in (53cm)

$700-725 24in (61cm)

Higher prices for unusual costumes

Deanna Durbin as Gulliver (Illustration 268) $800 plus (very few sample prices available)

Dopey (Illustration 264B) $800-100 (very few sample prices available)

Fannie Brice Flexy (Illustration 274, right) $225-275

Jiminy Cricket (Illustration 273) $250-300

Judy Garland (Illustration 270) $1000-1300 plus (depending on the condition of the doll)

King-Little (Illustration 273) $250-300

Little Bo Peep (Illustration 266) $350 up (very few sample prices available)

Mortimer Snerd (Illustration 274, left) $250-275

Peter Pan (Illustration 254) $150-200

Pinafore Doll (Illustration 285, right) $275-325

Pinocchio (Illustration 273) $250-300

Plassie (Illustration 284) $100-150

Precious (Illustration 280) $125-175

Sallykins is Growing Up (Illustration 281) $150

Shirley Temple (Illustration 89) $700-800 and up

Shirley Temple (Illustration 257) $750-850

Shirley Temple (Illustration 258) $575-650

Shirley Temple (Illustration 259) $650-750 up

$100-150 (trunk alone)

Shirley Temple Baby Doll (Illustration 261) $840-940

Shirley Temple Texas Ranger Doll (Illustration 262, left) $700-725

Shirley Temple Texas Ranger Doll (Illustration 263) $1100-1200

Snow White (Illustration 264A) $425-500 13in (33cm)

$500-525 18in (43cm)

Snow White (Illustration 265) $400 up (no sample prices)

Soldier (Illustration 276) $175-200

Strawman (Illustration 270) $500-600 (few price samples available)

Tickletoes the Wonder Dolls (Illustration 279) $100-150

Walking Mama Doll (Illustration 280) $125-175 (each)

IDEAL (MEXICO)
Mexican Lady (Illustration 286) $100-125

JOLLY TOYS, INC.
Girl in Blue Dress (Illustration 289) $100-125

KNICKERBOCKER TOY COMPANY
Dwarfs (Illustration 292) $225-250 (each)

Snow White (Illustration 292) $275-325 14½in (37cm)

$400-450 20in (51cm)

LEE, H. D. COMPANY
Buddy Lee (Illustration 293) $250-300

MAMA-PAPA DOLLS AND BABY DOLLS
Girl in the Yellow Dress (Illustration 295) $150-175 (in appropriate clothes)

MARCIE DOLLS (A & H)
Bride (Illustration 296) $35

MINERVA DOLL COMPANY
Darling Baby (Illustration 299) $100-125

Snow White Look-alike (Illustration 298) $100-125 (original)

MOLLY-'ES (MOLLYE)
Baby (Illustration 304) $200-225

Bridesmaid (Illustration 300) not enough sample prices

Glamour Dolls of 1940 (Illustration 302) $400-500

Modern Teen (Illustration 303) $350-400

Russian Girl (Illustration 301) $400-500

MONICA STUDIOS
Doll in Silver Net Dress (Illustrations 305 and 306) $475-525

Dorothy (Illustration 308) $400-450

NATURAL DOLL CO.
Brother Ritzie (Illustration 311) $100-150

MARGIT NILSEN STUDIOS, INC.
Thumbs Up Victory Doll (Illustration 312) $75-125

NOMA ELECTRIC CORP.
Halo Angel (Illustration 313) $35

P. & M. DOLL CO.
Patsy-type Doll (Illustration 314) $95-115

PRINCESS ANNA DOLL CO., INC.
Bouquet (Illustration 316, right) $35-45
Daisy (Illustration 316, left) $35-45
Girl Grouping (Illustration 317) $20-30

PULLAN COMPANY, EARL (CANADA)
Eskimo (Illustration 318) $175-225

QUINTUPLET DOLLS
ALEXANDER
Dionne Quintuplet (Illustration 320, center) $450-500 plus
Dionne Quintuplet (Illustration 320, left) $150-175 plus
Dionne Quintuplet (Illustration 320, right) $300-350
Dionne Quintuplet (Illustration 321) $900-1200 plus
Dionne Quintuplets Nurse (Illustration 322) $300-350
Dionne Quintuplets Toddlers (Illustration 323) $2500-2750 (set and up depending on condition)
Dr. Dafoe (Illustration 321) $700-800
ARRANBEE
Arranbee Toddlers (Illustration 325) $750-1000 (mint-in box)
$500 plus (without box)
Sunshine Baby Made by Arranbee but Dressed by Vogue (Illustration 325) $75-250 (depending on costumes)
FREUNDLICH
Quintuplets and Nurse (Illustrations 326 and 327) $900-1000 plus (in box)
JAPANESE QUINTUPLETS MADE FOR TRUCCO OF NEW YORK, N.Y.
Quintuplets (Illustration 328) $700 plus
UNKNOWN QUINTUPLETS
Quintuplets (Illustration 329) $350 plus
Quintuplets (Illustration 330) $500-550 (set)

REGAL DOLL COMPANY
Kiddie Pal Dolly (Illustration 331) $200-275

RELIABLE TOY COMPANY LIMITED (CANADA)
Baby Joan (Illustration 335) $125-175
Barbara Ann Scott (Illustration 334) $325-400 (in original clothes)
Hiawatha (Illustration 332) $100-150
Indian Squaw (Illustration 332) $85-110
Royal Canadian Mounted Police (Illustration 333) $300-350

SKOOKUM APPLES
Skookum Apple Indian Doll (Illustrations 337 and 338) not enough sample prices

S.F.B.J.
Bleuette-type Flapper (301) (Illustration 339) $150-200
French Provincial Lady (301) (Illustration 339) $150-200
French Provincial Man (301) (Illustration 338) $125-175

THREE-IN-ONE DOLL CORPORATION
Trudy (Illustration 340) $175-225
Trudy (Illustration 341) $175-225

TIPICA MUNICA MEXICANA
Mexican Boy and Girl (Illustration 342) $80-100 (pair)

TOYCRAFT, INC.
Denny Dimwit (Illustration 343) $250-275 plus

TOY PRODUCTS MANUFACTURING COMPANY
Lil Sis (Illustration 344) $125-175

UNEEDA DOLL COMPANY
Rita Hayworth (Illustration 346) $225-275

ALBERANI VECCHIOTTI
Girl in Organdy Dress and girl in Regional Costume (Illustration 347) $125-135 (each)

VOGUE DOLL COMPANY
Baby (Illustration 356) $200-250
Bo-Peep (Illustration 349) $275-350
Girl in Dress and Coat (Illustration 361) $275-325
Girl in Southern Costume (Illustration 360) $275-325
Make-up Doll (Illustration 363) $225-275
Military Dolls (Illustration 352) $275-350 plus (each)
Painted-Eye Doll with Blonde Hair (Illustration 357) $200-225
Pilgrim John Alden (Illustration 350) $275-350
Rosie the Waac-ette (Illustration 358) $225-275
Russian Boy (Illustration 355) $275-300
Toddles Brother and Sister (Illustration 353) $300-350 (each)
Toddles Girl (Illustration 354) $275-350
Toddles Policeman (Illustration 354) $275-350
Toddles Victory Gardeners (Illustration 354) $275-350
Two Make-up Dolls (Illustration 362) $225-275 (each)
Wee Willie Winkle (Illustration 350) $275-350

WONDERCRAFT
Swing and Sway with Sammy Kaye (Illustration 364) $100-125

IDENTIFICATION GUIDE
"Lil Sis" Boy (Illustration 388) $125-150
Anna Nitschmann Doll (Illustration 382) No sample prices
Black Patsy Look-alike (Illustration 390) $25-35 (in this condition)
$100-125 (in excellent condition with original clothes)
German Patsy Look-alike (Illustration 377, left) $150-200 (small doll in box with extra clothes)
German Patsy Look-alike (Illustration 377, right) $150-175
Girl with Slitted Eyelashes (Illustration 391) $135-165
Jeannine of Alsace-Lorraine (Illustration 375, right) $60-80 9in (23cm)
$75-100 13in (33cm)
Judy (Illustration 386) $125-150
Lil Sis Boy (Illustration 388) $125-150
Maizie (Illustration 385) $125-150
Marilyn (Illustration 369) $150-200 (in original clothes)
Mary Ann (Illustration 376) $50-65

Miss Italy (Illustration 375, left) $60-80 9in (23cm)
$75-100 13in (33cm)
Mitzie (Illustration 380, left) $130-160
Nancy (Illustration 371) $185-200
Patsy and Snow White Look-alike (Illustration 381, left) $85-120
Patsy Look-alike (Illustration 378) $100-125 (in original clothes)
Patsy Look-alike (Illustration 392, right) $65-100
Patsy Look-alikes (Illustration 389) $200-250 (each) (recent auction price)
Patsy Look-alikes (Illustration 392, left) $35-50 (in this condition)
Patsy-type Doll (Illustration 384) $95-115
Peaches (Illustration 372) $175-275 (depending on size)
Phyllis (Illustration 374) $125-150
Ritzi Girl and Boy (Illustration 383) $100-150
Sally Petite Brother and Sister (Illustration 370) $600-700 plus (pair)
Snow White Look-alike (Illustration 381, right) $65-100 (with original clothes)
Tootse (Illustration 387) $125-150
Tootsie (Illustration 380, right) $130-160

Index

207